BIG GAME HUNTING
101
NO ROOM SERVICE & OTHER
TERRIFYING REALITIES

FREDERICK N. KLOECKER

(A.K.A. FREDERICK ALOYSIUS WELLINGTON IV)

ISBN: 978-1-7335256-2-6

E3 Outdoors, Inc.
PO Box 1265
St. Charles, Missouri 63302

info@e3outdoors.com

Cover Image: Catherine Grandy Photography
Cover Design: Steve Parisi
Editing: Jessica Santina
Book Design: Sarah Katreen Hoggatt of
Lucky Bat Books

Printed in the United States of America

CONTENTS

HUNT #3: FALL OF 2003

THE MISSION

In this world of cell phones and video game consoles, which boast endless networking capabilities and have become the social life, the extent of social interaction, and practically the exclusive "classroom" of a generation, people have allowed a foundational cornerstone of the developmental process and formative rite of passage to all but disappear from the life experience.

Reduced, defeated, and replaced by multiplayer network video games and interactive apps, family relationships and interaction lie in ruin along with quality bonding time, adventure, and opportunities to participate in, and marvel at, the great outdoors. This breakdown comes at a tremendous cost that will likely fail to be entirely absorbed within one's lifetime.

I speak from experience. I never noticed the outdoors until I was nearly in my thirties, despite almost three decades of standing in the middle of it! I can tell you from firsthand experience that its discovery is awe-inspiring and profoundly life-changing.

A priority and, in fact, the primary mission of this book is to reintroduce the importance of getting in touch with nature and the great outdoors, encourage exploration, and reinitiate interest and curiosity in the most wondrous and enduring resource we have.

I encourage everyone — even beg you — to put down your tablets, smart-phones, laptops, and streaming devices. Set aside your virtual experiences and the practical addiction to the various electronics threatening to rob us all of our interaction with each other and the world in which we live. Experience life firsthand. Get back to nature. Return to live interaction and education through immersive on-site exploration using all of your senses.

The vast outdoors is waiting for each of us to notice, experience, and appreciate it. Don't let the opportunity slip away and become unable to see the forest through the ~~trees~~ technology. Please, for your own sake and for that of your children . . .

EXPLORE. EXPERIENCE. EVOLVE.

DISCLAIMER

All accounts in this book are certified to be almost entirely truthful. All names have been changed to protect what's left of the dignity and pride of the moderately impaired, indescribably shameless, devastatingly uncoordinated, and profoundly hopeless individuals that make up this merry little assembly of insolent, intolerant degenerates and inept social misfits. In other words, this stuff really happened and is being recounted to the very best of my memory — sans real names. I have also left the questionable language in the woods where it belongs.

To be fair, it should also be noted that while there was a great deal of assistance from others regarding the recollection of these sordid anecdotes, I will be taking all the credit.

Assuming that this collection of stories has been written correctly, most readers will laugh as they look ahead to all the fun that awaits them in the woods, or as they look back at similar instances in their journeys. But for those who allow the adventure to stoke curiosity and intrigue in the outdoors and influence them to explore it (further or for the first time), consider yourselves among the privileged few that got the most out of it.

As a final note, this book is, in part, to thank my very dear friend Jon for his unwavering patience in teaching me the art and skill of hunting. It is also partly in retaliation for everything he has pulled at my expense—not that I didn't deserve every last bit of it . . . . I'm just sayin'.

CREDITS

Assigning Fault: Jon, the one single person I can blame for <u>all</u> of this.

Source of Assurance: Dan Duffy, the author who gave me the courage and confidence to write.

Pre-Edit Editors: Kimberly Russell, a gracious friend who offered to be beta reader #1. And Emily Bremer, another generous friend who lent a very impactful, critical eye. I am truly appreciative.

Elk Photo: Steven Straub, a remarkable friend and exceptionally talented photographer.

Biggest Supporter and Champion: Elizabeth, my darling wife, who encourages me and loves me for who I am. She is obviously a saint — or completely off her rocker.

Author's Assistant #1: Kodiak, our sweet little Klee Kai Husky, who selflessly sacrificed her playtime so I could write.

Author's Assistant #2: Beringer, our indulgent black Lab, who dutifully warmed my feet and kept me company throughout the entire process.

I couldn't have done it without my "assistants," as they take great care and pride in protecting my sanity — a duty that is often placed in their capable paws. Elizabeth and I adore them both.

DEDICATIONS

I dedicate this book, my first attempt as an author, to my dear parents. They have given me a world of experience, the capacity to appreciate it and the passion to actively pursue more. I could not have asked for a more loving and generous pair to guide me or set an example for me as I try to find my way in this world. If I manage to become merely a shadow of who they are, with even a fraction of their love, integrity, loyalty, character, compassion, and understanding, I will consider myself extremely fortunate. Thank you, Mom and Dad, from the bottom of my heart and soul for all of the love and support. It has made all the difference in making me who I am.

Additionally, none of this happens without my dear friend Jon and his tireless efforts to teach me the art and appreciation of this wonderful experience called hunting. He was and remains available at any hour, for any reason, without exception or expectation. I thank him for being the close friend to me that I aspire to be to others. Jon is a truly gifted mentor with a unique way of offering carefully crafted support that forces people to demand more from themselves than what they knew they had in them. He brings out the best in others and allows them the opportunity to discover the best within themselves. Thank you, Jon, for taking the time to believe in me, befriend me, and have such a positive influence on me. I am and will remain forever grateful.

FOREWORD

I know hunting camps. Some would even say I am a hunting camp aficionado. I've savored experiences in about as varied a selection of camps all over North America as one could imagine, ranging from ultra-posh, five-star hunting resorts to bedbug- and spider-infested camp shacks and everything in between. Until last fall, however, I thought I'd experienced about everything one could experience in a hunting camp. My week in northern Utah showed me just how wrong I was, and then some.

After reading the manuscript for this humorous and mildly disturbing book, author Fred Kloecker and his partner-in-disaster Jon invited me to join them on Jon's ruggedly beautiful 10,000-acre family tract in northeast Utah for a rifle-season elk hunt and to experience its hunting camp firsthand. Having read the manuscript and noted the chilling monikers for certain locations within the property—The Bear Claw standing out in neon-illuminated significance at the forefront of my mind—I accepted with eager trepidation.

I recognize the oxymoron, but how else do you describe being excited to go somewhere new and obviously beautiful beyond description, hunt elk for the first time ever when it has been on your bucket list for decades, and also be nearly eighty percent certain you were going to wind up as aggregate holding together a pile of bear scat on the side of some remote mountain? The only stipulation: I could not say anything about the book nor let on that a book even existed. Fred and Jon wanted me to fully experience the camp and its colorful cast without bias or anyone putting on for the "camera." This was to be the real deal.

Everything was there, just like the image painted on my mind's eye by Fred's careful words. The Bear Claw was as I'd pictured it: rugged, thick, dark, and ominously quiet. Buzzards circled above just waiting for some naïve soul to wander in and find himself a stain in the crusting snow. The cabin, though much grander than I'd expected at more than 9,000 square feet, was set upon a ridge with a glorious view of the valley below and the endless peaks that continued well into Wyoming. Even the notorious outhouse loomed just fifty feet from the cabin and projected an air of foreboding that made gooseflesh rise.

And then there were the people. Though many of the cast were absent during the hunt, some were in attendance in all of their glory. My mind's caricature vision of them overlaid on real faces and became one.

I made fast friends with Boy Wonder (a character you will meet in the book), who was now grown, a father and one heck of a fine person, though his youthful and fit physical being nearly caused me my death on one hike into the bowels of Hades. We dove off of a mountain and trudged down, down, down, and still farther down, barefoot through thigh-deep, crusted snow. I embellished that a little with the barefoot part to garner your sympathy, but in reality, even with the best clothing, boots, and preparations, a long, agonizing death awaited with one slip and a broken leg or ankle.

We had great success once at the bottom and doubled on majestic 5x5 bulls just a half second apart—an experience I'll never forget, and which happened to be the origin of Jon and Fred's nickname for me—you'll have to read the next book to find out what that is. There also might be some references to a card game, but I'll leave that for you to discover. No spoilers. In my defense, however, I can count, just not add.

Falling solidly within the too-funny-to-be-fiction category, this book paints as accurate a picture of camp, property, events, and characters as to be envied by Whistler, his mother, and all of his cousins. I stepped into the book, and let the story take me along as it wended through the real and surreal of life on this stunning mountaintop.

As you read on, you'll involuntarily fall into the story too. Fred is a master at capturing even the smallest details of a setting and firmly planting the reader right in the center of it. His emotions transfer through the pages, and your heart will pound in syncopation with his own, your flesh will pimple with his anticipation, and your soul will lighten with his laughter.

Regardless of its name, this is not a step-by-step primer for the budding hunter. You will not learn which firearm and ammunition pairings are best for big bulls, nor what elk bugle or cow calls to use, nor how to field dress the horse-sized beasts. But this book is important for every hunter, regardless of age or experience, for its underlying but very relevant message: no matter where you find yourself, no matter with whom you share camp, cherish every second of the experience. In fact, this book is important for the casually interested who are considering a foray into it, as well as the experienced adventurer who wants to relive a personal journey. The story is even relevant for nonhunters who are curious about the deeper reasons why true hunters hunt. In the end, know that it's okay to question your abilities, to be afraid, and to laugh at yourself and your friends, but also to always be safe, ethical, and legal so you can look in the mirror and be happy with who's looking back. Bon appètit, but beware of the chili!

Matt Lindler

P.S. Full disclosure: Cinnamon Bears are cute, sweet little spawns of Satan.

HUNT #1

FALL OF 2001

1

THIS IS FUN?

It seems like not too long ago when I sat in a duck blind as a twelve-year-old boy taking instructions from my best friend's father while trying desperately (though not very effectively) to feign my excitement over the institution known as freezing to death . . . I mean boredom . . . uhh, that is to say, hunting.

This was an experience that was entirely foreign to me. My thought process was, *Why would one wake up at it's-still-dark-outside o'clock, in December (in Missouri, no less), to willingly go outside, slog through mud, wade through water crusting over with ice, and sit motionless and almost entirely unprotected from the wind and other elements in an open sardine can? And all to wait for a feathered rat to fly by and offer the slightest chance of a successful shot to certify the morning a success? Why indeed, when I could simply order the fully prepared conquest du jour from the country club's menu later that night without ruining my circadian rhythm, plucking feathers, or risking pneumonia?*

There you have it in a nutshell: my earliest outlook on duck hunting in general. Perish the thought that I could have an experience and actually appreciate it. I was entitled, lazy, and clearly not cut out for the outdoors, or anything else, for that matter, that inconvenienced me and didn't offer immediate gratification.

Lost on me, due to my tender age and complete lack of maturity or thirst for experience, were the beauty of the sunrise, the magic of witnessing nature wake from a night's slumber, the serene landscape as snow accumulated on the barren tree limbs, and the sight of the ponds beginning to freeze over as the ice crept out from the shore. Nor could I appreciate the hundreds of birds flying in formation across gray skies while we tried to call them closer. Even the big picture escaped me: that I might be learning useful lessons in life about patience, effort, planning, and reward. I couldn't see any of that back then. And why? Because it was fricking cold out there and I couldn't hear myself think over the sound of my chattering teeth!

It was no wonder we rarely saw ducks. I'm sure they could sense my restlessness in the blind, not to mention hear my incessant pleadings to my friend's father when I begged him to take us back to the warmth of the farm house. Not only did I crave the comfort of central heating and the round of sympathy I usually got from my friend's sisters once we were back inside, but the big breakfast that awaited was, indeed, also a relevant lure.

Hunting became a tedious part of the trips out to my friend's farm during duck season, where all the other activities were right in my wheelhouse: target shooting off the porch, building bonfires, watching movies, riding ATVs and exploring all the places we were expressly forbidden to go. But the hunting component wore out its welcome when I became increasingly aware that I wasn't patient enough for it, I wasn't even close to good at it, and there would most likely never be formal plumbing in the blinds or even a phone from which to order room service.

My early foray into duck hunting came to a screeching halt one day after an impossibly cold and personally futile day (why break a perfect streak?) during which I watched my friend kill three ducks right before I embarrassed myself in front of him and his dad, both of whom I looked up to.

The light was fading on the last day of the season, as was my optimism that I would learn to love duck hunting. (After all, a dozen hunts over several years with zero success is a tough way to breed interest for me.) We stood shivering in a blind to which the three of us had waded. There was nothing to shield us from the stinging wind but the small bunch of cattails that camouflaged the rigid edges of the metal box that had been submerged to the rim in the center of a flooded millet field. I was anxious, even a bit excited, as there had been some rare success on this day. I thought that maybe I would finally have an opportunity to shoot my first duck.

We watched the sun drop toward the horizon — often a time of day with many opportunities — and encountered not a single bird. And just when I had given in to the idea that, again, this wasn't going to be my day, the opportunity I had waited so long for was upon me.

A gruff voice broke the silence of the moment, and I heard, "Quiet. Don't move. Three o'clock."

I slowly turned to my right and looked directly out my side of the blind. My eyes caught a duck flying twenty feet over the cornfield directly toward me. His wings were cupped, his feet were down, and he was headed into the decoys we had set out around the blind. I was focused at that point on two things and two things only: my host's voice and that duck. My eyes were locked on it and my heart was pounding.

The voice behind me then said, "Wait . . . wait . . . now!"

I raised my friend's .410 shotgun and did exactly as his father had taught me. I concentrated on breathing and being steady. I put the gun to my shoulder, laid my cheek on the stock, looked down the rib of the barrel, and put the bead directly on the duck.

At that moment, the duck seemed to slam on the brakes. His wings were spread as wide as they could be, and his chest was pushed out and completely exposed, leaving the bird in a vertical position as he tried to radically change direction. He had slowed to nearly a hover in midair, not twenty-five feet from the tip of my gun, providing a target that, by most standards, was equivalent to the size of a highway billboard.

This was it. This was what I had waited for all these years. It wasn't just about the satisfaction of killing my first duck or giving me confidence that I could actually do it; it was about achieving the goal in front of my friend and his dad as I wanted to make them proud as well.

I remember being confident as I concentrated on following what I was told was the most important instruction of all: to gently squeeze the trigger.

In my excitement, I promptly closed my eyes and yanked the trigger back. I opened them in time to see the duck through the smoke from my shot, flying off just as healthy and intact as he had been before I pulled the trigger and almost certainly laughing at me with pity.

Not only had I missed the duck completely, but I was informed that I had missed a coveted canvasback drake (a rare and highly sought-after one-hundred-point duck as well as the end of your hunt, back when the limit was defined by points).

To their credit, my friend and his father never said a discouraging word about it. And when we returned to the house some thirty minutes later, one of the sisters remarked with a huge smile, "My goodness, Freddie, your lips really bring out the blue in your eyes."

We all had a genuine laugh about that, but I realized that this just wasn't the hobby for me. I didn't like waking up early. I didn't like being cold. I was entirely unable to sit still. And I couldn't resist the urge to talk. (While we're at it, I also didn't like the fact that vendors weren't selling hot dogs and popcorn.) But what I just couldn't tolerate was not being good at it. Thus began my first hiatus from guns.

Little did I know that as I would grow up, these days would yield a love for guns.

It was in high school, when I tried out for the rifle team, that I discovered a surprising fact. It turns out I had a genuine and natural talent as a marksman. I got back into shooting when I discovered that I could actually hit what I was aiming at—consistently and with my eyes open.

Now, I'm not talking about being able to shoot a can off a log with a pellet gun at twenty paces; I'm talking about competing nationally against tens of thousands of other individuals using .22s and paper targets with a bull's-eye smaller than the period at the end of this sentence. I became quite accomplished and was ranked nationally in the top two hundred, but I gave it up after four years when I entered college. Ultimately, shooting at paper targets on an indoor range became mind-numbingly boring, and I simply walked away from the sport.

This was the beginning of my second break from the world of guns, though I left with far more interest and appreciation for them this time. Roughly nine years later, a most unexpected event pulled me back into shooting for good.

After college, I moved back home into my parents' new house, where they had barely had enough time to unpack, get organized, and meet the neighbors. The neighborhood was affluent, just like the place from which they had relocated. It was similar to what I had been used to while growing up around all the country clubs, large estates, influential people, and old money. Their home was decorated with paintings and antiques, silver, collectibles of all sorts, and one of two sons, my older brother having already moved out.

The two of us never wanted for anything. (In case you missed it, that's where my spoiled attitude and entitlement mindset probably came from.)

I was minding my own business one evening when the doorbell sounded. My father was not yet home from the office, and my mother was elbows-deep in a box, unpacking some collection of knickknacks and dressed only in a house robe before having to get ready for a nice evening out to dinner. Naturally, I answered the door.

I had no way of knowing that the character on the other side of that door I was about to open would affect me so greatly, nor how badly my sides would hurt from laughing so hard for the next twenty-plus years and counting.

Let me attempt to paint a picture: I opened the door, and there stood the silhouette of a large man, backlit against the sunset, with his left arm at ninety degrees and something large on his hand. I quickly apologized, reached for the porch lights, and was rendered completely speechless (doesn't happen often) as I realized that this man of forty-something-ish years, had a huge red-tailed hawk tethered to his wrist, which was shrouded in a thick leather glove so the nearly one-and-a-half-inch talons didn't puncture his forearm.

"Hello," he said eagerly. "I'm Jon. I'm your neighbor."

I managed to stammer, "Uh, nice to meet you," as I was terrified at the realization that the only thing that separated me from his pet pterodactyl was a flimsy screen door.

Visions flashed through my head of this prehistoric chicken punching through the screen, clawing my throat wide open with its talons and snacking on my larynx while I watched in disbelief and gasped for my last breath.

Jon interrupted my horror with, "And you are?"

Calling the police! my inner voice responded. Thankfully, the audible reply was, "I'm Fred."

Before I could ask the obvious bird-related question, my mother rounded the corner into the front hall, adorned in her pale-yellow terry-cloth robe, and remarked, "Fred, who's at the door? Would you please—What is *that?* "she interrupted herself, stopping dead in her tracks and clutching her chest in unqualified panic.

At this point, I had come to my senses and realized that the bird was not a threat. However, knowing full well that my mother is terrified of birds in an enclosed environment—particularly those large enough to eat a Shetland pony in one sitting—I opened the door, invited Jon into the foyer, and announced, "This is our new neighbor. And this," gesturing toward Jon, "is its human."

My mother was just about ready to dissolve into an unbridled apoplectic episode when Jon eased back out the door with his hawk and apologized for scaring her. He promised to return without the bird and quickly disappeared across the side yard into the tree line separating the houses.

Mom and I looked at each other, not entirely sure what we had just witnessed, and wondered exactly how we would explain it to Dad when he got home.

True to his word, though much sooner than we expected, the doorbell rang again. Jon was now standing at the front door with a woman whom I would soon come to know as *the* woman. Figuring that it would be far less stressful on Mom this time around, I opened the door and invited them in.

Jon was laughing hysterically, face beet red, and could barely introduce his wife to us between attempts to breathe. Clearly, she was not amused and greeted my mother with a sincere apology for her husband's behavior. She explained that he was an idiot before punching him in the shoulder for continuing to laugh and then demanded an apology from him for my mother.

This only served to encourage his hysterics, which had now rendered me nearly paralyzed and doubled over in stitches. She scowled at him before guaranteeing that he was in trouble, as though he were a ten-year-old boy. (To be fair, that was way off the mark. I assure you he acted as though he was at least twelve!)

By the time my father came home, we were all fast friends and sitting in the library. Dad walked in, introduced himself to the neighbors, and offered them a drink.

Their response was a very polite: "No, thank you. We don't drink."

My father, who has always held social drinking in very high regard, looked squarely at Jon and said, "Well, what good are ya', then? Fred, pour me a Scotch on the rocks, please."

They stayed for an hour or so, and I don't think I've ever laughed so hard in one sitting in my life. Jon was as animated an individual as I had ever met and knew precisely how to push his wife's buttons. She was very soft-spoken, witty as the day was long, and totally in charge of Jon's universe. Sitting in the same room with them was like having a front-row seat to an experiment demonstrating how propane interacts with an arsonist.

As they were leaving, Jon asked me if I liked hunting. I told him the story about my humble beginnings in the world of duck hunting and of my utter lack of talent and interest in the arena.

He said, "Well, you're doing it wrong. I'll teach you. It will be a blast."

I then further explained several of the reasons why I wasn't a fan of it, namely that it was too cold, too early, etc., to which he replied, "I don't care. You're going."

With that they were out the door, leaving Mom, Dad and me to just look at each other and laugh.

"They're somethin' else," my dad remarked. Little did he know just how right he was.

Jon and I became the closest of friends, and since we shared a similar sense of humor (a frightening truth leaving most to wonder which one of us is more in need of therapy), our hunts became infamous among our sporting friends and often resulted in muted success due to the relentless jokes and laughter echoing off the levees and carrying down the sloughs.

However, I did listen to Jon, who attempted to teach me the finer points of safety, hunting, identification, stalking, reading the landscape and weather, as well as various techniques for selecting the proper areas to focus on to achieve a fruitful hunt. Apparently, I learned these techniques well as not only have they served me well over the years, but Jon has repeatedly invited me to continue hunting with him. Or perhaps he just likes having a constant source of humor and irritation at his side offering a seemingly endless ability to provide those you-must-be-kidding-me moments. What can I say — you have to be good at something, right?

2

SOOOOOOO NOT WHAT I EXPECTED

After a few years of duck hunting with Jon (that's a whole different book), he asked me if I had ever been big-game hunting. I admitted that I hadn't ever hunted anything that didn't fly, with the exception of the random opossum who made the grave error of crossing my path while I was diligently guarding the homestead with my new BB gun at age 15. He then insisted that I join him and his group for the annual mule deer hunt on his property in northern Utah.

I must admit that I was on the fence about this, as I wondered if I had the nerve to shoot something that large without being overcome by the but-it's-so-majestic-how-could-I-kill-it thought process. Then again, I already knew how much fun it was to hunt ducks with Jon, and I couldn't help but imagine how much fun a week in the mountains with his corrupted friends might be.

With caution to the wind and the promise of a brand-new rifle from my dear father, I accepted the invitation and thus sealed my fate as the recipient of a very large helping of ridicule and humility, as well as becoming a seemingly never-ending source of fodder and heir of abuse. I surmised that knowing Jon and how he entertains, I would have free license to be an antagonistic pot-stirrer, provided I recognized that this was a two-way street. In other words, I would be able to dish it out as long as I would be willing to take it in return—and often in larger quantities. I did, however, make one nearly fatal error in my assessment. I thought I would be protected by Jon and thus relatively immune to any serious abuse by the others. I would find out quickly that there was very little truth in that notion and that, in fact, he was often the primary instigator and almost always the one fanning the flames.

It started before we even left. Jon helped me pick out all the proper gear I would need to blend into the landscape (with the appropriate hunter-orange accessories) and not freeze to death: all critical elements to hunting, I was led to understand. He also spent quite a lot of time trying to put me at ease, knowing full well what I was used to with regard to travel.

Thanks entirely to my parents and the great opportunities they had afforded me growing up, I was exposed to the very best of everything, from accommodations at five-star hotels and resorts to the finest food, wine, and entertainment to be had. Travel was always first class, as was my general existence, for all practical discussion. Having gotten to know my parents as well over a period of time, Jon came to realize this, and the hazing began.

I became quite curious about what I had gotten myself into. I began to ask questions about Utah and where we were staying, what the weather was like, how big the hot tub was, etc.

Jon calmly and thoroughly described his ranch out west. "Well," he said, "the cabin is situated on ten thousand acres and is located about four hours from the airport and two hours from even the slightest version of civilization you can picture in your mind. The cabin itself sits at 9,500 feet above sea level, is positioned in the very back corner of the property and is protected by a crescent-shaped mountain, which rises out of a meadow directly behind the structure. We get anywhere from ten to thirty-five feet of snow every season, we cut our own wood to stay warm, we have no cellular service, and I do all the cooking. The topography of the property has everything you could want as a hunter: wide-open fields, rolling hills, spring-fed ponds and creeks, a river canyon, dense forest, sheer cliffs, rock formations of all types, and total seclusion. We have black bears, grizzly bears, mountain lions, bobcats, mule deer, moose, elk, sheep, mountain goats, porcupines, and a very unhappy spirit of something that stalks the woods at night. It has been seen many times but defies description, other than to say that it's frightening enough to take your very breath away and paralyze you with fear. According to various personal accounts, it has left even the bravest individuals motionless in their tracks."

My response to all that was, "I'm sorry, did you say, 'cabin'?"

All I could picture now was that six of us would be holed up on the mountain in a nine-hundred-square-foot tomb constructed of giant toothpicks with a fire pit outside, a tiny potbellied stove inside, and a single bed that we would all have to fight over. Then a terrifying thought crossed my mind: I had yet to even consider the bathroom situation. Suddenly this seemed like maybe not the best plan for an adventure that suited my comfort level.

But there was no turning back now, was there? I had already committed to Jon and taken a highly coveted place on his annual hunt, I had been given a beautiful (and profoundly expensive) custom hunting rifle by my father, and to back out now might cause perceived dependability issues. At this point, there was really no graceful way to cancel, and Jon knew it. So for nearly four weeks I was beside myself worrying about this trip and whether or not I was going to survive it. Naturally, Jon loved every minute of it.

To make matters worse, he was flying out a week ahead of me to meet another group before ours, so that meant I was flying out to Utah alone. Not that I'm opposed to flying by myself, but it just seemed a bit daunting given that I had never been to Utah and would have a significant drive once I touched down.

The plan was to arrive at the airport around noon, rent a Tahoe or something similar, and meet Jon and the others at his second house in Richfield, a town about three hours from the airport and, sadly, in a direction other than that of the ranch. (It was here where Jon and his family lived for part of the year while his son finished high school.) We would then head to the local high school as a group, to get to know one another and watch his son play in his last football game of the year. Immediately following the game, we would retreat to the house, pack up the three SUVs with all the gear and supplies for a week in the mountains, and start the four-plus-hour drive to the ranch.

Well, it all seemed easy enough in theory, but the day started with a bizarre turn, and I never fully recovered.

I arrived at the airport in St. Louis, Missouri, and approached the check-in desk as I had done so many times in the past. In one hand I dragged all my gear and clothing in an unusually large navy-blue duffel bag. It was stuffed beyond capacity and easily recognizable due in part to the neon-orange initials emblazoned on the side, but mostly because it looked and felt as if it had a dead body inside of it. In my other hand was an orange ballistic hard case containing my gun . . . a custom .270 Weatherby magnum, a gift I treasured dearly.

The gun was absolutely beautiful. I actually got to hand-select every component, including the piece of heavily grained, medium-brown walnut wood that the stock was to be created from. The grip and forearm were custom-carved and hand-checkered, utilizing six separate measurements taken of my hand alone for the integrated palm swell so that the gun felt fused into my hand when I held it. The barrel was heavily fluted to increase the surface area in order to disperse heat more quickly, and there was an exaggerated muzzle brake at the tip allowing redirection of the propellant gases to counter recoil. The bolt action was the smoothest action on the market and drew shells from a four-shot magazine holding the best custom ammunition money could buy. The icing on the cake was a remarkable scope, which, until just before assembly of this masterpiece, had been unavailable to the public and reserved for the elite sharpshooters of our country's advanced specialized armed forces. I had been given a surgically precise instrument which, in the hands of an expert, knew few limitations.

I placed (dropped) my duffel bag on the scale to check in my first piece of luggage. The counter attendant carefully noted the weight at seventy-eight pounds. (Thankfully, this was before airlines enforced weight limits for baggage — and so what if I pack like a woman, get over it.) She smiled, attached the claim tag to it, and then nearly pulled her liver out trying to move my bag onto the conveyor belt behind her. She awkwardly adjusted her back and then politely asked about my second piece of baggage, to which I responded, "This is my gun," gesturing to the blaze-orange hard case. "Do I check it with you or someone else?"

The gravity of what had just come out of my mouth hit me immediately, and with the same force of order-disrupting panic and polarizing fear as getting a call on one's cell phone during mass — right in the middle of one of the silent pauses of the Eucharistic prayer.

In the blink of an eye, I was surrounded by four very large, intimidating, and generally unamused men in uniform who seemed keenly interested in the orange case and why a rugged hunter type was dressed in a collared pastel-pink polo shirt, blue jeans, and loafers with no socks. (Apparently, preppie is not the new camo.) A fifth uniform stood directly in front of me and glared at me with awkward disdain as though I had just stolen his cocker spaniel.

He barked at me to put the case down, step away from it, and follow the four unhappy agents to the end of the counter. Naturally, I complied, right after I seriously contemplated soiling my shorts. I followed my escorts over to the corner of the main lobby of the airport, where they began interrogating me regarding the case and its contents.

Now please be aware that I am not entirely incompetent. I was smart enough to read about traveling with firearms the day before and had taken all the necessary precautions. I removed the bolt from the gun, packed the ammunition separately (disclosing same at counter), and locked the case with a pair of keyed padlocks. The minor detail I had forgotten was to advise the airline, prior to my arrival at the airport the day of departure, that I intended to travel with a firearm. (Oops . . . my bad. Everybody's so unreasonably sensitive.) I handed one of the officers the key to the padlocks so he could inspect the case and the gun inside. Then, while trying desperately to stop staring at his unibrow, I offered a very sincere apology to them all.

"Gentlemen, it was an honest oversight on my part, which I clearly regret now. This is my first time traveling with a firearm and, believe me, I have learned my lesson," I said.

As one of the officers pulled the gun out of the case and inspected the breech, I mused that at least I had remembered to leave it unloaded. He promised me that this was no time to joke around and that they were taking the situation very seriously.

It was right then that I realized two things: not even Moses could have parted that eyebrow and made it plural, and silence was the best option for me at that moment.

After a full inspection and a brief lecture about how differently this situation could have turned out, he placed my rifle back in the case, shut the lid, and closed the padlocks. He handed me the key, pulled a baggage tag from his back pocket (along with an "Officially Inspected" sticker), and affixed them to the case.

He sent me on my way with a stern warning to secure all dangerous implements as the law required. I wanted desperately to point out to him that, in fact, I had secured my firearm exactly as the law required. However, I felt as though I was better off swallowing my pride than getting into a semantics debate with someone who could make me miss my flight.

I cleared security, got on my plane, took my seat by the window, and waited for the rest of the passengers to board and get situated. As I often do, I was watching them all as they boarded, hoping, as usual, that a beautiful girl would sit by me, or possibly just a nice person with whom it would be entertaining to converse, or even, at the very least, just someone who believed in general hygiene who took up only their own seat.

As it often happens, the aisle seat was taken first. It was occupied by an average-sized, normally dressed young man in his twenties who promptly organized his belongings, pulled out his headphones, and went to sleep. This left the middle seat open, and as the plane filled up and the announcements were made that the aircraft would be completely full, something terrible happened. A gentleman in his late forties and pushing three hundred thirty pounds squeezed into the row and packed himself between the two of us already seated, displacing the college kid halfway into the aisle and me squarely into the window. He sat with both shoulders against the row of seats, leaving his left shoulder overlapping his assigned chair's real estate boundary and resting behind mine, forcing me to sit twisted at the waist as if I were in a permanent let's-look-out-the-window pose. (I'm twisted, all right, but I mean physically in this case.) And as if that weren't bad enough, the man smelled like the east end of a westbound goat.

Now I try (mostly) not to be judgmental, and admittedly I haven't the slightest idea why this man had a thick, putrid, green haze around him that was enough to make any self-respecting skunk tear up, but whatever the circumstance, one would think that some effort could have been made with soap, cologne, or even garlic. This bordered on criminal. The charges would have been trespassing (into my seat) and assault on my sense of smell. All I could think about was the looming three-hour flight to Salt Lake City, Utah, and the threat of permanent damage to my olfactory system.

Scared to begin any sort of dialogue with the man for fear he might breathe in my direction, I cozied up to the window as best I could and fell asleep — or passed out from the stench. Either way, it spared me from an agonizing in-flight experience.

I ended up sleeping most of the way but was jarred awake, not far from our destination, when the poster child for reinforced mattress springs returned from a trip to the lavatory and plunged into his seat with all the grace, delicacy, and precision of a nearsighted proctologist. He crushed my right side, which had fallen back into its natural position in his absence, and then had the nerve to look at me as though I were the one intruding on his space.

As we descended toward Salt Lake City's airport (and while I attempted to reestablish circulation in my right arm and shoulder), I began to take a bit of the day's inventory: I had woken way too early. I had almost been arrested at the airport for announcing the possession of a firearm at the ticket counter. I had been treated to a nasal nightmare the likes of which would offend a rotting corpse. My back was twisted and stiff from spending several hours contorted into a pretzel so that Shamu the killer inhale was able to rest comfortably in *our* seats. And now my right arm and shoulder (the one that I shoot from) had been pancaked by a thirty-eight-inch-wide person who had literally fallen into his nineteen-inch-wide seat without regard for the safety of others.

Now, for the most part, I can roll with the punches. But this was a far cry from what I had expected for the day to this point. What I had originally predicted was that the second half of the day would be the part that would get to me (i.e., arriving at the cabin and realizing that I was stuck, quite literally, in the middle of nowhere for a week). At this point I hadn't even arrived in the state yet and I was already regretting the trip.

The airplane landed, we all deplaned, and I headed for the baggage claim area, where I was to reunite with my overstuffed duffel bag and my implement of destruction. It was when I was standing at the carousel waiting for my bag that I realized I hadn't the slightest idea where my gun would be released to me. Dare I ask someone acting in any official capacity at the airport? After all, look what had happened the last time I announced that I had a gun in an airport. What was I to do?

I finally retrieved my neon-initialed bag and set off on the next adventure to find my gun case, which hopefully still had the gun inside.

I asked a fellow traveler where I would recover my hunting rifle, having checked it as baggage on our inbound flight. He looked intelligent, was well dressed, and seemed like he might know these types of things.

Without batting an eye, he turned to look over his shoulder, acquired an airport policeman's attention, and yelled across baggage claim, "Hey! Where can this guy pick up his gun?"

You can imagine my horror. In that split second, so many awful scenarios played out in my head. Here the only trouble I had really ever been in had been over a couple speeding tickets and getting caught lying to my parents as a teenager. Now, in the span of just five hours, I'd scrambled law enforcement at two separate airports over gun remarks!

To my complete disbelief, the policeman simply responded, "Oversized baggage. Skis and gun cases are over at number seven."

Once my heart started beating again, I picked up my case and headed to the car rental desk. Surprisingly enough, things there went off without a hitch — and if you think that's a good thing, you aren't reading that literally enough.

Everything was fine until I was shown to my brand-new (seventeen miles on the odometer) white-with-tan-interior Chevy Tahoe and the rental agent recognized the absence of the trailer hitch. It turned into this huge ordeal because the paperwork specifically indicated that this SUV had a trailer hitch and it wasn't anywhere to be found.

Suddenly an entire contingent of representatives was on a frantic mission to uncover the unknown whereabouts of a trailer hitch that allegedly had belonged to this vehicle at one time or another.

Now I could've understood the ruckus if the actual vehicle had vanished, leaving only a trailer hitch behind; that would be something to worry about. But the AWOL hitch affected me not even slightly, other than it was holding up my day. I became very frustrated after twenty minutes and felt it necessary to voice my honest, yet snarky, opinion on the subject.

"Call me crazy," I said, "but since I'm not worried about it and I'm the client, how about you let me leave and get on with my life while you resolve the Great Mystery of the Missing Trailer Doodad on your own time. It's simply not my problem, and I've got someplace I need to be."

I had four people, including the shift manager, stop dead in their tracks and look at me as though I had just revealed the winning lottery numbers. I could see the wheels turning in their heads, but I wasn't sure how this epiphany was being processed. Was I right? Was I missing some logical component that was leading me to an ill-conceived remedy? Or perhaps were they simply offended that I didn't appreciate their dedication to their jobs?

Finally, one of the porters just said, "That's fine, sir. You go ahead, and we will just make a note on the paperwork that the hitch was not on the car."

My immediate thought was "What else could happen today?" which, as almost all of you know, is something that should never be uttered or even silently considered by someone who is already, in fact, having one of those days.

At that point, I just loaded up the truck, jumped in, and drove away. I got as far as the gate to exit the rental car lot and realized that amid all the coupling hardware hoopla, I had failed to collect the paperwork from the Towing Accessory Detective. I wanted to cry. I explained to the gate attendant that I didn't have my paperwork, and offered to reverse out of the lane and return to the agents who had released the vehicle to me to retrieve it. But as luck would have it (which is to say, as *my* luck would have it) another car had pulled up behind me.

The gate attendant said, "Hold on. Let me get them on the radio."

He picked up his two-way radio, called for the team at the garage desk, and briefly explained the issue.

"I got a guy here who left his paperwork," he said.

The reply was astounding: "Is that the white SUV without a trailer hitch?"

I confirmed that indeed it was the very same SUV. The attendant responded affirmatively, and the guy said he would bring the papers right up.

Several minutes later, and with eight more cars in the queue behind me, their occupants growing angrier with each passing moment, Earl arrived with my paperwork and a broad smile caked with Oreo cookies. (I couldn't fault him for that . . . I've been there many times.)

He handed it over to the attendant, who stamped two sheets, tore one, passed me the stapled bunch, and raised the gate. I sped off in desperate hopes of leaving the airport grounds as quickly as was legally and responsibly possible in an effort to put the rather inauspicious traveling component of the day behind me.

To my shock and relative surprise, I cleared the airport successfully and without further delay or incident, only to discover that I had accessed the highway in the wrong direction.

Now, I started to realize that when this many things go wrong and the only common denominator among them all is me, it was only logical to begin looking inward and considering the notion that instead of the day being an all-out disaster due to a world conspiracy directed against me, it may simply be because I'm an idiot. However, that became merely a fleeting thought as I turned around and got back on course because, clearly, personal accountability is overrated.

Jon's directions to the house in Richfield were quite good, surprisingly enough, and I reached the destination somewhat on time. Naturally, I was the last to arrive and was greeted by Jon, now sporting a full beard, with a heartwarming, "You're late! Help us bring the groceries inside before we head off to the football game."

I looked to the Chevy Suburban parked in the driveway, and there was a steady parade of people emerging from the back end of the car with bag after bag after bag of groceries and heading into the house or to the gigantic cooler chest (which could comfortably sleep three) in the garage. I jumped into action (at least as much as I jump into anything) and began ferrying bags of groceries into the modest yet absolutely spotless, single-story home.

And when I say spotless, I mean that there was not a single flat surface of counter, floor, or furniture real estate that wasn't covered with groceries. It looked as though an entire Save-Rite had been liquidated and all the goods were being held here for later distribution to those in need.

I was amazed to the point that I was literally standing there, jaw slightly agape, staring at the expansive landscape of food. That is until I heard my host's delicate request to, "Move your backside, Fred! We got a timeline here. If we miss the start of my son's last game, the only thing we'll all be hunting tomorrow at the ranch is you!"

Well, this was just the impression I was hoping to make with the other guys I hadn't even met yet. I was (fashionably) late, appeared to be lazy and unwilling to roll up my sleeves and dive in, and I was already being threatened with bodily harm—it was the first day of summer camp all over again. After that, everyone felt the need to take a bite out of my hind quarters at their earliest opportunity.

Just then, Jon's wife slugged him in the shoulder and said, "See what you've done? You be nice to Freddie!"

Yes, I had an ally . . . and a loyal, dependable one at that. She had been sticking up for me since the day I met her, and I had admittedly taken full advantage of it as often as I'd been able.

I had come to know Jon's wife as a very warm and caring individual. She always looked out for others, particularly the underdog, and was relentless in her pursuit to make everyone around her feel important, loved, and appreciated. She was a pit bull when defending those she cared for, and had a walk-softly-and-carry-a-sawed-off-shotgun personality that one learned quickly not to get on the wrong side of. She was organized, determined, exceedingly intelligent, and quite strong-willed, although unless she let you see it, one would never know. She stood about five-foot-six and had long, straight, blond hair, piercing blue eyes, and one of the warmest smiles you've ever seen. For some reason, she adored me and protected me from her husband's sense of humor with unfailing and often violent resolve. I always felt comfortable, nearly invincible, when she was around. And why not? If Jon so much as looked at me sideways, she'd punch him in the shoulder or remove her shoe and swat him with it. The only problem was that she wasn't always there and paybacks were brutal in this league.

Clearly, the ribbing was all good-natured and, in fact, really fun once I started fighting back. I could tell I was just one of the boys right away, and I knew I was going to be just fine with this group as long as we could finish unloading the vast assortment of groceries in time for the kickoff.

It turned out that Jon had been to the grocery store three times that morning to collect a week's worth of supplies for breakfast, lunch, and dinner for six adults. He had also acquired ancillary provisions like first-aid kits, charcoal-starter fluid, etc., as well as snacks, which included, but were not limited to, half the chip aisle, a spectacular array of candy, and his own personal stash of roughly five pounds of Cinnamon Bears. (I'm a good host in my circles, but clearly I had no idea what went into hosting a hunting trip like the one we were about to embark on. I was entirely out of my depth.)

With all groceries safely accounted for, there was just enough time for a quick round of introductions before we were off to the football game three blocks down the road. We all walked to the game together and climbed into the stands just as it started.

Present in the immediate vicinity of the stands were Jon and his wife, some of their neighbor friends and I, and the four hapless misfits that made up our group of six hunters (whose actual names will be withheld in an effort to save what little dignity they may have left after this trip).

There we sat while Jon extolled the virtues (or lack thereof) of the head coach, who had, in his infinite wisdom and sports prowess, decided that he would only teach and run two offensive plays all season long: a rushing play and a passing play. Likewise, he would only teach and run two defensive plays:

one to defend a rushing play and one to defend a passing play. After all, his logic was fundamentally sound. If you practice only two plays, you should be able to execute them flawlessly each time out of sheer repetition and muscle memory. That is a solid plan until you take into account that the other team will recognize each of the two plays for exactly what they are when the offensive or defensive team lines up and then adjust accordingly.

Jon was beside himself even before the game started and often interrupted his own conversations with us to scream at the coach, who naturally thought of himself as a brilliant leader and enjoyed to the fullest extent all the power he felt he wielded.

And, of course, with each insult Jon hurled at the coach, the most recent being slightly more offensive than the previous, so went his wife's scolding of same, which eventually ended up with her shouting his name in outright anger (or embarrassment) and delivering a strong, closed fist to his upper arm.

Finally, the game started and the heckling was rampant and relentless from multiple sources in the bleachers. In fact, the pace of the jeering picked up markedly and the abuse escalated exponentially with each corresponding touchdown against the home team. The game was a blood bath by halftime, but the real casualty, besides the kids being let down so badly by their useless coach, was the coach himself. He had suffered (deservedly) countless direct vocal assaults to his ego, with some other, more colorful language suggesting his mother to be somewhat at fault.

The icing on the cake immediately followed the kickoff to begin the second half. The kick was promptly returned for a touchdown without even so much as a single defender reaching within ten yards of the ball carrier at any given point during the play. Jon lost it.

He stood up and yelled at the top of his lungs in front of the entire gallery watching the game, "Hey, Coach! You're worthless!"

Jon's wife was mortified, bless her heart. A severe look came across her face and she admonished him in a loud and decidedly serious tone, "Sit down this instant. Say something positive or don't say anything at all."

Jon immediately stood up again and yelled at the top of his lungs, "Hey, Coach! You're positively worthless!"

The entire section of the bleachers dissolved in laughter. Not even Jon's wife could miss the hilarity in that one, and she broke down and began to convulse with laughter. The place was up for grabs at that point and the coach was literally hiding among his players on the sideline.

The game finally ended (mercifully) with a score so lopsided it looked as though only one team had taken the field. The idle postgame chitchat was kept to a minimum as we all headed for the cars back at the house.

We packed up the three SUVs amid laughing fits over one thing or another, often taking time to mock Jon's comments at the game for the benefit (or torment) of his wife, who was helping us to get out on time for our four-hour drive to the ranch. We finally drove off at five p.m. in three trucks that were so overloaded that none of the drivers could see a thing out the back windshields. Between the people, groceries, supplies, gear, and, of course, Jon's candy, it was a miracle that the suspension didn't fail on any or all of the vehicles.

The drive was relatively peaceful, no doubt a product of waking early, traveling, and spending the afternoon outside publicly tormenting a high school football coach. (That can really take it out of a person.) Naturally, the guy I rode with slept nearly the entire way, so the benefit of having an opportunity to get to know him and identify a potential ally for when we arrived at the ranch was completely lost.

We made the haul with a driver and one passenger in each car and arrived in Coalville, Utah (the afore-mentioned "slightest version of civilization you can picture in your mind") at eight-thirty p.m.

A booming metropolis with a flourishing tourism component this town was not. Within the vast boundaries of its entirety, it boasted four official stop signs and one flashing red light suspended over an intersection. This would certainly indicate a small town. However, when I clarify that all four stop signs and the suspended red light were all part of the same intersection, you can now picture more accurately the size of Coalville. It had several buildings, including a motel, a couple of small fast-food restaurants, a taxidermy shop, a market, and what appeared to be a municipal structure—presum-ably to provide offices for the town's leadership and parking for their single police car. The place was a ghost town, and I'm sure they rolled up the sidewalks at dusk and declared curfew promptly at sunset.

We all pulled into a lot, exited our vehicles, and stretched our legs. We had a few jokes at one anoth-er's expense and then climbed back into the cars to make a push for our destination. Jon took over driving my Tahoe and relegated me to the passenger's seat, undoubtedly so he could lead the others to the ranch and harass me at the same time (two birds with one stone and all). He directed one of the other guys to drive his Suburban in the second position and the last pair to bring up the rear in the third truck.

We pulled away from Coalville and drove down a desolate road into absolute darkness with barely any other roads intersecting. Jon was telling me all about the area, its history, how he'd been coming to this ranch for years and years, etc., and I began taking note of how far beyond my comfort zone I was as Coalville became merely a mental footnote now far behind us.

Suddenly, Jon pointed out something on the side of the road. "Look!" he exclaimed as he pressed the brakes.

I looked over to the left shoulder across the opposing lane of traffic, which for the record had been empty for nearly half an hour, and I saw a mountain lion roughly the size of an Oldsmobile tearing at the flesh of a deer that had been hit by a vehicle earlier in the day.

Jon was thrilled at seeing such a thing. He became excited and overcome with new stories to tell me, none of which put me at ease. All I could do was stare off down the road ahead of us and wonder about the countless ways I could meet my demise on this trip.

I was terrified. I kept thinking, *This is no country club out here. I'm in the sticks. I am so not cut out for this stuff. Why was I not content going to Palm Beach, Florida, with my parents and eating crab salad sandwiches and lobster rolls on the beach while waiters brought me tropical cocktails at the wave of a hand?*

Jon finally uttered the words I thought I'd be happy to hear, but they had somehow recently developed a more ominous tone.

"Okay, we're here," he said.

He pulled off the main highway (which apparently is code in Utah for "paved road") and onto a large apron of dirt facing headlong into a metal gate with a cattle grate beneath it.

He got out, unlocked the gate with a key from his pocket, and swung the gate open. He then directed me to drive through the gate and stop far enough past it to allow the two trailing trucks to get through and then stop and wait. He closed the gate and hopped back into the SUV, instructing me to drive ahead and follow the dirt road.

At the time the instructions seemed pretty straightforward. How hard could that really be? Just as he said to slow down and watch the road for ruts, I hit one squarely at about thirty miles per hour. It jostled the car around and jolted its contents so hard that I felt my fillings rattle. Jon got a real charge out of that, and I got quite the wake-up call having bounced my head off the roof of the Tahoe and then into the window. Suddenly I was overly alert and paying such close attention to the road (and the knot swelling just over my left ear) that I was missing the bigger picture.

As I looked around, I noticed we were driving through herds of cattle. It was an amazing sight brought into immediate focus when Jon pointed out the multiple sets of glowing eyes peering out from the trees bordering the open fields as they reflected the light from our high beams.

He explained that those were predators watching the herds waiting for an opportunity to feed . . . probably mountain lions. It was quite surreal, fascinating, creepy, and riveting all at the same time. I reflected on a time when I was certain I was at the top of the food chain, as opposed to this moment when I decided that I wasn't entirely sure of that anymore—at least not in these surroundings.

After a couple miles we approached another cattle gate. Again, we stopped for Jon to get out and let the group through. I pulled forward, as did the trailing vehicles, before Jon locked the gate behind them and climbed into the truck again. I asked, "Are we almost to the cabin?"

He laughed and said, "We have one more gate. That will put us on our property, and then it's a forty-five-minute drive from there."

It was then that I started to grasp the enormity of this ranch.

Now, mind you, I couldn't see anything other than what the headlights illuminated, as it was approaching ten p.m. in the wilderness and pitch black. We stopped momentarily and shut off the engines to look up and marvel at the array of stars in unnerving silence. The sky was clear, and there were more stars above than I had ever seen, being so far away from the lights of the big cities. I had never seen the Milky Way so clearly defined outside of a textbook photograph—it was as if there were hundreds of thousands of pinholes in the blanket of night. The darkness was still and absolute, adding to the eerie sensation, and the occasional ghoulish owl hoot shattered the calm and sent chills up my spine.

We returned to the cars and headed for the third gate. Upon our arrival, Jon quickly realized that the padlock on the gate had been changed. His key no longer fit. So there we were about a quarter of the way up a mountain somewhere in northern Utah, it was ten-thirty at night, the closest place to sleep besides the cabin (in a bed anyway) was roughly an hour behind us in greater metropolitan Coalville (I could assure you I wouldn't be sleeping in the Coalville Motel!), and five of the six of us were searching the surrounding area for a Hide-a-Key. Meanwhile, the sixth was sitting in the car preparing to have a nervous breakdown. (Guess who that was.)

Suddenly, one of the guys emerged from the woods with a key. (Um, seriously?) Talk about finding a needle in a haystack . . . or, more accurately, a Hide-a-Key in the woods, in Utah, a quarter of the way up a mountain, at night, while undoubtedly being stalked by mountain lions and owls!

At this point, I was too relieved to dwell on the unlikely odds of having overcome this obstacle and too anxious to face my impending fear of having to stay in a cabin for a week without a spa or five-star restaurant in sight. I was exhausted, hungry, edgy, a bit scared, and quite whiny, if I'm being honest.

After the ritualistic parade through the third gate, the ceremonial locking of same, and the return of the key to the spot where we never should have found it in the first place, Jon took over at the wheel and I returned to the passenger seat for the remainder of the journey.

Just beyond the gate and around a bend, the road became suddenly narrow (as in one-lane kind of narrow) with imposing trees lining the road on one side and various obstacles like rock formations, other trees, and steep embankments, just to name a few hazards, on the other. And to make matters a bit more exciting (interpreted as treacherous and/or alarmingly troubling), it had recently rained, leaving the roads, which is to say mud paths, as slick as oysters. The vehicles were slipping and sliding all over, and the often-steep sections were presenting challenges for even the best and most experienced drivers—namely Jon. After a solid nerve-racking hour of some of the most dynamic driving I had ever been witness to, we finally arrived at the base of the last hill leading up to the cabin. We navigated a rather difficult section of muddy terrain, where the "road" had been partially washed away and remained submerged, split a dense tree line as if passing through a decorative stage curtain, and began to climb the final set of switchbacks to the plateau on which the cabin stood.

I watched as the headlights finally fell upon the "cabin," revealing the structure from the night's all-consuming grip. And, like the rest of the day, it was not at all what I had pictured or expected.

Directly in front of the car was a ten-thousand-square-foot cabin perched in a clearing at the base of a crescent-shaped mountain with an outline I could barely make out against the dark sky. Clearly I was relieved, and Jon just laughed, knowing full well he had tortured me by allowing me to believe that we would be just a step above camping outdoors for the week.

"It's a five-star cabin," he said with a smile on his face. "You're going to be fine. I swear it's true."

To be clear, Jon didn't lie—particularly when he swore it to be true. In fact, that's always been a big thing with him. You can BS with him all you want, tell stories, and even lie your pants off, but if he calls you out and asks you to swear that what you're peddling is really the truth, you'd best come clean or risk losing his trust. Even worse, you will face remarkably poor odds against ever getting that trust back. It goes both ways, but it is an unwritten rule with him. Lie to his face after you swear it's true, and you'll be lucky to salvage your friendship with him and his respect for you will be almost irretrievably lost.

Jon had another brief laugh at my relief over the accommodations as we jumped out of the car. The other four guys met us in the middle of the gravel driveway, and we all talked about the harrowing drive up from the last gate. We were all thankful to have arrived in one piece.

After a minute or two, we recognized, as we stood there in the night jawboning at each other, that we were, in fact, standing near the top of a mountain in Utah, in October, freezing our tails off.

Jon declared that it was time to unload the vehicles and get the cabin up and running. Everyone started scrambling to get the gear and the food into the cabin while Jon walked toward the generator to start it.

I yelled to Jon, "You said this was a five-star cabin, huh? So where's the bellhop to take my bags for me?"

He just shook his head and kept walking.

As if instinctively I knew what was good for me, I stopped while I was ahead, grabbed some gear, and started to carry it into the cabin.

3

THIS DOESN'T SUCK

It took us nearly thirty minutes to unload the SUVs and bring all the gear and supplies into the cabin. All of the items were placed in three neat groupings (at least as neat as six guys in the woods were concerned) just inside the main room of the lower level: food to the left, suitcases in the middle, and gear and guns to the right.

Now that everything was in from the cold, including Jon, who was kind enough to provide light by starting the generator, we realized that it was just as cold inside as it was outside. Jon tossed several logs into an enormous fireplace, arranged them just so, and set them ablaze. Within a matter of minutes, thanks to some prodding with a fire poker, the inferno was roaring inside the hearth. As heat spread slowly throughout the cavernous room, Jon declared it time for a tour.

The log cabin had two levels. The lower level was built into the side of a hill such that two stories were visible from the front of the cabin and only one from

the back. The entire lower level was carpeted and con-
sisted of a great room, which faced a wall of windows
presumably looking out at a marvelous view — not that
we would have known given that it was midnight and
we couldn't see our hands in front of our faces outside.

Centered on the back wall in this vast room was
the fireplace, which was almost big enough to stand in.
Behind that wall were two dormitories, one all the way
to the right of the room and the other all the way to the
left. Each slept fourteen guests comfortably in bunks,
and each dorm had its own bathroom.

Upstairs was considerably more formal. It con-
sisted of another great room, this one with vaulted
beam ceilings, and another colossal stone fireplace facing a wall of windows. Additionally, there was a dining
area, a small kitchen, a pantry, six small bedrooms,
four bathrooms, and a wraparound deck outside. The
floors were all hardwood with rugs, the walls were
adorned with mounts and nature-themed art, and the
chandelier in the center of the great room was made
from a massive old wagon wheel. The woods all had
a warm tone that was instantly inviting and calming
(not that I imagined there was ever a lot of stress out
here — other than mine — to begin with), yet even I was
put at ease, at least with regard to where I'd be staying
for the next week.

We were all to sleep downstairs in the dormitory
to the right of the fireplace, and we were told that we
could select our bunks after we got all the food up to
the kitchen. Additional instructions were to leave all
the candy on the table in the middle of the seating area
in front of the lower-level fireplace. Following that was
the warning that if anyone were to eat any of the Cinnamon Bears, it would likely be their last act in life.

By the time all the food had been put away, the candy had been put on the table, and the contents of the suitcases had been unpacked and laid out on the upper bunk of the bed each of us had claimed, it was nearly one a.m. We were all exhausted . . . all of us except Jon, who asked excitedly, "Who wants to go for a ride and see the property? We can do a little scouting for tomorrow."

We all looked at each other as if to confirm that we all thought he was insane. (We were unanimous, by the way. Everyone agreed that he had lost his last marble.) Three of the guys rolled their eyes and climbed into bed. The other two, myself included, decided against our better judgment to ride along and try to get some sort of idea just how big this place really was. We grabbed our coats, and Jon grabbed his new multimillion-candlepower portable sunbeam—expressly forbidding any firearms along for the ride. We drove off into the night leaving the safety, warmth, and comfort of the cabin. (What, in the name of all that is rational, were we thinking?)

Jon explained the layout of the ranch as we drove along.

"The cabin sits in the southernmost portion of the property," he began, "and faces due north. As we drive north off the hill from the cabin, we will run into an intersection offering three roads that all run, more or less, north and south. The East Road obviously runs down that side of the property, the West Road down that side of the property, and the Middle Road bisects the ranch."

Jon continued to point out areas and tell stories as we spent the next hour exploring the three roads at least as far as the muddy conditions would allow.

On this night, my brain starved for sleep, it was mostly impossible to get, let alone maintain, my bearings. Jon could've told us we were in the Bahamas and I would have believed him. But we continued to drive around, and when I asked why we were doing this instead of sleeping, he pointed out that we were searching for the two flocks of sheep on the property — each having roughly three thousand head within it.

"And why do I care about flocks of sheep?" I asked.

Jon explained that he wanted to locate them so he could identify which areas not to target for hunting over the next five days as deer never comingle with sheep.

Personally, I believed that he just wanted to give us a tour of the incredible property and show us something he was not only proud of, but something he knew we'd appreciate, having never seen anything like it before.

And speaking of things we'd never seen, during our search for the two flocks of sheep, we encountered a jackrabbit that appeared to be auditioning for the circus.

As we rounded a bend in the road, our headlights illuminated a small clearing with one tree in the very center. It looked a bit like a stage, on which a jackrabbit decided to give his all to impress us with an impromptu dance performance right as the lights discovered him. He was jumping around like he was on something and running in circles so fast it was enough to make our heads spin. The rabbit would jump six or seven feet into the air and twist and contort himself in the most unusual and unnatural ways, often landing on his head or his side, only to right himself again and start anew. The animal appeared to have issues. I tried not to speculate because it is often rude, but I offered up the explanation that possibly he had rabies, was somehow impaired, or just had a passion for onstage slapstick. Or maybe he was just in love. Regardless of the baseline problem causing the highly peculiar behavior, we laughed uncontrollably for quite some time at this creature's antics. To this day, none of us have ever seen a display like it.

Additionally, we saw a bobcat, an enormous porcupine, and literally over one hundred moose, elk, and mule deer. The animals were everywhere. It was clear that there was very little pressure here and the animals were thriving.

All in all, it was utterly fascinating, but eventually a lack of sleep caught up with all of us, and the consensus was reached to return to the cabin with our personal energy tanks on empty. Well, maybe not completely empty. It seemed that there was just enough residual emergency vigor remaining to mess with the guys who had elected to stay at the cabin and sleep.

Those of us who were returning from the drive walked into our dorms as quietly as possible so as not to disturb the sissies, I mean fellow hunters, who had been too lame to go with us and were completely unconscious by now. Mind you, our stealthy entrance wasn't at all out of consideration for our comrades who were sound asleep; it was merely to take advantage of an opportunity to be in the right place at the right time and enjoy a cruel prank.

Jon turned on the lights and announced that it was time to wake up for the hunt—which he did at a decibel level most likely not healthy for the average human eardrum. I can assure you that Jon is neither a subtle nor even remotely quiet man, so when the lights came on with a blinding flourish and his voice rang out falsely announcing morning's arrival while he beat a kitchen pot with a metal spoon, the pandemonium that ensued was riotously funny and well worth the risk of bodily harm, at least for those of us on the right end of the joke.

Those poor clowns jumped out of their skins, eyes blazing red after having slept for only an hour, and were completely disoriented. We had to peel them off the ceiling, which, for the record, was hard to do while we were laughing as hard as we were.

At that point, as things settled down, it was time to go to bed. Now that the sleeping three were wide awake with adrenaline surging through their bodies, the remaining parties climbed gently into our racks and drifted calmly off to sleep (after we stopped laughing) to choruses of choice expletives flying around the room. It was the perfect scenario. We knew that retaliation wasn't even remotely possible given the exhausted condition we were all in. Most of us slept like babies until morning really did arrive (which was way too soon), and we were awakened by Jon in a similar manner to what we had witnessed only four hours prior.

For the record, it was not nearly as amusing this time as last, being that I was one of the poor clowns on the wrong end of it. It's amazing how an individual can go from being labeled hysterically funny to being thought a callous agitator, within mere hours — and all for the same behavior. (I find it amusing that with regard to similar conduct, the conclusion becomes simply a matter of perspective.)

"To my credit," Jon said almost half apologetically and in a tone slightly ridden with guilt for waking us, "I have already made breakfast." And just as we were all taking that statement in and processing it for the positive concept that it was, he said, at the top of his voice, "So get your sorry butts out of bed and come tell me how good it is!"

If I'm being honest, this was not the same experience as a gentle wake-up call from the front desk at the Ritz-Carlton. It wasn't entirely without its own merit, but the idea of being permitted to awaken slowly didn't seem to be high up on our host's list of priorities.

We scrambled to our feet, threw some clothes on, and headed out into the main room to go up the stairs when we were all caught off guard by the stunning view through the wall of windows looking out over the ranch.

It was breathtaking. Visibility was easily thirty miles, and the vista included a mountain range off in the distance and rock peaks to the right, giving way to a tree line and a medium-dense coverage of pines, spruces, and other evergreens with the occasional outcropping of rock and granite. Fields and meadows spread out to the left past clusters of forest, with a creek and another log cabin in the distance. An expansive vista of rolling land straight ahead vanished into quaking aspen timberland replete with yellow leaves that created a remarkable, quivering tapestry on the landscape. We were all speechless . . . and all in trouble for letting breakfast get cold.

Jon called down the stairs, no doubt concerned about our well-being.

"Are you pinheads coming up for breakfast, or did I get up early for nothing? My gosh! Doesn't anyone appreciate effort anymore?" he bellowed.

We heard him chuckle before his hefty six-foot-something frame, along with his well-intentioned sarcasm, walked across the hardwood floors back toward the kitchen. We figured our attendance at the table before he stopped laughing would be entirely appropriate, if not advisable and beneficial to maintaining our health. With that in mind, we quickly migrated upstairs for a bite to eat.

We sat at the table and were each served a plate with one piece of bacon on it and a glass of orange juice. Jon then finally sat down and placed in front of himself about twenty pancakes, the remainder of the two pounds of bacon he'd cooked, freshly scrambled eggs, warmed syrup, butter, and half a loaf of toasted bread. He then asked us all point blank if we planned to be late for breakfast in the future. When we all agreed not to be late for breakfast again, he kindly passed all the food around the table. He had made his point very clearly, though I should mention that he made one other point just then. I was seated to his immediate right, and he had passed all the food to the left.

As it came around the table and back toward me, he said, "Freddie doesn't get any."

When I inquired as to why with my best, whiniest, most sympathy-seeking voice, he responded with, "All these guys promised they wouldn't be late to breakfast again."

"As did I," I offered.

And he replied, "Yeah, but I know you're lying. You haven't gotten up before 10 o'clock since you graduated high school."

The insult war was on.

I remarked that I was shocked he knew anything about high school, as I was under the impression that schooling of any kind had been developed well after his childhood. The bonding-through-abuse ritual was off to a spectacular start, and breakfast was one good laugh after another.

At this point, I finally knew these guys a bit, so I feel that now is the time in my story when proper introductions are in order, though the nicknames may not make much sense until later.

Jon, or Grizzled Adams, as he became known (only because "den mother" didn't go over too terribly well with him), was the jack-of-all-trades on the trip. He knew the property better than anyone, and his knowledge of the game on his land was second to none, which made him perfectly suited as the guide. He was clearly the best cook among us (which doesn't really give him proper credit as he is a pretty amazing cook by all rights anyway), which also permitted him to claim the designation of chef. And he claimed responsibility for everything, from our experiences to our absolute safety, which earned him the title of babysitter — particularly in my case, as I had never been big-game hunting nor had I ever been in the mountains, unless you would count skiing in Vail and greater Summit County, Colorado, in between massages, hot-tubbing with Champagne, and decadent dinners.

Beanpole was a somewhat shy young man from southern Missouri who was in his early forties. I had first met him a few years prior to this trip, and I'd learned then that he owned a feedlot that sold food and other supplies for livestock. He had a slight build, appeared to weigh in at about a buck-eighty, and just so happened to be nearly six-and-a-half feet tall. It looked like the guy would blow over in a stiff wind like an unassembled cardboard box leaning against a portable fan. He was clearly articulate with a mind for business, had a heart of gold, and would do anything you asked of him, yet he could not maintain his concentration during card games to save his life. He could be an integral part of the conversation and not remember why he was holding cards, or he could be paying close attention to the game at hand yet fail to realize he was the only one left sitting around the fire. It was truly amazing. He was one of the nicest guys I had ever met, but I'm not sure I'd ever endorse him as the poster child for multi-level awareness.

The Great White Hunter was the eldest member of our troop at age sixty-sevenish. He owned a very successful sporting goods store in St. Louis, Missouri, which had a nationwide customer base, and he had been all over the world hunting every animal you can imagine. He had more stories than any of us, some of which may have even been true. He was a real character, a wonderful storyteller (when he wasn't falling asleep in the middle of them), and was the one who had the most to complain about (aches, pains, bad knees, age in general, life issues, business, etc.), yet he never did—not even once. I don't think I ever saw him without a wad of chewing tobacco in his cheek or walking around without that repulsive spit cup. It was a particularly nasty habit when you took into account his coarse and tangled gray beard, which often caught a portion of the purged tobacco saliva on its journey from his mouth to the cup. He had reached the point in his life and hunting career when he was full of knowledge (among other things) and wanted nothing more than to pass it along to younger, less-experienced hunters in an effort to help them succeed in this wonderful tradition that he had cherished his entire life. He was one of those people who would have been far happier and gotten more out of watching someone else take a trophy than take one himself. He was a real woodsman, though probably a bit too long in the tooth to go out wandering alone anymore. But as far as an ambassador for hunting and the great outdoors, there was truly no one better suited.

Stunt Mouse was also from Missouri and someone I had been introduced to a couple years prior. He was a tremendous guy who, at first glance, looked like he was in his twenties, though after hearing about his wife and children and asking his age just to qualify everything, we discovered was well into his forties. His hair was cut very close to his head; he wore round, thin-rimmed glasses and looked as though he was standing in a hole when next to Beanpole. Stunt Mouse was a scant five-foot-five, give or take (though, for his sake, hopefully give), and was a heavy-equipment operator. He drove bulldozers and backhoes, likely perched atop a phone book or two so he could see over the controls. He didn't seem like someone to be afraid of until you saw him without a shirt. The man was cut and solid as a slab of granite, but he had a mild demeanor and couldn't have been more helpful had he tried.

He was the go-to guy for seemingly everything, and he answered the bell time after time without even so much as rolling his eyes. His personality was of the determined type, and he was the problem solver of the group. He always took the initiative before anything became an issue and expected no credit for heading the problem off at the pass. I also liked him because he always seemed to have the underdog's back. So often the underdog was me, so he and I got along famously.

Boy Wonder was the youngest of the group. He was the nineteen-year-old son of another friend of Jon's. Wonder had signed on as the whatever-we-needed guy.

In other words, we had a workhorse. He was a great kid from Salt Lake City, Utah, who, let's just say, could've benefited greatly from some mentoring by Jon. Boy Wonder was a good-looking kid who obviously spent time in the gym. He was fit, full of energy, happy to respond to most requests, and always almost intolerably polite . . . with the exception of when he wasn't.

He reached his limit a few times and became a bit too big for his britches, showing his shortcomings in maturity and underscoring the need for time with Jon. I remember Boy Wonder as a great guy. We got along very well, and he was often my guide around the property as he had been there many times before and knew the art of hunting, stalking, and tracking while always maintaining his location related to the cabin. He was also very gifted in the area of situational awareness and was adept at collecting visual clues from all over the landscape at a simple glance to make decisions. This gift came in handy several times. Overall, he was a bright young man with unlimited potential who was just a bit undercooked in the maturity department. And since he was nineteen, none of us were too quick to call him out on it. Nineteen is nineteen, and we all understood that.

As for me, I think most of my background has been made clear. However, to be fair-minded about this, I should disclose that I am six feet tall and, at the time, weighed a meager two hundred twenty pounds. I was shaped like a pear and exercised regularly — once every decade or so just to be safe but not overdo it. I was about as fit as an overly ripened cantaloupe and as eager to face and conquer physical challenges as a sun-warmed housecat on Ambien. Finally, I should also add for posterity (and with a small amount of shame) that my camp nickname was Frederick Aloysius Wellington, IV (no doubt a sarcastic tribute to my entitlement) or Peach Fuzz for my inability to grow any substantial facial hair. I was the only one of the bunch who, in addition to having a baby face at the tender age of twenty-nine, couldn't grow a beard if my life were exclusively dependent upon it. I'd love to say that that was my only flaw, but then I'd be suggesting that I don't snore like a freight train, which, as you can imagine, went over like a pregnant pole-vaulter during the night when everyone was trying to sleep. Other than that, though, I'm perfect. (Or not.)

Breakfast was fantastic, but the cleanup in the kitchen was daunting. Given that I had been brought up to be a courteous guest, and due to the fact that I felt I didn't know Boy Wonder well enough to order him to do it, I volunteered to clean the kitchen. (That is to say that Jon said, "I will cook for you nimrods, but I will not clean up the kitchen. Freddie, you're elected.") Had I known that because of this "gesture" the duty would fall to me for the rest of the trip, I may have decided to find something else important to do, like count my socks and refold my long underwear. But everyone at one point or another "claimed" their roles and duties, and it simply became the natural order around the cabin.

As I was finishing up the rather extensive kitchen restoration project (so-called because Jon practically destroyed it making the first meal of the day), my stomach began to settle. Breakfast was pushing on the Subway sandwiches we had eaten in the cars on the way up to the ranch the night before. So as nature persuaded me to find a bathroom, I calmly made my way downstairs and walked through our dorm and into the attached bathroom for a quick shower and the morning constitutional. I shut the door, started the water in the shower, disrobed, and hopped in.

My entire body convulsed immediately and involuntarily as I screamed and fell into default panic. The water was so cold that it rivaled swimming in Lake Michigan . . . in February! My vocabulary in that instant was surely enough to make a sailor blush, and the goose pimples that resulted were for the record books.

I quickly turned the water off, got out, and immediately dried and wrapped myself in a towel.

As the pace of my cursing and jumping around like the Easter Bunny to try to reestablish blood flow to various parts of my body slowed down, I dropped the towel, walked toward the commode, and sat down for the morning purge. I will simply state that it was productive and provided significant relief. (That should suffice.)

Just as I stood and flushed, an announcement rang through the entire structure that would certainly change my life forever: "By the way, the bathrooms are off limits until further notice. The water pipe has frozen and ruptured. It is completely disabled."

I looked on, pretending not to have heard the warning while desperately praying that the system would work this one last time..

Everything appeared normal and I glanced upward and thought to myself, *Thank goodness!*

You can't imagine my relief, at least until I realized I still had a grave problem: we had six days left and the bathrooms were out of commission.

I wandered out to the main room where everyone was gathered to receive news of the dreaded solution.

"The outhouse is just out this door and thirty steps across the ridge," Jon declared. "Make sure to check for raccoons and the like before just walking in."

Oh, how I longed for the Four Seasons resorts and modern plumbing! I nearly broke into tears.

As I was overcome by anxiety, all I could say to myself was, *An outhouse? Really? Is this truly happening?*

The notion of using an outhouse (one that was possibly inhabited by a vicious, man-eating, abominable porcupine) was distressing, to say the very least. Further, it hit me that it was very cold outside (Utah. October. Mountains. Duh!). And then I got it: the full mental image of me trekking outside at three in the blessed morning, bundled inside my heavy hunting parka, jeans, and, yes, boots, to walk thirty paces from the sanctuary of the warm cabin—in the freezing October cold—toward the forsaken Den of Horrors, which had actually become a legitimate destination. Then to have to first clear the structure of any threat from carnivorous fauna before inviting pneumonia and hypothermia by disrobing what I had just, moments ago, put on to protect myself from same, all for the opportunity to relieve myself, was ludicrous. Moreover, the thought of having to perform the re-dressing ritual before risking life and limb, yet again, to return to the cabin was just too much. I was about to have a psychotic break. It made me realize just how much we take for granted the privilege of being able to discharge indoors without having to risk frostbitten appendages or being mauled by a bear!

Finally, to grasp the fact that we had no showers pushed me completely over the edge. My world had somehow spun uncontrollably off its axis. I was in my own personal hell. I wanted my mommy . . . or at least a five-star hotel and a wine list.

To myself I thought, *I liked being here a lot more when I liked being here.*

4

LET'S GO KILL SOMETHING

Granted, we were off to a late start on the first day. And by late, I mean it was noon. This aggravated our host, but you can't rush into these sorts of things — at least I couldn't. I'd never been hunting like this before. The boys were all ready within ten minutes, and there I sat on the edge of my rack still trying to unknot my long underwear, find my long socks, and figure out what gear I would actually need to bring along. After another twenty minutes, I was finally ready to embark on the first hunt of the trip.

I had layered sufficiently and felt relatively comfortable, coat over one shoulder and rifle strap slung over the other, and walked out to the waiting group in the SUV.

I opened the front passenger door, set my rifle inside, directing my barrel toward the floor of the vehicle as I had been taught, climbed into the seat, and looked over at Jon, who was sitting behind the wheel looking impatient.

"Well, what are you waiting for?" I said as I shut the door. "Are we going hunting or not?"

Jon simply took a deep breath, put the truck in gear, and drove down the switchback, through the thick patch of timber, across the mud bog, around the field to Grandmother's house . . . . (Sorry, wrong story.)

We reached the intersection for the three roads and turned east. The road took us around a beautiful pond, turned back to the north, up a couple hundred feet in elevation, and then led us into an expansive, open meadow that seemed as though it had no end. The field's western and northern boundaries were heavily wooded, and to the east was a significant foothill with patches of thick timber all the way to its crest. The road wandered for a half mile across the meadow before giving way to a winding route through the woods that became denser with each bend. For fifteen minutes we weaved in and out of the forest, up and over crests and across ridges and small open areas. Then, just over a rise in the road, we found ourselves beside a breathtaking, spring-fed stream bordered entirely by woods and rock formations. The leaves of fall adorned the edges, and the reflection off the surface of the water was a combination of the surrounding trees and the blue sky speckled with wispy white clouds. As we looked ahead down the road, we saw a rather hazardous passage requiring well-above-average driving skills and concentration to cross safely to the other side. The ride was exciting, and I found myself struggling to capture everything at which I was looking — the anticipation of what I would see around the next turn was intense and disruptive, but there was so much to take in, I simply couldn't help it.

We crawled at a snail's pace over naturally smoothed sheets of granite, shale, and silt, avoiding large rocks and boulders, all while trying to navigate the road, which was just under the surface of the water. In one instance, on a higher section of the track and halfway across the obstacle, a fallen tree wedged firmly in place by a rock blocked our way.

Before the car even came to a full stop, Stunt Mouse was out of his seat and walking through the water toward the tree to assess the situation. Jon rolled down the window and suggested returning with a chainsaw a bit later, but within moments, Stunt Mouse had a plan.

He told Jon, "Watch determination at work," and began to relocate a sizable rock (nothing I could've even budged, much less moved somewhere else), putting it next to the tree that lay across the road.

Stunt Mouse then summoned Beanpole and asked him to find a strong branch. He borrowed a small saw I had brought with me to cut branches should I have needed to improve my view from where I would be hunting. Within 5 minutes he had shaped the end of a substantial branch into a wedge, which he then forcefully jammed under the tree to use as a lever.

He positioned the heavy rock directly behind the branch so he could utilize it as a fulcrum, then pushed and pulled on that lever until he freed the tree from nature's stubborn grip.

He and Beanpole then "simply" pushed what had to be a four-hundred-pound section of tree trunk to the side, securing our passage. What could I say? I was really impressed. If it had been my show, I'd have had to call a professional tree-trimming service. I am far from a do-it-yourselfer and could no sooner think out of the box like that than change the oil in my car. (Sad, but true.)

We were moving again, and we emerged from the water hazard none the worse for wear. We drove ahead for what seemed like forever and finally popped out into an opening that allowed us to see for miles in almost every direction.

To our left (west) was a downward-sloping hillside covered in tall grasses that gave way to sage and tumbleweeds. The elevation eventually dropped off at a steep angle into the natural valley on the property known as Deep Canyon—a gorge cut by running water over millions of years that created an elevation difference from where we were driving to the bottom more than 1,400 feet below. Looking straight across the 900-yard-wide chasm, one could see clearly over to the west side of the property and beyond to a mountain range some thirty-five miles away. Looking straight ahead, the road hugged the crest of the hill and then cut sharply to the left and continued down a somewhat gradual grade and disappeared around another hillside. And to the right (east) the grade fell off rapidly into a wickedly dense forest called the Bear Claw.

Jon explained that it was off limits to everyone for now because, in part, it was very hard to keep your bearings inside. He advised that it was a very disorienting place with a surplus of wildlife, most of which was extremely dangerous.

"Incidentally," he continued, "the Bear Claw got its name from the way bears claim and mark their territories. They stand and stretch their front paws as high up a tree as they can reach and mark the tree by deeply clawing the trunk before they urinate at the base of it. Any other bear wandering into this territory will attempt to mark the tree above the previous scratch, and if he can't, he will know he is not the dominant bear and will move on. There are hundreds, if not more, of these marks visible to the naked eye all over the area, and most of the marks are relatively new."

Despite real effort, I couldn't see more than ten feet into the woods. I then made a mental note that, based on Jon's description of the area and the name alone, it was unlikely, at best, that I would ever voluntarily set foot in there—ever.

We drove to the end of the ridge where the road turned ninety degrees to the left. There Jon stopped and let me out of his black Suburban. He directed me down a path straight ahead, then right into the woods at the marker, and said I would find a fence line about three hundred yards into the trees running east-west. He explained that there was an opening cut for the fence that offered about fifteen feet of open ground on either side of it, and deer often cross the property line there.

"Sit at the top of the hill and watch the fence for deer jumping over. Take a shot if you can get one down. I'm going to head down the road and drop the rest of these guys off. Get on your way," he coached.

My head was swimming. The nonstarters in that pile of instructions were staggering. My nervous (and completely justified) rant started at the top and ran down the list.

"Are you even close to serious? I've never been big-game hunting, period, and you intend to send me into the woods alone? You're going to send me in so deep that I won't have any roads for reference? What if I get lost? And if I'm not mistaken, this is the bear thing! Have you lost your mind completely?"

Jon smiled and, trying to calm me, said, "Freddie, relax. The Bear Claw starts two hundred yards to your southeast from where you'll be, and sits at a lower elevation. As far as getting lost, you're walking a thousand yards due south down this two-track," he said as he pointed to a trail directly in front of where I was standing, "and then turning east, or right, at the neon-orange marker on the tree branch. That's the property line. Walk straight into the woods three hundred yards and you will see a fence. Sit down and shoot at any mature buck on the right side of the fence — just don't shoot any on the other property. If the deer gets over the fence going north, you can't chase it or collect it. And as far as getting lost, just stand up, turn around, and walk straight out the way you went in until you see the orange marker again. Then turn and follow the trail up to this spot. I'll be back in three hours."

Besides being confronted with confusing words in his directions, like "south" and "east," now I had to worry about ethics, sportsmanship, and survival — without any help — for three hours! I was in so over my head it was scary . . . literally. So off I went knowing full well I wouldn't be able to find my way back and accepting the likelihood that I would be spending the night out there in very close proximity to the Bear Cage, or whatever the heck it was, where people get lost regularly and are often chased and consumed by predatory monsters lurking in the Northern Utah version of the Bermuda Triangle.

Obviously my imagination was getting the best of me as I walked down the seemingly endless trail. I was sweating, though I wasn't sure whether it was because I was hot or terrified, and all I could think about was why I had signed up for this nonsense. I could have been home right at that moment in St. Louis, Missouri, in weather just as cold as this was, but with the option of staying inside and watching TV shows about people getting lost in the woods and eaten by heaven-knows-what rather than actually being one of those fools in real life.

I looked up and there it was: the orange marker. It was a small piece of hunter's ribbon tied to a branch on a sapling which was only about five feet tall. While it sounds innocuous enough, it may as well have been the Grim Reaper himself standing over me pointing down the path to my certain end. I took a deep breath, adjusted my big-boy pants, and took ten brave and deliberate strides directly into the timber, which to me at the time may as well have been like wading into the River Styx. I stood there defiantly for a moment, drew in another deep breath and took just a brief inventory of the situation.

I thought, *I'm in the woods, alone, with zero confidence, zero experience, and no bartender or servers in sight. But I am armed, so I guess that makes it all okay.*

I began walking as I was told, in an effort to locate the fence line. After what seemed like an eternity and well more than three hundred yards, well past when my mind had started to believe that I had missed it somehow and was hopelessly lost as I'd expected, I walked right up to the landmark as though I had intentionally marched straight to it with the precision of GPS — which, by the way, wasn't even a thing yet.

Well, as you may imagine, I was pretty impressed with myself. Granted it wasn't as if I had just led troops out of harm's way thanks to my keen directional aware-ness, but I had accomplished something I'd never thought I could. That was a big moment for me. So I took my rifle off my shoulder, sat down next to a tree, racked a cartridge into the chamber, and diligently watched the narrow clearing for sets of antlers with every confidence that I would not only see a shooter, but that I would get my first mule deer right there.

I was seated at the crest of a hill that fell away in front of me at roughly a 5 percent grade. It was fifty yards to the bottom of this hill and about the same up the other side to the top, beyond which I could see nothing. I had a great view of anything trying to cross that divide for a hundred yards, and I was excited.

It didn't take long for me to become somewhat disenchanted as my confidence waned with the lack of game. I watched that fence for two hours and didn't see one living organism. To make matters worse, the silence was deafening until I really started listening, at which time every single noise I did hear fed my paranoia to the point that I was driving myself (already a bit unstable) completely bananas. I just tried to remember to breathe and calmly think about what I was going to do to Jon if I made it out of there alive.

I was considering pulling his toenails off one by one with pliers, pouring syrup on his back and pushing him onto an ant hill, or possibly just forcing him to drink from our colleague's spit cup. The options were endless and, admittedly, both a welcome distraction and an amusing source of entertainment.

With that I noticed movement in the tree next to me. I calmly looked up and saw a red squirrel darting through the intertwined branches above me. I watched him for a strong five minutes as his antics were quite riveting. When I finally looked back down at the Alley of Stillness and Boredom, there was something distinctly different about the view. A short way down the slope at forty yards was a mule deer peering out from the woods on the in-play side of the fence. I could only see his face and limited portions of his rack as he was still tucked into the trees.

My heart started pounding and I slowly raised my rifle and looked through the scope. It was a buck, all right, but I couldn't yet see how mature he was or even get a good angle for an acceptable kill shot. I waited patiently for a time, and then, as if he'd played this game before, he dashed from the cover of the trees, jumped the fence, and then stopped and quartered toward me as if to say, "I saw you the whole time and know you can't shoot me over here."

He stood there patiently staring at me for a moment, as though he were flaunting his mental superiority over me. As contempt brewed inside me, I noticed he was a mature eight-point with some serious mass and tall brow tines. Clearly, he hadn't gotten that old by being careless.

The buck then turned and calmly strutted into the woods on the neighboring property, knowing full well that there was nothing I could do about it. That was the end of that.

This is just an aside, but what in the name of Kelly's corset is with Utah hunters and how they count points? Boy Wonder kept correcting the group when they spoke of "eight-point bucks," saying that they were four-pointers, as you only count one side. That makes no sense to me. And what if it's atypical? Would a five by four be called a four-and-a-half? This counting-only-half business was just senseless. And seriously, if someone told a Utah hunter that he'd started dating a gal with a fantastic pair of legs, would he assume she had four of them? He'd think the guy was dating a Picasso! With the present standard in place, if a Utah hunter told me he had shot a five-point deer, then I really wouldn't be that impressed, when, clearly, he would be expecting a much better reaction. So can we please just get on the same page and learn to count all the points? If it's a schooling deficiency, maybe we can write a letter to the school board and have it cover counting one to ten a bit more thoroughly.

So back to my story. The deer was gone, yet I had previously played that scenario over in my mind, and now I was stunned at the different outcome when faced with the reality of my reaction. I would've thought that I'd be really disappointed to watch a deer get away like that. But to tell you the truth, it was a magnificent sight to experience and a snapshot in time I will remember forever. I sat there for another hour or so hoping to see something else, but that was not to be. I glanced at my watch, unloaded my rifle, and walked back out of the woods.

As I was walking up the trail to meet Jon, I thought to myself how fun the afternoon had been and how impressed with myself I was over what I had been able to accomplish. To tell the truth, I was proud of myself and even had a story to tell.

I reached the orange ribbon and turned back up the initial trail. It was a long walk before I rounded a bend and could see Jon standing waiting by his truck, just as he'd said he would be. As I got close enough to hear him, he shouted, "So how was it? Did you see the big eight-pointer?"

I stopped, tried to process what I had just heard and yelled back with genuine confusion, "How did you know about that?"

He said, "I snuck in and watched from about thirty yards behind you in case you had any problems."

It was then that I understood that he hadn't left me alone in the woods—he wasn't going to let anything happen to me, and he was going to teach me, one way or another, to expand my comfort zone, gain some self-confidence, and learn how to hunt.

I continued up the trail and hopped in the car after what I considered a very successful day, and off we went to explore the rest of the East Road. It was miles and miles of winding road weaving in and out of stands of trees, ponds, and open fields with seas of sagebrush and patches of forest that looked impenetrable. Then came a steep grade in the road, one that maintained a very discomforting angle. The road, which used to be ten feet wide with space on each side for pulling over, shrunk to eight feet wide with, instead of a shoulder, a rock face on one side and a sheer drop on the other.

Jon slowed to a crawl, rolled his window down, and paid close attention to keeping the driver's side of the car on the road by looking down out of his window. Only occasionally did he bother to look ahead through the windshield. I was uncomfortable, to say the least, as the road was still quite muddy and slick. Jon pointed out that these were the switchbacks and that each tier, which accounted for a straight stretch of roughly forty yards, equaled a drop in elevation of about eighty feet, with turns that were remarkably sharp and treacherous.

There were six straight sections and five one-hundred-eighty-degree turns, all of which had to be executed precisely, with virtually no room for error. The sixth turn was a hundred degrees, which then put you on the floor of Deep Canyon (the shallow side) in front of a small river, which we drove across gingerly through eight inches of running water. From there it was a slight turn to the right and a steep, straight climb back up the opposite bank to the top of the four-hundred-foot-high ridge. The only concentration level that could surpass that of Jon's as he navigated this stretch of road was mine as I was quite focused on my well-being and safety. While I'm sure we were concentrating on different things at the time, we both went through a very intense fifteen minutes. When we got to the top of the ridge, I was obviously relieved. And when I told Jon how scary I thought that stretch of "road" was, he just laughed and said, "Live a little, Freddie. It won't kill you. And by the way, you're driving next time."

The ride grew suddenly quiet as we continued down the road to collect the other malcontents who were waiting at various points along the drive back to the cabin. As we picked them up, each one had a story about his first afternoon hunt. They included Stunt Mouse and Boy Wonder, who'd hunted together and actually seen two shooters but passed on them. I was quite pleased thinking that none of their stories had even come close to how well mine had turned out. I was hooked and ready for it to be tomorrow morning already.

True hunters know that the next morning comes quickly enough—most of the time right as one settles into a sound sleep. And as eager as I was to get back out there and hunt, I was told that the rest of the day would surprise me as well.

We arrived back at the cabin, and indeed we were all surprised when Grizzled Adams (Grizzly for short) realized that he had inadvertently locked us out. A couple of us circled the building to check all the doors.

We had hoped to find one unlocked, but all returned with bad news. As we all stared at each other wondering who was going to throw a rock through a window to gain access, our dedicated problem solver shimmied up one of the poles supporting the deck on the upper level. Once he climbed over the deck's railing, he pulled a credit card from his wallet to disable one of the locks on the rather antiquated windows and simply opened it before crawling inside and appearing moments later at the door to let us in. We all applauded him, to which he responded that it was no big deal and, also, that he did all his own stunt work. Well, that, along with his diminutive stature, earned him the name Stunt Mouse. And it stuck despite (or because of) his rigid objection.

We all poured inside to get out of the cold and changed out of our layers, whined and complained about the lack of ability to shower, and gathered around a roaring fire to tell stories, play cards, eat candy until we were almost ill, and abuse one another without mercy. The bonding among hunters (a strange breed, those folks) had hit its full stride, and I had to admit that this was every bit as fun as being in the woods and trying to harvest a deer.

The gloves came off quickly and the insults flew. Sarcasm ran rampant, jokes were obscene and slipping in social acceptance at an alarming pace, and we all laughed until we were ready to cry. We sat around the fire for a few hours getting to know one another and began to play a card game called "Ninety-nine."

For those unaware, in this game, all players place three tokens (pennies, buttons, or, in this case, pieces of candy) before them on the table. The dealer then delivers each player three cards. As the play goes around the table, each player puts down one card. The point total starts at zero and each card adds its face value in points (e.g., a six is worth six points, a face card is worth ten points) except for specific cards that have special values or implications: seven reverses play and does not change the total number of points. An eight is a pass and does not change the total number of points. A nine takes the point total to ninety-nine, or keeps it there if one has already reached ninety-nine. A ten subtracts ten points from the total. And an ace adds either one or eleven points, announced by the player who plays it. After each card is played, the player announces the new total to the table and draws a replacement card. Each player must play a card from his hand without sending the total number of points higher than ninety-nine. This is very easy in the beginning, but play becomes more complex as the total climbs. If a player cannot play a card that keeps the total at or less than ninety-nine, then that player loses the round and forfeits one of his tokens into the pot. The cards are then shuffled and re-dealt, and the process begins again. Players are eliminated when they lose their last tokens, and the overall objective is to be the last player with at least one token remaining. That remaining player is the winner and receives the contents of the pot.

It seemed easy enough for a bunch of educated people, particularly when none of us were drinking. Well, for some reason, Beanpole just couldn't stay focused. Either he was participating in stirring the pot and provoking people, along with the rest of us, and unable to concentrate on his turn coming around, or he was so focused on the game that he would utter unintelligible things under his breath, ostensibly in response to an insult that had been hurled in his direction. Of course, then no one understood what he was mumbling about, which would provoke the question, "What are you talking about now?"

Inevitably, he would get so focused that he would forget to draw a card after playing one, and then he'd suddenly announce that he was out of cards.

This happened multiple times, and he always looked so confused as he sat there with empty hands. It was like watching a ten-year-old getting overly tired — he'd look so sad, as though he had just flushed his goldfish.

It turned the rest of us inside out with laughter each time it happened. Here was a guy who owned and operated his own successful business that grossed many hundreds of thousands of dollars each year, so we all knew he was smart. Actually, he was brilliant, which is what made this so funny. It was entirely out of character, and we were simply amazed. It was inexplicable. He could add and subtract the values of the cards quickly and accurately (not like it was advanced trigonometry, but still), yet he just couldn't grasp having to maintain a total of three cards in his hand. Much to his chagrin, we sat there taking side bets with spare candy in another pot on how many times in a given game he would forget to draw a card after his turn. It became so bad that, more often than not, we were all watching the cards in his hand more than the game we were supposed to be playing. The snickering persisted, and he became so self-conscious that the poor guy began to wonder if he had a real problem. (With friends like us, who needs enemies?)

It was time for dinner, and we were all starving. The chef headed upstairs to prepare dinner, and we all remained downstairs. Occasionally, we would wander up to see if we could assist, though we were really more interested in antagonizing Jon. While he did send us out to the spring with two coolers to collect water for dishes and hygiene practicalities such as brushing teeth, I really had to hand it to him. When he was in the kitchen working (and I mean *working*) he was unflappable and able to multitask to solve problems before they even became issues. Not only could we not get to him, but he was a master of balance as he was able to pick us apart while managing not to burn any one of the dinner's components — and there were plenty of them, to be sure.

To our collective disbelief, when dinner was served, we were each presented with a fresh green salad and dressing as a starter, followed by a complete steak dinner (eighteen-ounce ribeye steaks) served at a perfect medium-rare with loaded baked potatoes and fresh corn on the cob. Dinner was outstanding, and the conversation around the table was all about the day's experiences and what to expect the next, which included the itinerary from our fearless leader.

As dinner was winding down, he advised us that we would be getting up at four a.m. for a quick breakfast and commanded that we all be dressed and ready to leave no later than five. (There's that part about mornings arriving quickly.) The table was adjourned, we all thanked our camp leader for a spectacular dinner, and I commandeered Boy Wonder to help me clear the table and clean up the kitchen. We carefully and respectfully fired Jon (temporarily, of course) and banished him from the upstairs to relax with the group by the fire downstairs. After all, he had earned the break.

Boy Wonder and I then managed to knock out the cleanup detail with relative ease and in short order. We made a good team, mostly, I believe, because he laughed at all my jokes and told me repeatedly that I was hysterical — indeed my most coveted compliment. (My favorite thing in the world is to make people laugh.) I thought he was a really nice kid, and he seemed to look up to me and thought I was the funniest guy in the world — which, of course, I am. We were off to a good start as we all spent the remaining hour of consciousness talking around the fire.

Then, one by one, we dropped like flies. We'd stand, stretch, announce our exhaustion, and head toward the bedroom. At that point, all that was left to do was brave the frigid wind on our way to the outhouse for what we all hoped, when our turn came, was our last visit there for the night. We all survived and managed to avoid being crippled by exposure or devoured by forest-dwelling creatures. We then collectively fell asleep in sixty seconds and slept like logs straight through the night.

5

SURE GLAD I WORKED OUT (THAT ONE TIME TWO YEARS AGO)

The day started out in typical fashion. Jon arose at absurdly early o'clock and was none too quiet about dressing, wandering outside to "read the newspaper," vocalizing his displeasure with how cold he had become "reading" said "newspaper," and finally stomping up the stairs to make breakfast for the rest of us who were still trying, unsuccessfully, to cling to our REM cycles.

Naturally, given yesterday's antics at breakfast, I felt as though I had to be the first one at the table to show Jon that my promise really meant something. I donned my socks, jeans, and a shirt and charged up the stairs at the speed of sloth, earnestly trying not to fall asleep in mid-stride. I arrived at the table, hair sticking straight up and with my eyelids at half-mast. As planned, my arrival preceded the rest of the pack.

Jon took notice and, when all were present, was sure to kick off breakfast with a quick note that I had, in fact, been first at the table. Just as I was basking in the rays of superiority, he continued by dismissing it as a sad attempt to suck up. Yes, the derision had begun earlier than anticipated, but we had to get as much in as we could because today we were going to be spending much more time hunting than degrading one another. We were just making the most of our time together.

Breakfast involved another amazing spread. This time there were eggs, toast, hash browns, sausage patties, and other accoutrements, which made for another sensational start to the day, or whatever label you'd put on this hour. It was, after all, hard to tell as I looked out the window to discover it was still as dark outside as the inside of a casket that had been shut, locked, and buried.

As per usual, the morning report was announced. It included the weather, the approximate pickup times, and details about who was hunting with whom and where. I was assigned to a mountainside hunt clear down at the northwesternmost corner of the ranch near Box Canyon with Jon and Boy Wonder.

Box Canyon, as it was known, was exactly that: tall mountains with rough terrain surrounding a low point with only one way in and out. The mountains were tall enough that most game stayed nestled within, especially because the hunting pressure was low there due to the time-consuming journey to get there and the tough conditions that corner of the ranch was known for—both unstable weather and rugged topography. The landscape was very rocky and barren above the tree line and evenly dotted with parcels of trees below. And the single road in and out of this magnificent geological formation entered from the southwest corner and literally just ended in the fields. It was a strong twenty-five-minute ride down the West Road on a four-wheeler to get where we needed to be, though we stopped just short of entering the canyon.

We pulled off to the side of the road and were nearly frozen despite being dressed for a stroll on the polar ice cap. I had ridden on the back of Jon's ATV while Boy Wonder followed on his own four-wheeler. The sun hadn't risen yet, but you could see morning's predawn light glowing behind the mountains.

Jon explained, in a quiet tone, that we were going to walk a thick patch of trees, north to south, and look for game. I was to climb to roughly fifty yards shy of the top of the foothill that rose out of the ground right next to the road we had just ridden in on. Boy Wonder was to walk up roughly halfway, and Jon would stay close to the bottom. After we reached our positions on the hill, we would then all make eye contact and walk slowly into the woods after seeing the appropriate hand signal—me first, then Boy Wonder five minutes later, and Jon five minutes after that. We were told to walk very slowly through the woods at an even pace. I was instructed not to shoot past a ninety-degree downslope angle, and Boy Wonder was told not to shoot uphill.

I turned around to look at this "hill" that Jon had just instructed me to climb and realized I stood in the shadow of a titanic elevation.

"You expect me to climb *what*?" I asked in utter shock and disbelief. "You have got to be out of your ever-lovin' mind. Whatever you're smokin', don't let the game warden catch you with it!" (This is even funnier when you know that Jon doesn't smoke anything, ever.)

"Freddie," Jon whispered, with a certain amount of encouragement, "Move it . . now! You need to be up there before the sun comes up in fifteen minutes. Don't make me chase you up there!"

I began walking straight up the embankment. (See? All I needed was just a little friendly intimidation.) My eyes were focused on the top, and my mind was focused on when I was going to collapse in a heap of asthma-induced semiconsciousness. Much to my surprise, I was where I needed to be right at the time I was supposed to be there. My heart was ready to explode and I felt searing pain in my quads, but at least I wasn't complaining about it—only because no one was there to listen. I looked down at the two of them, and they signaled me into the trees.

I quietly racked a round into my rifle, held it at the ready, and, once again, bravely and confidently stepped toward the thick brush and disappeared into the woods with my thumb prepared to disengage the safety at a moment's notice.

I was trying to walk on top of the fall leaves as delicately as I could, and I was mindful of my pace so as not to run through the trees and beat the guys to the other side by an hour. The light slowly brightened, and as I began to look around, I was struck by the beauty of all the colors on the trees and under foot on the forest floor. I was amazed by the sound of chirping birds and the calm, interrupted only intermittently by a short breeze that rustled through the trees. It was hard to know at that point whether I was there to tour the scenery or to seek game. I stalked my way through the woods, often having to contend with massive tangles of underbrush and fallen limbs. Other than that, and the fact that I had yet to see anything resembling life on four legs other than a couple of squirrels, it was a fairly pleasant walk.

After about half an hour, I came across a huge mass of thorny vines that had grown together for what must have been a decade. I attempted to scout a way around it and found only one way without having to climb farther up the hill. It was through a very shallow and thankfully dry creek bed under an enormous tree that had fallen across the trench. I couldn't go over the tree as the tangled mess of thorns blocked any reasonable passage. Thus I carefully knelt down and passed my gun through the opening first, then got on my stomach and pulled myself forward. I moved my gun forward a second time, placed it gently on the ground, and pulled myself across the leaves once again.

I repeated this several more times until I was finally on the other side. I stood up with my rifle only to find myself standing in the fork of another large tree that had fallen. As I looked around for the easiest way over or around this obstacle, I noticed a rather large figure in the woods. Upon closer observation, there stood a cow moose with a calf in tow, no less, standing about twenty-five yards away and looking directly at me. Now, I was already quite aware, through warnings from Jon, that cow moose are often extremely defensive, particularly around their young. I was also aware that they would charge if they felt threatened.

I quickly took stock of the situation and reacted (which is to say panicked). I threw my rifle up to my shoulder, disengaged the safety, steadied the gun across the fallen tree, and glared through the scope. I saw nothing. Once I realized that the lens cover was still closed, I flipped it open and tried again. There she stood, staring straight at me.

Now, I wanted to pull the trigger — partly because I had never killed a moose, but mostly because I was scared entirely witless. I was aware that she wasn't in season and that killing a cow and leaving her calf to die alone is, by every ethical hunter's standards, poor form. (I also knew that if I shot an animal out of season without a really good reason, this would certainly be the last time I ever hunted with Jon, who spent a lot of time teaching me integrity, ethics, and safety over success at taking game.)

Those facts did not, however, relieve any of my angst regarding my own safety. As a result, the cross-hairs stayed squarely on her chest. I figured I would just wait her out and eventually she would continue down the hill and become Wonder's problem.

But minutes later, the standoff was still raging. She stood resolutely in place, looking at me and preparing to defend her calf at the slightest provocation while I remained paralyzed by fear and prepared to wet myself if she so much as blinked at me. I didn't know what to do. I figured that if she took one step toward me, I would be justified in shooting her as I was truly frightened for my well-being. But provided she remained standing there, I had no intention of harming her or putting her calf at risk.

Out of sheer terror, I called out to Boy Wonder. I figured he would come to my rescue, but there was no response. *Certainly*, I thought, *he can hear me.* I tried again with a deep breath and a holler. Again, there was nothing. I then realized I was so scared that my voice, which I heard screaming in my ears, was barely an audible whisper to even someone standing next to me in a library. She heard me, though, and offered a rather unfriendly grunt in response. I froze in outright fear.

I could feel chills creeping up my spine and the flood of adrenaline in my body. My knees were weak, and I was shaking noticeably. She grunted again, louder this time, as the fur on her shoulders began to rise and the hackles on the back of my neck stood straight out. I held the rifle as steadily as I could. She grunted one more time and my finger tightened against the trigger. My eyes were fixed on her through the scope, and I could feel the moment of decision rapidly approaching. She glared at me with that "watch-yourself; I-know-where-you-live" look and simply trotted away down the hill.

I went completely limp, having been on high alert for what felt like hours (three minutes, tops). I collected what was left of my composure, re-engaged the safety, climbed over the dead tree, and began pushing forward again while I seriously contemplated what it was I thought I was doing out there.

It was about two and a half hours from the beginning of our stroll through the woods when I popped out the other side into the clearing. Shortly thereafter, I saw Boy Wonder emerge, and as I walked down to meet him, Jon came into view at the base of the hill.

We met near the road and reported to one another what we had seen. Jon recounted an uneventful experience, as did Boy Wonder. I then regaled them with my story of how I faced off with an irreverent cow moose and her offspring, nearly soiling myself in the process, and all while calling out for someone to help yet unable to utter an audibly perceptible syllable. I was nervous again just telling the story. They, on the other hand, were doubled over and unable to breathe while they made fun of me.

We jumped on the four-wheelers and headed back toward the cabin, stopping halfway there to push through another strip of woodland. Jon had Boy Wonder follow him a couple miles down the road to leave one of the ATVs there and brought him back to where I waited. The two of us were directed three hundred yards into the woods and then told to turn south and walk to the ATV down the road. He advised us he was returning to the cabin to cook lunch and would see us there in a few hours. Given that we were huge fans of eating, we let him go and started our hike through the timbers.

Just nine steps in, my thighs were screaming. I hadn't had this much exercise since Field Day in fourth grade, not to mention the fact that we were at high altitude, where the air is thinner and I was laden with twenty-five extra pounds of clothing, gear, and firepower. (*Where's my sherpa? This sucks.*) But Boy Wonder and I pressed on—he much faster than I, given that he was roughly two-thirds my age, just over half my weight and possessed the energy and stamina of the Energizer Bunny (show off!). We trudged three hundred yards in and turned right to begin our trek to the ATV.

We began walking again at a slow pace, all the while keeping a keen eye out for happy woodland creatures to send into the next world. Boy Wonder was also taking account of rubs on trees, areas where animals had bedded down recently, as well as droppings (called sign) indicating the presence of the aforementioned happy creatures.

I thought this was fascinating and started bombarding him with questions—at minimal volume, of course.

Finally, he turned and asked, "Do you want to interview me or hunt? You can't do both. With all this chatter we may as well have brought a radio to see if we could tune in to a football game or something."

The point was well taken, so I did my best to limit the conversation while still trying to learn what he was doing and why he was doing it.

At one point he stopped and looked at a tree rub and mouthed the word, "fresh" to me while pointing at it. Ten steps later, he pointed to an area where all the grass had been stamped down in a small circle with fresh sign only feet away. He looked at me and, with two fingers, pointed at his eyes and then pointed off to our left. I looked over, and about thirty yards away in a small clearing stood a buck with two does.

Boy Wonder began to walk stealthily toward them and indicated to me that I should follow in his exact footsteps by pointing down to his impressions as he walked. Ever so slowly, we inched our way closer to them, the wind directly in our faces, using the trees to mask ourselves. Once we got to within twenty yards of them, we stood there, each behind a tree, and watched them. We were almost close enough to count their eyelashes with the naked eye, and they were beautiful. I was thrilled with the encounter and amazed we were able to get so close. After a few minutes, we backed away from them and left them in peace (so we could go in search of one of their older relatives to shoot) and resumed our long march southward. A bit disappointed at having reached the end of the trees without seeing anything else, we jumped on the ATV and drove off toward the cabin.

We took a brief detour when we saw Beanpole waving us down from the side of the dirt road. We stopped and killed the engine so we could hear what he needed. He began telling us a story and was notably confused.

"I spotted a huge mule deer across the field just inside the tree line. I shot at it but missed. I shot again and it didn't fall. I shot a third time and nothing . . . it didn't even move. Will you guys come take a look at this? I just don't get it."

Boy Wonder and I rolled our eyes at each other and immediately thought Beanpole was a couple sandwiches short of a picnic. We followed him over hill and dale, crossed a small creek, passed through a wooded strip, and stopped on the edge of a field. He pointed across the flats to the opposing tree line and asked us if we could see the deer. Boy Wonder and I both looked through our binoculars and could not see what he was talking about.

He looked through his and described where we were supposed to search.

"Okay," he explained, "starting at the tall dead tree right on the edge of the field . . . got it? Now, look to the right five trees, and there's a rock. Okay, now, just to the right of the rock is what I'm talking about. See?"

Boy Wonder and I still didn't see a deer. But as I looked more carefully, I understood the situation and began to laugh. At first, I was looking for a deer, and clearly there was nothing of the sort out there. Then I started looking for anything that Beanpole could have mistaken for a deer, and it jumped out at me right away. The scrawny tree next to the rock was about five feet tall, and the leaves had been picked off the top two feet, revealing two branches that Einstein cleverly deduced were antlers.

Having forgone the hunting rule that says you're supposed to positively identify your target before shooting at it, Beanpole started peeling the bark off the tree from 325 yards away and just couldn't understand why it hadn't dropped dead.

I mustered up just enough strength between fits to explain it all to Boy Wonder, and now the two of us were stumbling around at the field's edge ready to wet our pants. Expectedly, Beanpole suddenly became defensive.

"No. That can't be it," he argued. "It had legs. I know I saw legs."

This put Boy Wonder and me over the edge. I seriously didn't know if I was going to make it back to the cabin. I was crying, I was laughing so hard.

"I don't know how to break it to ya', Big Guy," I said as I put my hand up on his shoulder. "It is what it is . . . and it's a shrub."

He was devastated, and Boy Wonder and I were dumbfounded — this guy was an experienced hunter. We laughed all the way back to the ATV before the three of us hopped on and made our way back to the cabin. We arrived at about eleven-thirty, and, naturally, Boy Wonder and I double-timed it up to the kitchen to find Jon elbow-deep in some horrific concoction sitting on a burner.

"You've got to hear this one," announced Boy Wonder with me by his side. "This is epic. Tell him, Freddie."

I articulated the story to Jon as he diced onions and threw them in the giant soup pot on the stove. Jon gave the occasional eyebrow raise in disbelief, which eventually gave way to an audible, "You're kidding." That was then followed by the raising-of-head-with-jaw-slightly-open look, which finally culminated with a, "Seriously? Swear it's true?" that we were only too eager to affirm.

Jon dropped his knife and laughed so hard I thought we were going to need to resuscitate him. Just then, Beanpole arrived upstairs and walked toward us with lips pursed to begin offering an excuse, at which time I spoke as if to "defend" him and mocked, "Really, Beanpole should be commended for his remarkable identification of the rare and elusive topiary mule deer—a bush that more closely resembled a Vegas showgirl's feathered headdress than an actual game animal. He should be celebrated and his ID and reasoning technique should be taught in schools: 'Don't be fooled by something standing with its four legs so close together that they resemble a tree trunk. Don't be misled by something with fur that emulates that of a Chia Pet. If it has pointy things sticking up from the top, you should start shooting at it and figure the rest out later.'"

Realizing that there was no chance of avoiding the full treatment on this one, Beanpole simply turned on his heels and went back downstairs without so much as a single word. Meanwhile, the three of us left in the kitchen were in hysterics—fueled even more by Jon's revelation that he'd cut his finger when he looked up during the story. He had been bleeding all over the floor for five minutes and hadn't had the slightest inkling.

Shortly thereafter, our attention turned to all things edible. What can I say? I was starving. It appeared that the mile-high deli sandwiches which were carefully stacked on the cutting board behind Jon were slated for lunch. However, we were also curious as to what the science experiment in the pot on the stove was.

Jon smiled broadly and said, "Chile con Grizzly. It's a tradition from which recovery is doubtful—or at least agonizing."

He explained that the pot's contents were scheduled to steep and percolate until dinner, at which time we would all draw straws to see who got the use of the outhouse first after eating it.

It sounded like a perilous endorsement if I'd ever heard one, but it didn't frighten me too badly as my stomach is rather strong and I happen to like spicy food. I really didn't give it much more attention than that because I was far more focused on the sandwiches. I assisted Grizzly in getting lunch on the table, along with the chips and drinks, and then proceeded to round up our merry little band of lunatics for the midday chow down.

Lunch was a raucous affair. It began with a celebration of Beanpole's vicious and relentless assault upon a defenseless deciduous hedge and continued with barbs about my encounter with the cow moose and bets as to whether or not I actually had to change my outfit when I returned to the cabin. In other words, it was pretty much business as usual.

That was until Boy Wonder discovered a splinter from his exploits in the field. This was a minor distraction in an otherwise totally discombobulated lunch experience.

Everyone was trying to talk over everyone else to get their insults officially logged and approved with laughter from the group while Boy Wonder's splinter declaration went almost entirely without sympathy.

Jon excused himself from the table and disappeared out the back door off the kitchen. He'd been gone for a solid fifteen minutes by the time I went out searching for him and found him standing in the middle of the field behind the cabin in the shadow of the crescent mountain. I walked out to him, and as I got closer noticed he was on his cell phone. When I asked if everything was okay, he nodded and explained that the only place on the entire property that had cell reception was this very spot in a three-foot-by-three-foot square. He then mentioned that he was on the phone with his wife and that he'd be right in.

I couldn't resist the opportunity, so I asked if I could say hi. He handed the phone to me, and we began a short conversation. She asked me how I was doing, and in my best sad, lonely, and pathetic voice, I whined, "Jon's being really mean to me. I don't think my self-esteem will ever recover."

Meanwhile I had a grin on my face from ear to ear, and when I looked at Jon, he knew instinctively that he had just gotten played.

"It'll be fine, Freddie," she said. "Put him back on the phone, please."

With that I reverted to my energetic, happy self and answered, "Okay — miss you!" and handed the phone back to Jon.

As I walked away, I could hear her yelling at the top of her lungs, "You be nice to that boy or you're going to be in big trouble when you get home!"

Jon was literally holding the phone away from his head, and I could hear her threatening him as clearly as if she were standing right beside him.

That was truly a laugh worth having, or so I thought until I realized that once Jon hung up that phone, she couldn't save me from him. Admittedly, my pace toward the cabin and the witnesses within increased.

Once we were both back inside at the table, Jon's ear still red from the scolding he'd received from his wife, Boy Wonder mentioned his finger again and closely examined his digit with a pained expression on his face, adding that it really hurt.

By now, lunch was largely over and we were waiting for our fearless leader to tell us where we would be hunting for the afternoon. After he made a point to dismiss Boy Wonder's incessant whining about his wounded limb, Jon paired us off and sent Beanpole and Stunt Mouse down the Middle Road and told them to find a place that looked good. They were both experienced hunters, and Jon was clearly not concerned about them getting lost or doing something unsafe. Then he sent Boy Wonder and me to a picturesque point atop two draws that came together looking over a sprawling vista of quaking aspens reaching as far as the eye could see.

There were open patches with watering holes and small clearings scattered about to our right, and our vantage point provided an amazing view of the hillside falling away to our left. Before us, we could peer through the canopy of leaves and spy any game wandering about the forest. We sat toward the edge of the point, loaded our rifles, and started to glass the countryside.

It wasn't long before we saw our first mulies. There were four of them, two bucks and two does, padding among the aspens on their way across the ridge to our left. Over the course of an hour, they cautiously made their way down the hill to the edge of the draw below us. They were shielded by the cover of the trees and only visible for a moment as they disappeared beneath the point. We slowly stood and, in an effort to improve our view, repositioned ourselves thirty yards to the right so we could see them emerge from the protection of the rocks and make their way to the watering hole.

Boy Wonder watched through his binoculars, and I lay down on my stomach, rifle at the ready, observing through my U. S. Optics scope. (If any of you are curious about whether or not there is life on Mars, be my guest to look through a U.S. Optics scope to find out. They are incredible pieces of optical hardware.) Some twenty minutes later, the foursome emerged. I had an unobstructed quartering shot at either buck, but, sadly, both were small six-pointers (or three-pointers, for those of you keeping score in Utah) that had paused briefly to graze. We decided to let them walk, but what a sight it was. We watched them all the way to the water and saw them drink and then stride into the timber again as they headed for Deep Canyon.

Boy Wonder and I didn't see much the rest of the afternoon, but, again, the experience was magical for me. I started to appreciate the notion that a hunter doesn't have to actually kill something, or even fire a shot, to have a successful hunt. Aside from being cold, this was turning out to be an incredible adventure.

We gathered our things and walked back through the woods to the road, where we sat and talked about what our loved ones were most likely doing back in the real world while we had the privilege of experiencing this remarkable week. I bet we chatted for an hour before Jon made his way from the cabin to pick us up.

When he arrived, the Great White Hunter was with him, spit cup at the ready, and they were jawboning about the first dead deer of the trip.

Apparently, the Great Hunter had killed it just down the road from where we were, but on the other side of the ridge and well down an embankment near the edge of the dark and mysterious Bear Claw.

All the way back to the cabin, we had to listen to the old codger tell us how easy it was and how, "If you young'uns would just listen . . . blah, blah, blah," we'd have already filled a tag of our own.

The way he told the story about killing his deer, you'd think that there had been a spectacular hand-to-hoof combat bout from which he had finally emerged victorious by rolling over on top of the deer and strangling it with his bare hands. It was clearly a shameless ploy to impress the green city guy and the young kid, although we were both old enough to recognize a load of meadow muffins when presented with one. I never doubted for a moment that he had killed a deer, but I guessed that the more accurate version of the story was that the deer walked near where the Great Hunter likely was napping under a tree and expired in its tracks upon being rendered disoriented and eventually incapacitated by the stench of the tobacco-laced saliva emanating from his drool repository.

Regardless of the details—which, by the way, changed every time he told the story throughout the trip—he had the first deer down, and it was a dandy. In fact, Jon claimed that it was the largest deer ever killed on the ranch. It was a stocky, broad-shouldered old mule deer with perfectly symmetrical antlers boasting six points per side and unrivaled mass at the base. The inside spread looked like you could drive a car between the antlers, and their height was quite significant. The buck was a monster and truly one to behold. The Great Hunter really set the benchmark for the trip and the ranch. (To this day, that deer mount hangs proudly on the wall at his store.)

When we returned to the cabin, there was, in fact, another deer hanging from the beam under the deck.

(The dead animals were hung in this fashion so the meat didn't rot.) As it turned out, Beanpole was on the board as well. I surmised that he had taken aim at another ten-point piece of vegetation and mistakenly dropped the unseen deer that was standing behind it.

While my guess was a realistic one, the real account was much more exciting. He claimed that he took the buck (a rather thick deer with a solid eight-point rack sporting some serious brow tines) with a five-hundred-plus-yard shot that felled the deer with a double-lung pass-through shot. Stunt Mouse was right there to corroborate the entire story and credited BP with a great technical shot. In the end, we were all happy for our two friends, but even happier that we were now officially prepared to donate food to the Salt Lake City pantries benefiting the less fortunate during these cold months. This was, in fact, part of what we had come to do.

We were off to a fairly good start, but we all had multiple tags to fill, so there was still a lot of work to do.

Jon pulled me aside and said, "There're still two hours of light. Let's go see if we can make something happen."

The two of us piled back into the Suburban and drove back down the East Road to a stretch that bordered some thick woods, which Jon promised me was not the terrifying Bear Claw.

The idea, he said, was to put me in the vicinity of a known watering hole that remained largely untouched by human traffic throughout the hunting seasons because it was remote and difficult to reach.

As we exited the vehicle and collected our gear, Jon tried to allay my reservations about walking so far into such isolation. Naturally, he casually left out that he would be leaving me by myself in the woods to watch the sun set into oblivion, but that's a different tangent.

We walked into the woods together, Jon with all the confidence in the world, and me on the verge of wetting my camouflage overalls. It was a forty-minute hike through the dense, quaking aspen thickets and patches of dark timber. Grizzly was mindful of pointing out fresh cat tracks to heighten the already mind-numbing fear that I was going to be eaten at any moment, while also suggesting how quiet and tranquil it seemed. My anxiety was at an all-time high—that is, until we arrived and he told me that he was going to be waiting a hundred yards away "over there" (as he pointed off in some direction that I failed to notice through my blind panic). My anxiety's all-time high was surpassed by an alarming margin just as quickly when he disappeared over a small hill and into a shroud of evergreen. I found myself alone in the timber with nothing but my camo gear, my required orange, my new rifle, and a cataclysmic sense of dread.

I sat on the damp hillside in a small clearing surrounded by aspens, with a curtain of evergreens shielding my view of the watering hole. Every noise commanded my full attention, and I felt as though my head was on a swivel.

The aspens swaying in the breeze, squeaking and crackling all around me, raised the hairs on my arms (and everywhere else) and only underscored the fact that I was alone in a desolate, cold, and unforgiving environment just waiting to be dismembered by a mountain lion or some other terrifying creature.

The more alone and helpless I felt, the more convinced I became that there was something watching me and lying in wait.

And then, as if I weren't paranoid enough already, off in the distance I heard a blood curdling sound. It was the sound of women screaming in horror and of demons laughing and mocking their intense fear. The sound grew closer and louder, and I began to hear the rustle of leaves as this ghostly force danced through the woods just beyond my sight.

My body was a shivering mass as I sat waiting for a glimpse of whatever was floating through the darkness. It was as if I were trapped in a scene that was a cross between *The Blair Witch Project* and *The Hound of the Baskervilles*. I had goose pimples in places I didn't know you could have goose pimples. And as quickly as it approached, it was past and gone again; the howling, huffing, and wailing were in the wind again as the pack of coyotes I never saw ran back into the depths of the forest.

More terrified and excessively alert than ever, I laid my rifle across my lap again and looked desperately for Jon, who was nowhere to be seen. And just as I made a decision to call out to him, I heard a small branch snap in front of me.

It popped with a determination and certainty that made me realize that it wasn't just the wind or ambient noises playing tricks on me. No, this was something else altogether . . . it was *something*.

My concentration snapped into focus directly in front of where I sat with my rifle. I glared under the evergreens with acute awareness and within moments began to hear deliberate footsteps in the leaves layered over the rocks. Four legs appeared behind the trees and slowly walked from left to right toward the end of the row of pines. A cold bead of sweat ran down my back, and immediately I was flooded with adrenaline for the second time in minutes. I slowly raised the rifle stock to my shoulder, removed the safety, and followed the legs through my scope in great anticipation of what was going to emerge from the cover. The legs reached the end of the row of trees and left me entirely unprepared for what I saw.

From behind the evergreens stepped a majestic six-by-six bull elk. He was twenty-five yards away, and my crosshairs were locked on his leading shoulder. He was so close I could literally count his nose hairs and watch his nostrils flare as he breathed. His steps were carefully measured, yet resolute, as he stepped into the open. He walked twenty yards ahead and paused to carefully pick something up in his mouth before casually turning and walking up the hillside to my right. He would pause every few steps to survey his surroundings and then continue. When he reached a point where he was ninety degrees from my position, he paused again, turned to his right, and began pacing forward. I was directly in his path and he was stepping toward me without a clue I was there.

It became clear that I was going to have to do something. The real dilemma was that I knew elk season had ended several days before, so this animal was not legal to shoot. But I figured a couple more steps in my direction would constitute a situation where I was in danger and therefore authorized to fire. The bull stepped closer and closer still until he was literally twenty-five feet from me. With my heart nearly in my throat, I counted to three inside my head and spun ninety degrees to my right (still on my butt) to face the bull head-on holding my gun steady, with the crosshairs precisely positioned in the center of his neck. My finger was inside the guard and pressed against the trigger. Pressure started to build on the lever that would release a shot certain to kill this beautiful animal and potentially label me a poacher and poor sportsman in the eyes of a personal friend and hero. Indeed, it was a predicament that had me weighing my safety against my perceived (yet coveted) integrity — I would always know I had done what I had to do, if in fact I had to shoot. But without any witnesses, I was fearful of what others would think.

The bull stopped in his tracks when I spun around. He looked at me for a moment, trying to figure out what exactly I was. We made eye contact and both shared what I felt was a moment of mutual fear and respect, and then, with a quick turn and a burst of speed, he ran four or five strides and stopped again. My rifle still on my shoulder and my eye still looking through the scope as I kept the crosshairs true, he looked back over his shoulder at me one last time and then ran into the woods.

I was breathless. I was shaking. I was sweating. I was exhilarated. And I was an honorable hunter. I called out for Jon, who walked over the hill and approached me. "Did you see it?" he said.

I couldn't speak. "I . . . he was behind the trees . . . and then he was right there . . . and he looked at me . . . it was less than ten yards . . . and my gun . . . and WOW! It was incredible!"

I could barely get the words out, and Jon was truly excited for me. He could tell I had had an amazing experience, and I was sure he was eager to hear about it once I remembered how to talk.

"Was it a big elk?" he asked.

"Of course it was big!" I exclaimed. "Are you kidding? It was enormous! It's the first whole one I've ever seen!"

We hiked back to the car in the fading light, and the walk through the woods this time seemed to fly by. I suppose my mouth was flapping nonstop trying to tell Jon what had just happened to me, and naturally I couldn't wait to tell my story to the guys back at the cabin.

The drive seemed shorter than usual as well. We returned to the cabin as the very last bit of sunlight disappeared beyond the horizon — and I was still talking.

We went inside, changed, and got a roaring fire going so we could all sit down and share our adventures of the day. As we settled into the supple leather couches in anticipation of some great hunting stories, we heard Boy Wonder pipe up and say, "Gosh. My finger still really hurts. That splinter is a bad one."

"Again with the splinter?" queried Stunt Mouse. "You are such a weenie. It's a splinter! Let me look at it." He grabbed Wonder's hand and examined the tip of his index finger, palm side up.

"I don't see anything," Mouse grumbled.

"It's right there near the bendy part, under the knuckle," Wonder whined.

Stunt Mouse got a look of horror on his face and exclaimed, "You mean that huge sliver that's nearly two millimeters long just under the skin? My goodness, what a terrible wound! Jon, come look! Do you think you can save his hand?"

We all burst out laughing, which set Boy Wonder off down a dangerous path as he barked back at Stunt Mouse, "Well, at almost two millimeters top to bottom, it's bigger than you are!"

Stunt Mouse stood up and invited Boy Wonder to do the same, and things got a bit too serious for my liking.

"Settle down, Mouse. I'd embarrass you," said an overly confident and completely misinformed Boy Wonder as he stood to confront the instigator.

Wonder went to wrap up Stunt's arms, but in the blink of an eye, Mouse went low, took him down, and, with the agility and speed of a rodeo cowboy roping and tying off a calf, rolled the kid and twisted him into a pretzel, leaving him without use of a single extremity. It was over before it started, yet there was Wonder, tied in a knot on the floor, gasping for air while Mouse had not even changed the expression on his face.

He let Wonder up with a friendly warning, saying, "Let it be over now," as he extended his hand in peace.

Wonder said, "Next time I'll just take you outside and beat you to death there."

Mouse handled it about as well as I could've imagined. He smiled and remarked, "Your mouth is still flapping because I'm guessing you didn't learn anything from being body slammed and pinned the first time. For your own safety, please don't make me teach you the lesson again. Just be smart enough to shake on it and let it be over. We're all friends here."

And to both their credit, that was the end of it . . . until, of course, we all started mocking the exchange.

Having served as an EMT in one of his previous lives, Grizzly promised to take a look at Wonder's finger after dinner. He then stood up and said we were all to be at the dinner table in fifteen minutes and excused himself to walk upstairs.

We all washed up and wandered upstairs to the table, where Jon was stirring a huge pot of Chili con Grizzly with a giant wooden spoon. He had a look on his face that worried me as I had seen that look years prior in a duck blind just before he'd perpetrated a vicious prank on one of his friends.

"Gather 'round, my sheltered minions," he said. "It's time to partake in a tradition here at the ranch. I hope you enjoy your first experience with Chili con Grizzly." (I half expected to hear that evil laugh so prevalent in the spooky cartoons I used to watch growing up.)

With that, we were each served a healthy portion — and when I say healthy, I mean huge. It was like eating out of a Roman bathing vessel.

As I waited my turn for a bowl, I couldn't imagine there was anything healthy about what I was about to introduce into my system.

"Is it hot?" I asked.

With a grin and a sinister tone, Jon responded, "Fire goin' in — napalm comin' out."

The mixture being ladled into the bowls was a dark brown sludge with the consistency of semi-dried stucco with ground beef, onions, beans, and corn visible to the eye. The smell was unique, boasting a high concentration of spices — likely salt, black pepper, chili powder, and cayenne pepper used in a quantity one would expect to find in pepper spray. But the proof was in the taste. After all, it was a tradition. But the mystery was whether it was a tradition that people enjoyed or one a person needed to endure and survive in order to be inducted into the club. I mustered the courage with the attitude that there was only one way to find out — that, of course, and the fact that I was starving and there were no other options.

I courageously put a spoonful of this experiment-gone-wrong in my mouth and was pleasantly surprised. Sure, it was as hot as a dragon's breath during a bout of heartburn, but it was actually pretty good. In fact, we all said that it passed the taste test, and some of us even went back for seconds.

We asked how it became tradition, whose recipe it was and how it had evolved. Jon laughed and explained that over the years it had taken many forms; one year, he left it unattended, and everyone on the trip decided to walk past the pot and add their own special surprise ingredient. He mused about how, in addition to the cereal, pancake syrup, and can of Dr. Pepper that had at one time or another found their way into the pot, a touch of dishwashing soap had also been added to the mix on one occasion.

We were all horrified. Jon was in stitches as he recounted the fits of diarrhea it had caused within the group, the worst case ironically belonging to the half-wit who had added the soap.

He digressed and said that he would not divulge the secret recipe but was very happy that we all liked it.

I then made the mistake of asking what I thought was a pretty innocuous question: "Why did you put corn in a chili? I've never seen that before."

Again, he smiled and explained, "I use the corn as an indicator."

When I asked for what, he replied, "This stuff tastes good, but it does remarkably terrible things to your system. I will put this as delicately as I can: when you stop seeing corn, all your troubles have passed . . . literally."

He started laughing, and we all put our spoons down, realizing that the inevitable was merely hours away and we had only one outhouse.

We all stood up from the table and, as I cleared it and moved to the kitchen to clean up, Jon summoned Boy Wonder and his throbbing finger to a pair of chairs at another table with a good lamp nearby.

Wonder sat in the chair opposite Grizzly and offered his hand so Jon could see what all the fuss was about. Jon adjusted his readers at the end of his nose and then, from an old zippered pouch, pulled a pair of tweezers, a straight pin, and an old pocket knife before declaring that he would get the splinter out one way or another.

A gallery of onlookers collected around the pair while Jon adjusted his glasses again for maximum effect and began to dig persistently into Boy Wonder's finger, all the while trying to calm him with soothing comments like, "Stop being such a whiner," "It doesn't hurt that bad," and "Hold still, you coward!"

The compassion was boundless. We all decided that we would give Jon a chain saw as a thank you in case another guest ever got a splinter, so he could offer faster and less painful treatment. Meanwhile, we all took special pride in ribbing Wonder for the rest of the night, telling him how lucky he was that he hadn't lost his arm in the horrible incident.

After fingers and egos alike were bandaged, we all adjourned to the fire downstairs, where we offered three more logs to the fire gods and settled in to play cards while Jon hoarded his Cinnamon Bears. It was another night of levity, and we finally got to hear the hunting stories we had hoped to hear earlier in the evening before the wrestling match had broken out.

The conversation quickly switched courses from hunting stories to haunting realities as one by one, each of our digestive system's resolve was tested and the chili made its presence known from within.

The Great White Hunter silenced the room with a resounding, low-toned, evenly paced emission that halted all conversation as though someone had ripped the needle across an old vinyl record spinning on the turntable. We were all stunned momentarily and then began to laugh. (C'mon, we're a bunch of guys up in the mountains who have hall passes to act like teenagers. Of course passing gas is funny!)

Things deteriorated rapidly as each of us began to process the lava we had consumed just hours before. Within minutes, you could cut the haze with a machete, and the noxious fumes were debilitating.

Finally, Stunt Mouse stood up and declared that he needed to be excused to the sandbox before he had a serious mishap. "Pretty soon," he said, "one of these isn't going to be the casual bit of gas I expect it to be."

He turned around, took three steps toward the door, buckled at the knees, and fell to the floor clutching his stomach.

"I think I'm gonna have a problem," were the exact words that floated across the room in the direction of the group, which, at this point, was laughing uncontrollably.

Jon's immediate comment was, "Not on my carpet, you're not! Get outside!"

We all just laughed harder rather than help the poor guy. He struggled to his feet and ran out the door to the fun house, leaving a virtual smoke trail behind him. (For the record, we never figured out whether the smoke trail was from his exiting pace or a rear-facing orifice already under severe duress.)

While Mouse was having his life-altering moment out in the freezing cold, Boy Wonder decided to mess with him a bit by taking a single log off of the pile next to the fireplace (stacked three deep, four long, and eight or more high) and placing it inside Mouse's sleeping bag all the way down at the foot. We all laid bets as to whether or not he was tall enough to find it and then waited for his return, which, by the way, wasn't for a solid twenty minutes.

Mouse finally returned from his traumatic experience and declared that he had survived round one, but that round two was not far behind.

"I think my lower intestine is disintegrating," Mouse uttered. He wiped the sweat off his forehead and walked closer to the group around the fire to address us, suddenly slightly agitated, inexplicably demanding to know where the missing log was and gesturing emphatically at the wood pile.

We were all caught completely off guard. Who would notice something like that? Seriously?

"There's a log missing from the stack," he said with conviction as he gestured toward the pile again.

What could we say? He was absolutely correct in keenly observing the log's absence, but that didn't make it any less bizarre. Beanpole casually remarked that we had put another log on the fire, but Mouse, not believing him for a second, demanded to know what really had become of the log. We all shrugged our shoulders, branded him a paranoid and certifiable nitwit, and resumed our card game while he marched around the room looking for this piece of wood as if it were his wedding ring that he had misplaced.

He finally gave up after searching high and low for five minutes and announced with a great deal of frustration and doubt about our explanation that he was going into the other room. "You're all a bunch of liars! I'm going to bed."

After what couldn't have been more than a minute, he ran from the bedroom with the log in hand declaring excitedly that he *knew* he wasn't crazy — which pretty much clinched it for us that, in fact, he was.

"I knew you were all liars! I've got it right here," he shouted as he stood in the middle of our group in his underwear holding up the log over his head as though he had just won the U. S. Open trophy.

Anyone who's that neurotic about a piece of firewood and that proud of finding it in a sleeping bag ought to be fitted with a white jacket with long sleeves that tie in the back and left in a padded cell for at least a minute or two.

When he asked why we'd put it in his sleeping bag, Boy Wonder spoke up and said, "Because, in all honesty, we didn't think you were tall enough to ever notice it."

We howled at Mouse's expense and got back to the business at hand, which was playing cards, burning firewood, eating candy, and suddenly jumping to our feet to sprint out the door so we could pay homage to the chili spirits.

It was a long, long night — with many cold, cold trips outside, which left us all very, very tired in the morning, and so, so raw — and we were all terribly, terribly sorry we had ever, ever consumed Chili con Grizzly.

Oh, the humanity, the indignity of it all. Can you even for a moment imagine walking all over creation the next day as chafed as we were? I thought we were all going to need skin grafts and sphincter transplants.

6

FROM WITCHES' THIMBLES TO THE LION'S DEN

As had become expected, the four a.m. wake-up holler arrived altogether too quickly, particularly when taking into account the two or three trips each of us had made to the outhouse in the middle of the night. Waking in a cold sweat from a dead sleep only to realize that we had roughly thirty seconds to get boots on and sprint for the "Loo with a View" before permanently ruining our sheets took quite a toll on our quality of rest. Our eyes were swollen from a lack of sleep, our attitudes were merely a shadow of what they had been only hours before, and our stomachs were reeling. (And that's to say nothing of our hindquarters. I can only speak for myself, but I will tell you that there was a pain and tenderness there that I was certain I would never forget—and haven't.)

Breakfast was another crowd pleaser that included two pounds of freshly made bacon, a mountain of toast with butter and jam, and enough scrambled eggs, of all things, to feed an army — which was just what a group of guys suffering from intolerable flatulence needed. (As if the stench wasn't rancid enough.)

People were still occasionally running from the table in the aftermath of last evening's chili festival, which continued its damaging rampage through our intestines. And thanks to Jon and his indicator, we all knew the battle was far from over.

We were slow to get outside that morning (at least for the hunt anyway).

Each time we thought we were ready to leave, someone fell victim to a last-minute emergency requiring his immediate and undivided attention in the outhouse. It was a frustrating process, but one to which nobody was immune.

We were finally on the road, but over an hour past our target time. Jon had sent Beanpole and Stunt Mouse to Box Canyon and asked them to drop off Boy Wonder anywhere down the West Road at a place of his choosing. He sent the Great White Hunter to the halfway point of the Middle Road, where Jon advised him to walk east into the aspens until he could see Deep Canyon. Then he was to watch the game trails, which intersected just before descending into the chasm. This left Jon and me to hunt together for the first time since we had arrived on the ranch.

We took an ATV and headed down the Middle Road a bit more than halfway to the gate and pulled into the grass on the side of the road. We collected our gear and walked westward down an embankment, across a small creek, and then up a hill into a patch of trees. We navigated the thicket and walked out onto an amazing open field that Jon called Bluebell Flats, named after a flower also referred to as Witches' Thimbles, which, when in bloom, painted the entire two-hundred-acre field in a stunning array of blue, violet, and lavender hues. A small bit of the color remained, literally frozen in time. But it being October, nearly all of it had surrendered to the elements.

We walked all the way across Bluebell Flats and into a dense tree line that was merely a thin ribbon separating Bluebell Flats from another open space.

Settled at the base of a tree, Jon pulled out his binoculars while I got situated against another with my rifle at the ready. We were positioned just inside the tree line and dressed in full camo and the required orange accessories. The ground in front of us sloped away into a pasture with a grassy foothill rising up out of the pitch. The tall grass was golden in color, and there were only a few trees for hundreds of yards. We glassed the scenery but saw nothing, at least for the time being.

We got to talking about whether or not I was having a good time, if I was getting along with everyone, and whether I was learning anything besides never to eat his chili again—all the things good friends would talk about when one of them is the other's host and genuinely trying to make the trip something special for them. We laughed about all the times we had shared in the past, how close we'd become over the years, and even about how little I had known about hunting before I met him. (At that point, I had no concept of how much more there was to know or that I would still be learning even two decades later.)

We must have yakked for an hour before I noticed two bucks had walked right into our view at about one hundred sixty yards. They were just padding along, grazing every few steps, completely oblivious to our presence. Jon quietly told me to set up on the trailing buck as he continued to look through his field glasses. He reminded me to take the safety off when I was ready to shoot, breathe, and slowly squeeze the trigger when I was certain I had a good shot.

Also running through my mind just then was what he had warned me of several times before, which was how comical mule deer look when they run.

He warned that they look just like the skunk from the old Warner Brothers cartoons, and if I'd never seen a mule deer run before, I would likely miss any follow-up shot if it started to bolt because I'd be laughing too hard to shoot.

Wouldn't you know it, just as I was removing the safety and lining up the crosshairs behind the buck's front shoulder, he winded us and started to flee. I watched with my jaw hanging as this animal started to bounce across the field. He looked absolutely ridiculous. In an instant, I realized I had missed my chance and looked at Jon with frustration.

Jon pulled his rifle up to his shoulder and said, "The good news is that they're not terribly smart."

With that he yelled, "Hey!" and the deer froze, turned broadside, and looked directly at us as if to say, "Was someone calling me?"

BANG!

Jon's shot rang out and the deer fell into the tall grass. We gave one another a high five, and he said, "I told you they look funny. You'll know better next time."

We waited twenty minutes and headed over to tag the deer, field dress it (which, as a city slicker who hates the sight of blood, I told Jon over and over again I could never do), and drag it back across Bluebell Flats to the road. It was a nice-looking ten-point with tall antlers and a wide spread. He had a few scars from fighting, and one of the tips of his brow tines had been broken off. But he was a bruiser.

When we returned to the cabin, two more deer had been added to the beam beneath the deck, with Jon's soon to make three for the day. Within moments we had five hanging, and with each member of the group possessing one buck tag and one doe tag when we started, that meant we still had another seven to go.

The Great White Hunter got his second deer of the trip and had limited out. He had spotted a nice-sized doe right where Jon always told us to look for game: on a game trail. Stunt Mouse had limited out as well with a doe, leaving Boy Wonder and me holding two tags each and wearing the proverbial badge of shame. Wonder didn't seem to be too anxious about it, but I was becoming discouraged. Here I had this amazing new rifle that I was dying to shoot, had already passed on a few shots, and blown an opportunity an hour ago with Jon. I could still appreciate that the hunt wasn't necessarily about the kill, but I wanted to do my part for the food pantry, and I also wanted to take home a trophy. I became more determined than ever, which as seasoned hunters know is usually something that doesn't work in one's favor, and swore to approach the afternoon hunt with a renewed sense of passion and dedication. And once I found out I was paired with Boy Wonder for a hunt in the Bear Claw, that passion and dedication turned to outright distress. I finished lunch feeling a bit queasy and not knowing whether it was the chili again or the anticipation of walking into the lair of the unknown.

My mind was flooded with horrible imagery. It was as if all the horrors of Dungeons and Dragons were mixed with a collection of the most frightening scenes I had ever watched in scary movies over the years.

I was in a bit of a daze as we were dropped off by the side of the East Road roughly fifty yards from the edge of the mysterious Bear Claw. The terrain fell away from the road at a steep angle and the descent looked intimidating, especially with the woods looming as a backdrop. Boy Wonder and I walked toward it, one of us full of confidence and excitement and the other looking as though he were being led to his own funeral.

As we breached the boundary of the forest, still walking down a steep grade, I could feel the temperature drop, and the light was reduced to a fraction of what it had been only steps before. The tree canopy was about eighty feet above the forest floor but was incredibly thick and blocked out almost all of the natural light outside. It was only about two in the afternoon, but within this foreign world, it seemed that night was approaching and there were only minutes of useful light left in the day.

I was so scared my knees were literally weak, and I had trouble catching my breath as I looked around frantically to see what might be sneaking up behind me. This was going to be a long afternoon.

Boy Wonder assured me that I'd be fine and that all I had to do was stay close to him and do what he did.

While that seemed simple enough, my mind began playing tricks on me as we stepped deeper into the dark timber. *Did I really just hear that? What was it that I just saw out of the corner of my eye? There's something right over there; I saw something move.*

I was a walking bundle of nerves and couldn't seem to get a grip. My imagination was running wild with dread, and the intensifying, self-inflicted torment was reaching a merciless pace.

The woods were so thick in there that three hunters could all be separated by just thirty feet and never know the others were present. So when my trusty guide told me to spread out and walk parallel to him at about twenty paces, I told him he was out of his freakin' mind and he needed to either get used to me shadowing him like a second skin while I tried not to vomit out of sheer terror, or find someone else to hunt with who actually enjoyed taunting the Prince of Darkness and his forces of evil.

Eventually he got me to separate from him by about ten feet to his left (which felt like eighty), and every time he passed behind a tree and I lost sight of him, my heart skipped a beat. It happened often given how thick the woods were, so you can imagine how uncomfortable I was. Between trying to stay close to him and maintain situational awareness, I was quickly becoming mentally exhausted and unable to focus on the multitude of things causing my extreme discomfort.

Suddenly Boy Wonder froze at full attention, and my heart started to beat through my chest. He looked over at me, put two fingers up to his face, one to each eye, and motioned to look to my eleven o'clock. I slowly turned my head forward and noted movement in the foliage ahead of me, but I couldn't yet make out what was lurking behind the underbrush. And then, directly in front of me at no more than twelve yards, were a cow moose and her calf passing from left to right.

All I could think was, *Oh, come on! Not again!*

The rifle went to my shoulder and the safety came off in a flourish—though I was shaking so uncontrollably at that point that I would have almost certainly missed the shot, even at less than forty feet. I was so close to these enormous creatures that I could hear them breathing. I leaned a touch to my right to steady myself against a big tree (and also to give me something to put between me and the two of them) and prayed for a peaceful outcome. The calf was oblivious, but the cow knew exactly what the score was. She locked eyes with me, and then with Boy Wonder, and grunted a few times with obvious purpose. My finger tightened against the trigger, and at that point I didn't give a flying rat's backside as to what Jon might or might not approve of.

Thankfully, she and her calf just casually walked past us and down the trail. Apparently, scaring the wits out of me was satisfaction enough for her.

Just as my relief began to set in, Youth Blunder, the crowned King of Bad Ideas, decided that it would be fun to antagonize the moose. He walked out onto the trail behind them, cupped his hands over his mouth, and imitated some bull moose vocalizations. I couldn't believe it! Frankly, I was tempted at that point to shoot him, and based on that behavior, I felt that no court would ever convict me.

Luckily, the moose maintained their course and disappeared into the forest down the path. I was relieved on one hand, but quite angered that he had done something like that. I didn't feel it was terribly sportsmanlike, but even worse, it was not a smart thing to do in terms of general safety, particularly knowing that I was a beginner with zero experience and already scared out of my mind. With that on the forefront of what was left of my overly taxed brain, I decided to risk life and limb to have a chat right there in the heart of Mirkwood in Middle Earth, seemingly after the shadow of the Dark Lord Sauron had fallen upon it. (Actually, we weren't in the extremely scary and profoundly evil forest from the *Lord of the Rings* trilogy by J.R.R. Tolkien, but it sure felt like it.)

I called the Wonder over and said with as much grace and restraint as I could possibly muster and in a tone that wouldn't scare animals (in Canada), "Now, listen here, you lunatic. That couldn't have been a smart thing to do. You only succeeded in causing me to destroy a perfectly good pair of boxers! If your purpose today was to scare the living daylights out of me, then your goal has been achieved and we can head back now. However, if the idea is to show me a good hunt that's maybe just only a light year or two beyond my comfort zone, one that may give me an opportunity to actually shoot something, then let's get serious about this and stop trying to force me into cardiac arrest. This is not fun for me!"

I knew Boy Wonder was a bit of a character, but actually pursuing a cow moose with her calf in tow and attempting a verbal interaction seemed borderline insane to me and altered any opinion I had already reached about him.

I usually try not to rush to judgment, but that may have exceeded any comfortable limitations I had established. I was excited to be in the woods learning how to hunt, but now I felt as though I had been paired with a maniac. (At least I was armed, I suppose.)

Apparently, I got through to him. To his credit and my surprise, he offered me a sincere apology, which may very well have saved his life. If I had told Jon about the encounter, he'd have had a cow. Jon is entirely intolerant of harassing behavior toward animals or humans. Well, at least toward animals.

The rest of the trek through the Bear Claw was actually pretty amazing once my butt cheeks weren't so tightly clenched. The animals were everywhere, though none were in season. We saw elk, young deer still with their spots, and even a pair of mountain lion tracks, which were, admittedly, intimidating, but the experience was incredible.

We tracked the cats for about ten minutes (clearly an activity that I hadn't voted for) until the prints stopped at the edge of a shallow depression filled with water. There were claw marks on a tree trunk nearby and a sudden and highly suspect absence of other wildlife in the immediate area coupled with a palpable lack of noise in general.

Looking across the puddle and about ten yards past, there was a cluster of fallen trees and thick underbrush with a conspicuous void (as in a hole) in the tangled mess. Boy Wonder calmly pointed out that it was most likely a mountain lion's den. I then not so calmly pointed out that I was ready to leave, turned on my heel, and began walking at a modified and somewhat urgent pace in the only direction I seemed to care about anymore—toward the road. I figured I'd get a head start in case Captain Dipstick decided to taunt the carnivores who were hopefully still enjoying their afternoon slumber.

We hiked out of death's grasp (at nearly a dead run) and ascended the grade to the road where we awaited our extraction team. Shortly thereafter, we spotted a rapidly approaching Suburban followed by a dust cloud. Grizzly arrived and stopped abruptly, letting us take the full brunt of his personally engineered dust storm. After the dirt cloud settled, the two of us looked as though we had just hitchhiked across the

Sahara. (This was particularly special for me, knowing that there was no shower waiting for me at the end of the day.) We both spit the dust out of our mouths and climbed into the car before ruffling our coats and brushing our pants off. (What can I say? We were taught to share.) Jon was not amused as the cloud of dust spread throughout his truck.

I wouldn't exactly say that I'd conquered my fear of the Bear Claw, but I'd survived it and was able to see a truly amazing place unlike any other I had ever come across. And while I was still without a kill, I felt like I'd had, by far, the best experience of the trip. As a bonus, Boy Wonder and I understood each other a bit better than we had when we'd all woken up that morning. All things considered, I would mark it down as a significantly better-than-average day.

When we arrived back at camp, the dinner preparation was already underway. We were having grilled double-cut pork chops, applesauce, mashed potatoes and gravy, and canned green beans. I was excited right up until the part of the menu when I heard green beans. (The canned detail would have been a massive deduction on its own, but was irrelevant given the fact that I didn't like the fresh ones either.)

Chef noticed me turning up my nose at his green beans and assured me that I would like the way he prepared his version.

But being the entitled little food snob that I fully recognized I was and unabashedly embraced, I uttered under my breath, "I doubt it."

Jon's response was simple and to the point: "Actually, I don't care one way or another, but you're going to eat them regardless, so you may as well decide right now to enjoy them."

With the understanding that, firstly, he is an exceptional cook, and that, secondly, he is much larger than I am, I offered that I would at least try them with an open mind. And when dinner was served, all that was on my plate was a mound of green beans. Jon said, "Try them and you can have the rest of your dinner."

I was suddenly not afraid. In fact, I was quite eager to dive right in because Jon had leveraged bacon to elevate the simple green bean. And he'd leveraged a lot of it — three whole pounds for four cans of green beans. I demolished those things and went back for more. The chops were amazing, as were the potatoes and gravy, but the star of the evening's feast was clearly the bacon, sprinkled lightly with canned green beans.

There was good news all around the table as well: no one had seen any indicator since the morning ceremonies. It appeared that we had survived the Liquefied Intestines Disorder, and were all ecstatic that we would no longer have to worry about the Summit County Two-Step.

By now I had the clean-up process down to a fine science and could have the kitchen spotless within forty minutes. This may not seem like an impressive feat, but understand that Jon cooks like an octopus with reckless abandon and shows no regard for the aftermath or the poor slob who has to deal with it. (For the record, no complaints here — keep bringing me food and I will gladly clean the kitchen!) Therefore, returning the kitchen to its organized and workable condition is not the easiest thing to do, period, let alone within forty minutes. (Pardon me, I think I just pulled a muscle patting myself on the back.)

I wrapped up my custodial duties and joined the gang downstairs for cards by the fire, where, again,

Beanpole was still struggling to count to three cards. (I could've really fogged his glasses trying to explain how Utah hunters count antler points, but that could have resulted in permanent drain bamage.)

The game continued, as did my barrage of jokes. The laughter persisted despite my obvious social issues and highly distorted sense of humor. And when all was said and done, the logs all accounted for by the self-appointed Deputy Wood Marshal, the supply of Cinnamon Bears almost entirely depleted, and the embers in the fire cooling to a dark orange glow, we all stood and headed to our racks to rest up for what everyone hoped would be a big day. We had six tags yet to fill.

The lights went dim, the room fell quiet for two minutes, and then one voice in the darkness kicked it off, and none of us could resist:

Boy Wonder: "Goodnight, Beanpole."

Beanpole: "Goodnight, Stunt Mouse."

Stunt Mouse: "Goodnight, Peach Fuzz."

Peachfuzz: "G'night, Great White Hunter."

Great White Hunter: "Goodnight, Boy Wonder."

Collectively: "Goodnight, Jon Boy!" followed by a smattering of laughter.

Jon: "Will you hopeless juveniles shut up?" he groaned with a notable lack of patience. "This isn't *The Waltons*. Go to sleep."

7

DON'T THINK I WON'T SHOOT YOU

Morning arrived and was ushered in on the gruff notes coming from the top of Jon's voice: "Time to feed those who are less fortunate. Get up, get dressed, and let's fill those tags—except for you, Freddie. We know you're saving yours for your scrapbook." (I'm sorry, was that a gauntlet being thrown down, or was I just unabashedly insulted?)

Well, whatever the intention, the comment didn't feel particularly good, so I was hoping that it would serve to motivate me.

It took a bit longer to get dressed after four days and nights of clean and dirty clothes comingling on the top bunk, not that it made any difference as none of us had showered since we had arrived, but eventually I made it to the breakfast table on time, thank you very little, for another signature Grizzly breakfast. We were all treated to the best version of biscuits and sausage gravy from scratch that I have ever eaten to this day.

(I'm tellin' y'all, Jon doesn't mess around. After all the hiking and hunting was said and done, I think we each still gained ten pounds.) We sat down and gorged ourselves. The biscuits were light and fluffy, the gravy had fresh cream in it, and the sausage was nice and spicy — giving us all reason to question whether or not we wanted to punish our stomachs again. In the end, though, that risk was happily taken to enjoy this classic dish on a bitterly cold morning.

The day's weather called for sunshine with little to no cloud cover. The breeze would be minimal and blow from north to south, with zero chance of precipitation. Despite the sunshine, however, it was shaping up to be another showcase day for polar bears. (These are the kinds of days that are so cold, lawyers have their hands in their own pockets.)

Given that I was focused on having a productive day, I really didn't pay attention to the fact that Jon had dispersed the tagged-out crowd to various places around the ranch to scout for opportunities on my behalf. I didn't even notice that none of them had taken their guns out until someone pointed it out to me after the hunt. But Boy Wonder and I were paired together again and were headed to the top of Deep Canyon to sit amid the aspens and watch the game trails for mule deer walking into or out of the gorge.

We all left the table in gluttonous agony but were somehow happy in spite of it. We wandered downstairs to assemble all our layers for the day and put them on before meeting on the gravel driveway, where the vehicles would be warming up. Once we were all present and accounted for, my hunting partner and I took a vehicle and were on our way — this time with me in the driver's seat.

Now that I was familiar enough to know my way around and be trusted to head out without the chief supervisor, it felt like I had passed the initial tests. While I viewed it as a compliment, it put an added bit of responsibility and pressure on me that I really didn't need. I was, however, flattered to have it nonetheless.

We drove down the hill away from the cabin and sloshed through the washout as the vehicle slid almost completely sideways. The only image I had in my head was Jon and the rest of the group appearing five minutes later to find me stuck and thus incapable of being left to my own devices.

I was simply not going to let that happen, and I fought to keep the car headed in the desired direction. Of course, comments from Boy Wonder that I drive like a girl didn't help much but were received for what they were and quickly dismissed as I began to doubt whether I could get through the bog. I knew that if the vehicle stopped moving, I was in trouble. I threw the truck in low and carefully manipulated the accelerator. Just when all seemed lost, I regained control and cleared the muck by the closest of margins. Naturally, I was relieved and felt quite accomplished, at least until Beanpole and company came down the hill and powered effortlessly through the quagmire.

He pulled up alongside, rolled down his window, and said, "You're still here? Is everything okay, or did you two daisies get stuck in the mud?"

Just as I opened my mouth to offer a retort, he simply laughed and drove away, showering the Tahoe with all the loose mud from his tires. I vowed revenge and swore that his action would be something he would come to regret.

After that, Boy Wonder and I spent the entire rest of the commute conspiring and orchestrating our retaliation. (Of course, it's infantile. We're boys trapped together in the woods. What did you expect?)

We stopped in a small clearing to the side of the Middle Road and prepared our gear for the walk to our spot. The sun had not quite risen, but there was diffused light beginning to creep past the reaches of the mountain peaks on the horizon. We were able to enter the timber with just the slightest bit of visibility.

(As an amateur outdoorsman, I can tell you that these morning hikes into our hunting spots were, at least for me, a test of will against fear and anxiety.)

As we walked deeper and deeper into the woods, another evil thought took root in my mind and seized my imagination with a sinister and stubborn grip. Naturally, it had to be the thought of the spirit thing that Jon was kind enough to share with me. I didn't doubt that the story could be true, and I couldn't keep my mind from racing and picturing some wicked and unearthly creature behind every other tree. I had Jon to thank for that and vowed to myself that I would exact my revenge at some point for that as well.

As the light increased, thoughts of terror were replaced by the business at hand. I was ready to hunt and, possibly (finally), have an occasion to shoot my rifle at something other than a paper target for the first time since I'd gotten it. Boy Wonder took cover under an evergreen fifty yards up the trail from where I'd decided to set up. As I got situated, I looked around and had a beautiful view of three game trails converging at the edge of the gorge.

I settled ten feet off one trail inside the leaves and branches of a recently fallen tree. I became virtually invisible — except for the orange hat and other required colorful apparel that made me visible from northern Idaho. I made myself comfortable using another tree trunk to sit against, propped my rifle up in the direction of the intersecting trails, and waited for the moment I knew in my heart was coming.

I was so certain that good things were going to happen that, as the time slipped by, I was never cold, bored, tired, or even tempted to move from my spot to stretch my legs. I just sat in anticipation of getting to fill my first tag.

I'm guessing it was about ten a.m. when I heard a faint shot well to the east of us. It was barely audible, but there was no mistaking it if you knew what to listen for. And just as I started to wonder who had shot what, another shot rang out just up the trail to my left. I readied my rifle in case something was headed down toward me and watched intently as nothing happened.

I waited ten minutes or so and left my spot to see what the commotion was all about. I walked away from the trail about a hundred feet or so and then turned uphill toward my hunting partner.

A short walk through the trees revealed a very happy Boy Wonder, who was on one knee cutting his tag for the large doe just off the trail. He had dropped her with one perfectly placed round.

He asked, "What do you think?" as he gestured proudly toward the hundred-pound food donation.

Without missing a beat, I responded, "I think you shot my deer!"

We had a good laugh before he reminded me that we had a bit of work to do.

Clearly, he had not read the program, or at least the part that advises everyone that I don't do blood.

"What's this 'we' stuff, pal?" I said. "I'll supervise and make sure you're doing it right." As if I had the slightest idea what "right" was when it came to field dressing a deer.

I did help, which is to say I stood there without purpose and told jokes while watching the process from a safe distance. I then walked out with him carrying his rifle as he dragged the deer along. He placed it next to the Tahoe, and then we headed back in for the remaining hour of the hunt. I found my spot again and settled in. I sat motionless in anticipation for a deer that, despite my conviction, would never walk by. I ended the morning hunt as the only hunter on the trip who hadn't filled either of his tags. I was assured by Boy Wonder that this was why they called it hunting and not killing, which didn't make me feel entirely good, but at least a little better than I had. I still had the afternoon hunt and tomorrow morning's hunt, so all was not lost to despair.

We headed back to the cabin for lunch, and the ribbing pointed in my general direction was relentless. Having heard from Jon that I was a true marksman who had skill and surgical precision, as well as a rifle that was second to none, their expectation, I suppose, was that I would tag out almost immediately. Apparently, I got no credit for having never hunted big game. Honestly, I had only hunted birds before this experience, and I wasn't particularly proficient at that either. So I was battling uphill during lunch and drawing fire, albeit friendly, from every direction.

The beam below the deck at the cabin was decorated with eight deer now, and the only hunters who had tags left were Boy Wonder and me. The pressure was on, and I began to doubt that I'd get a deer on this trip.

After the midday feast of freshly smoked venison, a meal that was absolutely spectacular, I was once again paired with everyone's favorite punching bag, Boy Wonder. The poor guy simply attracted abuse because he never knew when to zip his trap. Although he had been relatively good since the night Stunt Mouse had tied him in a knot and slammed him to the floor, he still had just a bit too much to say. Jon must have figured that I was least likely to strangle and bury him in a shallow grave.

When we all got up from the table, Grizzly casually announced that by the time we all returned from the hunt, there would be another group at the cabin. He said it would consist of about four or five guys who were coming up to the ranch to close out the season.

"Let's make sure things look presentable downstairs before you head out this afternoon."

After the verbal beatdown I'd received over lunch, I tried to adjust my pride while helping to straighten up the lower-level common area. Once things were presentable again, we got suited up and walked out to the vehicles. This time, Boy Wonder and I drove down the East Road and parked at a trailhead. We walked down a familiar path and finally cut into the woods well north of the Bear Claw.

We hiked for about thirty minutes and stepped out of the woods into a clearing with patches of scrub oak and a few evergreens. To our left was a valley that looked somewhat barren and had only sagebrush scattered about erratically on the hillside. We walked a hundred yards across the ridge of the embankment and then turned to our left and wandered down the steep hillside.

I could see there was a creek nestled in the very bottom of the three-hundred-foot ravine. As we neared it, Boy Wonder began sidestepping down the gulley while warning me to watch my step and stay alert. I really didn't understand the need for drama since we could see in all directions. There seemed to be no danger of any predator, as we could've seen them approaching from a mile away. (Again, this is why nonhunters or newbies in the forest should always have a guide with them. Greenhorns stand a much better chance of surviving their own ignorance and carelessness when an experienced guide is there to babysit them.)

By the time we reached the bottom of this lovely pit, I was nearly spent. I thought the only thing worse than climbing down this three-hundred-foot elevation would be having to hike right back up the other side after crossing the creek in front of us.

I reluctantly asked, "So are we following the creek downstream?"

"No," he said. "We're climbing the hill in front of us to get into that expanse of timber at the top."

I think I knew the answer to the question before I asked, but was still frustrated when I heard it out loud.

I snapped. At this point I was simply wondering how much more I could endure. Clearly a lack of patience and fitness was showing through, even though I tried to remember that maturing afield is a process in its own right.

Boy Wonder replied, "Trust me, you're going to love what we get into at the top. And today this is the only way there."

I told him, "There had better be another way out, because if I have to cross this chasm again, I think I'll wait to be airlifted out by a helicopter."

He assured me that there was another way out but that entering from that side with the wind would have scared any game out of the area we were attempting to reach.

There we were, trudging up the hillside with our rifles slung over our shoulders and sweating profusely under our coats, when just halfway to the top, Boy Wonder stopped, hastily reached inside his coat, and pulled a 9mm Glock pistol from his waistband. He racked a round into the chamber and said, "Get right behind me."

Given his tone and my already-heightened sense of fear, I covered the distance between us in a flash and stood directly behind him just as he had ordered.

He was looking intently at something; however, I couldn't see it because his body was blocking my line of sight. He stood up and pointed ten feet beyond the sagebrush before him and said, "That's a problem."

I looked down and saw, to my horror, what was left of a sheep that had obviously met a very violent end. Boy Wonder noted that the bloody carcass had been devoured to the point that all that remained were the head, the hooves, and a few of the larger skeletal structures like the ribcage, spine, and pelvis. All the meat had been stripped from the bones, which had marks on them from the assailant's teeth and claws. In the dirt around the remains were perfect prints of a large mountain lion's paws, and the worst detail of all he saved for last: the blood was still sticky.

"This is a really fresh kill, and whatever ate it is probably napping not too far from here. We need to be elsewhere," he continued. "Let's go — keep up with me!"

Off went Mr. Fitness like he was training for an Ironman competition. He charged straight up the grade, which was steep by anyone's standards but may as well have been the wall of the Grand Canyon as far as my physical ability was concerned. I took ten steps in a highly motivated manner and was soon sucking wind like a politician during a campaign speech.

At this point he was twenty steps ahead of me and still going like a house on fire. I had slowed to a humiliating pace and said, "Don't leave me behind. I just can't go that fast."

He turned and looked over his shoulder and said, "C'mon! This is no joke. We need to get out of here."

Then he joked he could probably slow down a bit because all he had to do was outrun me. "That doesn't appear to be a problem," he said with a smirk.

My response was simple: "Antagonize me all you want, but don't think I won't shoot you to save myself."

I then pointed out that he was the one with the handgun and should be behind me watching our backs while I led the charge up the hill. (It was more like a geriatric crawl with a lot of whining, but you get the idea.)

We reached the top and he turned to survey the hillside below. He saw nothing and breathed a sigh of relief. However, while we were standing there catching our breath, I pointed out that the cat would probably seek shade and shelter if he were going to nap. I further suggested that since the hillside offered neither, the animal was probably snoozing under a tree in the very woods into which we had just run.

Well, that was a sobering and thought-provoking theory that left us both staring at each other in profound situational discomfort.

After brief but careful consideration, we made our way out of the highly secluded area at a notably increased pace. Despite the promise of a good opportunity to shoot something, our presence became more of a liability than an adventure. In other words, we tucked our tails between our legs and ran as fast as we could. We scared anything that may once have been a target clear over to the next property, literally miles away.

I realized that an outdoorsman I likely was not. An athlete, I definitely was not. But I lived to tell the tale, and that had to count for something. It was certainly better than the alternative.

Boy Wonder and I hunted several swaths of timber as we walked up the road and saw plenty of, well, other trees — but, sadly, no animals. The afternoon turned to dusk and another unsuccessful hunt was officially in the books. We drove back to the cabin and noticed something a bit unexpected upon our arrival.

Contrary to the heads-up we'd received that there would be four or five new people at the cabin, now there were nine or ten new cars littering the driveway and the lawn behind the cabin. It looked like the carnival had rolled into town.

We walked in, and it was quite clear to the guys in our bunch that I was in no mood for the cruel abuse that was coming to me. It was almost as if they sympathized with me . . . almost.

Actually, it made absolutely no difference; they pounced like rabid foxes. And now there were new people in the mix who didn't want to miss out on any action, so they wasted no time jumping in and chiding me about my lack of success as well.

Now, as you may well imagine, I was only moderately prepared to tolerate it from the guys I had come to know, in part because we had all taunted each other equally and there was a brotherhood of sorts there.

But these new people — all 20 of them — had never even met me. So I wasn't about to endure their barbs and criticisms without a bit of resistance, attitude, and retribution. However, for the time being anyway, I played the good sport and gracious guest, but only until my opportunity presented itself.

As the afternoon turned to evening, I already had some of these guys' numbers. I was a psych major back in college and could read some of these halfwits like a bad novel. I will stipulate that the majority of them were very nice people with whom I had very pleasant exchanges, but there was an obvious clique among four of these guys, and they were like bullies on the grade school playground. They would intentionally start trouble and then sit back and watch it unfold as though it were entertainment. They would egg it on when the intensity subsided and seemed only too happy with themselves when they were able to turn friends against each other. Their egos were insufferable and completely without virtue, and you could measure their insecurity with a pocket ruler. These guys were thundering buffoons with few, if any, redeeming qualities whatsoever.

Their ringleader was the most insecure of them all. He was a balding man in his late fifties who stood about six-foot-three and tipped the scale at a cool three hundred twenty pounds. He tried to let everyone know that he was the absolute authority on hunting — every aspect of it — all while talking down to anyone he deigned to speak with, purporting to know more about their areas of expertise than they did. He made a fool of himself on several occasions while trying to impress people and just couldn't stop while he was behind. The evening became nothing more than a one-upmanship display, by which I was entirely insulted, as was the rest of our group. If we had to endure one more story that started with, "Oh yeah? Well, I . . . ," I'd be convinced we were in grade school.

I remember one instance in particular, when a member of this little playground faction was mingling around and marginalizing everyone else in the room. This guy was a slender individual, about six feet tall, with a dark beard and fringe ringing a prominent bald spot on the crown of his head. Watching him work the room without ever separating more than a foot from the ringleader, he reminded me of a jackal in the wild — an animal that reveres his benefactor, the lion, only for what he can gain from him, while the lion merely tolerates his presence. One could tell immediately that this guy was nothing more than a user.

At this point, our group was attempting to interact politely but felt that we had targets on our backs. We were certainly not part of the "in" crowd and began attracting quite a lot of insolence without any provocation whatsoever.

The upstairs living room was packed with the busload of people who had been allowed to descend upon the ranch, despite the clearly worded, posted, and openly displayed rules of the property forbidding a single member from bringing to the cabin a group that exceeded a certain size. (I know about this because, as guests, we were all required not only to sign a waiver, but to familiarize ourselves with the rules of the ranch and promise to abide by them to the letter. Naturally, we felt obligated to adhere to the rules, but mostly out of respect for Jon, our host, and we were happy to do so.) But this clown didn't feel that the rules applied to him, and Jon hinted, in a not-so-subtle way, that this individual was known for ignoring the rules. Apparently, he was one of those guys who believed that the rules only applied to everyone else. We've all met the type.

As the new group just stood around waiting for things to be done for them rather than actually pitching in and doing it themselves, two members of our group, Beanpole and Stunt Mouse, dropped everything they were doing when they noticed that there was no wood for a fire next to the upstairs fireplace. Again, out of respect for Jon and the new group, and for camaraderie in general, they ran outside to gather wood for the stack next to the upstairs hearth so that we could all enjoy a fire.

They must have made fifteen trips down the stairs and out the door to stack six to eight logs in their arms at a time and then bring them back inside, up the stairs, and into the living room. There, they neatly stacked them for use. They must have stacked nearly two hundred pieces of wood over the course of thirty minutes to fill a firewood box six feet square and four feet deep, without being asked to do it. Oddly, they didn't even get a thank you from the other group's host, although Jon noticed their efforts immediately and pitched in to help stack. Then, just as Beanpole and Stunt Mouse sat down in front of the fire, each exhausted and holding a cold bottle of water (and a well-deserved one at that), one of the Fabulous Four walked up to them and suggested, "Hey, why don't you guys go make yourselves useful and fill the Coleman lanterns with fuel."

Beanpole and Stunt Mouse looked at each other, got visibly irritated, and simply stood and walked off. Meanwhile, the jerk who'd said this settled comfortably into the opening that had been left in front of the fire without guilt or hesitation. Our group stood together at the hearth and saw the whole thing unfold. Frankly, I was surprised that Stunt Mouse didn't just stand up and deck this pretentious goon. But even better than that was when an unlikely defender stood up for Beanpole and Stunt Mouse before they got two steps from where they had been seated.

Boy Wonder appeared through the crowd and berated this dope in front of everyone. Rather tersely, he said, "You ought to go make yourself useful; get off your tail and fill your own lanterns. Do you even know those two guys? That was just rude."

Now, clearly, Boy Wonder had overstepped his boundaries and let his mouth get away from him, but the idea that he was standing up for those two only a few nights after being bested on the floor by one of them spoke volumes about our group's bond and loyalty to each other.

Was Boy Wonder's comment ill advised? Debatable.

Had he exceeded his role as a guest? Maybe.

Was it ill-mannered and discourteous? Probably.

But was it a display of real character? Absolutely!

We were all shocked and angered by this guy, but Boy Wonder really took it personally. He was genuinely worked up over it all and wanted blood. When he walked away to go talk to Mouse, his ears were visibly red.

Then the icing on the cake was when Dopey looked up at us from his cozy, ill-acquired spot in front of the fire and said, "Well, at least they brought in some firewood for us."

Jon looked at him and said, "You wouldn't know courtesy or class if it bit you."

While that was bad enough, it didn't match the conceited ringleader, who was still flitting around and calling attention to the fact that he knew the least about the most of anyone in the room. He was constantly trying to insert himself into conversations by interrupting those involved in them with statements that were entirely inaccurate or opinions based on things he was clearly making up as he went along. And each time he was essentially pushed out of the discussion, he would simply turn around and offer his unwelcome and erroneous viewpoint to whoever had the misfortune of standing in his line of sight. He was even too stupid to realize that he ought to have been embarrassed for himself. Truly there was a village somewhere missing their idiot.

We decided we had been hospitable enough and figured that before one of ours killed one of theirs, we had better head downstairs and keep to ourselves.

We settled into our nightly ritual and built our fire, played cards, lamented the lack of Cinnamon Bears which had finally run out, and relaxed until dinner.

As the alert for the evening meal sounded, we all stumbled upstairs, pushed through the crowd and dropped into our chairs at the table. Our bodies were sore, our beards were three quarters grown in (except for mine, of course — I still looked like a molting hedgehog on Rogaine), and all of us had stories to tell but no energy to tell them.

There were many toasts of camaraderie and friendship at the "last supper," which was fit for royalty. Thanks again to Jon, we had a full tenderloin, grilled to a flawless medium rare. The baked potatoes were served with the works, and two pounds of delectable bacon adorned the top of the green beans. Naturally, the highlight was a heaping portion of humble pie, which we all got to enjoy at one another's expense. It was the fifth dinner-to-end-all-dinners in a row . . . and the food was good too.

Meanwhile, the new group was in front of the fire. They were busy lying to each other about the sixty-two-point buck one of them had shot from a thousand yards with a slingshot last year, which was only outdone by another guy who'd shot his sixty-four-point buck with a bow and arrow while hanging upside down from a helicopter. It was just like camp — when we were ten.

Our group headed downstairs to burn one last pile of logs before bed, and Boy Wonder and I cleared the table and stacked the kitchen sink a mile high with remnants of the dinner preparation. The kitchen looked like a war zone, and the casualties were many. There was debris all over the kitchen. The chives Jon had been chopping littered the countertops, and bits of bacon crunched underfoot. There was sour cream on the cabinets from when he'd dropped the container, and the stovetop was a disaster with various foods burned onto the surface. It was a mess.

Just then, Dopey and the Village Idiot walked into the kitchen and wanted to know how long we thought it would be before everything was put back together so they could get dinner going for their group. I smiled, looked at Dopey, and said, "It shouldn't take long if you set your mind to it. Make yourself useful."

With that, I draped the dish towel over his shoulder, and Boy Wonder and I walked out of the kitchen and down the stairs to the card game in front of the fire.

"Deal us in," we requested.

No, it certainly wasn't the right thing to do, but on some level it still felt good. And to be perfectly honest, the guy had it coming. Someone needed to put him in his place. Boy Wonder told Jon and the rest of the group what had happened, and Jon didn't say much.

I apologized to Jon and told him that I hoped I hadn't put him in a bad spot. I offered to go up and take care of the kitchen if he wanted me to, but just about then, the undynamic duo came down to have a word with Jon.

He quickly addressed the issue before they even opened their flannel traps. "I know why you're here, and you're on your own. Consider it the right thing to do after enjoying all the wood our guys brought up for you without any help or a single word of appreciation."

And it was over that fast. They went back upstairs and we never heard another word about it.

As we all sat in front of the hearth to wind down our last night on the hill, there was a lingering thought in my head that I simply couldn't shake. I reluctantly brought it up to Jon during a lull in the banter. I asked about The Spirit, the property's terrifying and apparently supernatural resident. I was curious about who (or what) it was, why it was there, and whether it was watching over us or meaning us harm.

The question draped a sinister shroud over our customarily animated conversation and ushered in some distinct discomfort. The laughs dissipated and the attention turned to Jon while we all anticipated his answer.

All he would say was that there were a number of stories that he had heard over the years — none of which he was willing to repeat. Whether they were unverified or simply true was also never disclosed. (Frankly, I'm not sure which scenario would be worse.) But what he did say sent a chill through all of us and left me with something to think about for a long time.

"Freddie," he said, "as any experienced hunter will tell you, there are things that we see, hear, or feel when we are in the field that simply cannot be rationally explained. Even you will come to understand that firsthand if you continue hunting. As in life, be prepared for, and even receptive to, things you don't understand. It will broaden you as a person and, in some instances, may even protect you."

He then abruptly announced bedtime and excused himself from the group.

None of us were particularly satisfied with his response to the mystery. We looked at each other with a certain degree of unease and bewilderment before rising from the couch and chairs and heading for our beds.

As we crawled into our bunks, Jon announced that he would be waking us at the normal time and sending us on our way, but that he would not be hunting with us. Instead, he told us he'd be sleeping in since he was anticipating a long travel day with many hours on the road. We cared, but were just too tired to address it and figured we'd fight about it in the morning. We were all asleep quickly, or at least I was. And, thankfully, my fatigue overpowered any nightmares that I certainly would have had about creepy things that Jon clearly didn't care to talk about.

I didn't move a muscle until the dreaded alarm (Jon) went off at four a.m. I woke with one thought in my mind: whoever invented mornings ought to be sacrificed to the ghoul in the woods or simply shot . . . repeatedly.

8

THE FIRST LAST DAY

The morning began with Jon verbally detonating most of us out of bed before we were fully conscious. I said most of us because I remained horizontal. Every bone and muscle in my body ached. I hadn't gotten enough sleep for five nights in a row and had come to the general conclusion that I simply wasn't going to kill anything on this trip. Having reached a certain peace with that, I elected to sleep in as well. I voiced my reasoning and turned over to go back to sleep. Evidently, that was not what Jon wanted to hear, nor was it something he was particularly prepared to accept.

"Freddie, you're going. Get up and get dressed."

I resisted and remained in bed, muttering something along the lines of, "You can't make me."

Of all the ill-advised things I have ever articulated in my lifetime, this certainly remains near the top of the list — definitely a top-five contender. And the guys all knew it too. I could hear a collective gasp followed by dead silence, and nobody was moving around the room anymore or getting dressed. The stillness in the room made me acutely aware that something bad was about to happen. I could feel the eyes of all five people in the room burning a hole through my back as I lay on my side, facing the wall. And then it happened.

Jon said very calmly, with conviction and certainty in his tone, "Freddie, if I don't hear your feet hit the floor by the time I count to three, I'm going to come over there and crawl into your bunk with you! One . . ."

I can tell you with absolutely faultless recollection that by "two," I was on my feet and completely dressed, and that by "two and a half," I was out in the car waiting patiently for the rest of the group. I put on-call firemen to shame that morning and seem to remember scorching a trail in the carpet under my feet as I ran out of the room.

To this day, Jon says that it was the fastest he's ever seen anyone get ready for anything.

The hunt was short because we all had to pack our gear and clothes, load up the trucks, and head into Salt Lake City to donate the meat that we had harvested. Beyond that was also getting everyone to the airport for their flights home. We figured we had about three hours after first light before we had to call the hunt for good. Everyone rallied around me, and we all went out in a calculated effort to get the last tags filled and my first kill logged.

We headed down the Middle Road, parked near the lookout post, and set up on a game trail in an area we hadn't yet hunted. The lookout post (or the Weather Station, as it was often called) was a small wooden hut raised on four tall timbers. It was enclosed with a little roof on it, accessible only by a rope ladder that had long since rotted away. It was used, I supposed, as a hunting stand or a lookout for game back in the day. It sat on an open hillside of sagebrush surrounded by aspen trees, and there was a well-traveled game trail that traversed an open field diagonally from one edge of aspens at the top of the hummock to the other wooded boundary at the bottom.

We all got in position just inside the opposing tree lines and waited for the sun to come up.

We sat with baited breath, and five minutes after first light, a gunshot pierced the morning silence. Stunt Mouse stepped gingerly out into the open and glassed up the hill to see Boy Wonder celebrating the punching of his last tag. Now it was down to me, but for the remainder of our time in the woods I saw nothing.

Time ran out on our adventure and I never got to shoot my gun. But as we walked up to the trucks, I realized this had been one of the most fulfilling weeks I'd ever experienced. We all rode back to the cabin, where we scrambled to pack and load up gear and deer carcasses for our drive back down the mountain and into Salt Lake City. We got everything ready to go and left our dorm spotless—mostly due to Jon's "sleeping in" that morning. (Unless he sleepwalks with dust rags and Pledge or rides a vacuum cleaner in an unconscious state, my guess is that he'd spent hours cleaning the cabin while we were all out having fun.)

We all bid a sad farewell to the ranch and caravanned down the mountain. Jon and I were in my Tahoe with all the gear and most of the bags while the rest of the crew had the remainder of the luggage and all of the harvested deer. I was talking to Jon all the way down to the gate about what an incredible time it had been, even though I would have liked to have shot my first big-game animal.

"That's hunting," Jon said. "I don't know what to tell you. But don't worry, next year will be different. You'll definitely get 'em next year."

I was elated to know that I was going to be included again the following year, although I understood I would most likely never be able to call myself a real outdoorsman. There was a reality there that I recognized: even as fun as it was, it was no Ritz-Carlton. But then I thought, maybe that's what I liked about it in the first place. Not that it was better or worse — just a different experience entirely.

Shortly after we hit the smooth, paved road beyond the series of gates, the hum of the tires on the highway lulled me to sleep in minutes. I woke up at the donation point for the deer and helped switch all the bags and gear around so everyone was organized for the airport run.

Somehow the four people flying that day were all headed to St. Louis, yet we were all on different flights with slightly varying departure times. The four of us said goodbye to Boy Wonder and Grizzled Adams, and then to each other, and sped off toward the car rental return at the airport, the three of them together for one concourse, and me on my own for mine. I pulled into my car's lot and drove to the front of the corral. I was greeted by a decidedly professional young man who was obviously into his job. I rolled down my window and he directed me with an unexpected level of excitement.

"Please pull up to the white line, sir. Leave your window down, put the vehicle in park, and turn your engine off. I'll be with you in just a moment. Thank you."

He wasn't Mr. Personality, though aside from his robotic demeanor, the potential was there. His look was eclectic and included, but was not limited to, thick, black-rimmed glasses, an oxford shirt buttoned to the very top, and a haircut that would have made him a ringer for the fifth Beatle. I unloaded the gear from the Tahoe and stood by the driver's door with my gun case and duffel bag at my feet.

The agent approached and circled the SUV.

"How did the vehicle perform?" the agent asked as he was finishing his routine inspection for dented body panels and missing hubcaps.

"It was great," I responded.

"I'm glad to hear that, sir," he said without looking up from his check-in device but as though he were actually listening.

"Did you return the vehicle with an empty gas tank or a full gas tank?" he asked.

"Empty. I prepaid the gas," I said.

"Very well, sir. You're all set. Here's your receipt that details the charges, which I will now review with you before getting your signature."

He handed me a clipboard with a printout of my charges attached and began to go through the document. He pointed with his pen to the charges, in order from top to bottom, as he explained them one by one.

"This is your daily fee for rental of the vehicle. This is your discount for a full week's rental. This figure is what you were charged for prepaying the fuel upon return. Your insurances were included so this line is no charge. And this is a $649 charge for the missing tow hitch, bringing your total to this figure here."

I felt the blood race to my face, and in an instant, I lost all composure.

"I can't believe we're still dealing with the hitch!" I shouted. "What is this company's obsession with the &#*%@^$ towing hardware? You're killin' me!"

I took a deep breath and pleaded, "Please get me a manager; I don't have time to explain this fiasco more than once."

After speaking with the manager, I was finally able to put the tow hitch calamity to rest and the charge was taken off my bill. I was then able to make it into the airport and succeeded in checking my gun and duffel bag through, without incident, before proceeding to security. There, I passed unscathed through that series of unpleasantries as well and began to walk down the concourse. With fatigue from the week's adventure setting in, I breathed a sigh of relief, reflected on my improbable accomplishment of survival, and began to feel a certain sense of achievement.

Then the boarding announcement for my flight interrupted my thoughts just as I approached the assigned gate, marking the first time that my timing had been on point since I was twenty-one and happened upon a SCUBA diver in distress at a depth of forty-five feet and saved his life.

I walked on board and quickly found my window seat with two empty spots to my right. I sat calmly, watching as the rest of the passengers filed onto the plane and took their seats, hoping I wouldn't be afflicted with another neighbor like I'd had for my outbound flight. Truth be told, I actually prayed for the seats to simply remain empty.

Of course, that ended up being too much to hope for as the aisle seat was eventually taken by an older gentleman (read: ancient) who appeared to have already passed away. If it weren't for the occasional clearing of the phlegm in his throat, I'd have called for a coroner.

As I sat dreading what was obviously going to happen next—the inevitable cramped existence that would occur once the middle seat was occupied—the cruelest of things occurred.

(Now. keep in mind that I was newly and quite happily married, not to mention entirely and unequivocally not in the market.)

I looked up and saw a beautiful young woman walking down the aisle. Just as she was about to pass by the row, she stopped, looked at her boarding pass, and excused herself as she sat down between me and Moses.

The look behind her green eyes was immediately disarming and her radiant smile could likely melt ice cream at twenty paces.

I was silently rejoicing that I wasn't stuck next to someone who was twice the size of their seat, nor would I have to make polite conversation with the cadaver on the aisle. And for the bonus: she appeared to be somewhat easygoing should the occasion for a conversation arise. I was suddenly looking forward to my flight home—such a departure from what usually happens to me regarding a flight neighbor. (And now for the cruel part.)

Just then, it hit me like an anvil: I hadn't showered in a solid week. I had hiked miles up and down mountains for five straight days, had been sweating like a pig in heat inside all my hunting gear, and had consumed enough garlic in Jon's cooking to ward off a vampire from two nautical miles. I bet I smelled bad enough to knock a buzzard off a manure wagon from fifty yards away, yet here I was sitting right next to, well . . . her.

I apologized profusely and explained my circumstances. I felt genuinely bad that I had subjected her and the surrounding passengers to my odiferous state, but the reality remained that I had no remedy for the situation until I arrived home. (It also changed my perspective regarding my outbound flight neighbor and his possible circumstances. Humility is such an important virtue and yet often such a painful one to acquire.)

She was very understanding and tolerant of the matter, unlike I had been just a week prior, and even graciously talked to me all the way back to St. Louis. Of all the times to get the cute girl seated next to me on a three-hour flight, it just had to be this one.

And speaking of home, we touched down in St. Louis after the time on the plane rushed by. I had arrived after my harrowing hunting ordeal in the mountains, and my wife, the cutest girl of them all, was eagerly waiting for me as I walked out of the terminal.

When she saw me, she smiled and rushed toward me. But just before we embraced, she veered off like a bad shopping cart.

"Whoa, buddy, keep your distance," she said. "You need a shower."

I was speechless. I had come all this way and I couldn't even get a "welcome home" hug.

Then again, I could hardly blame her given my pungent condition. It worked out, though — the hug post shower was quite a bit better and well worth the extra wait.

What can I say? It was nice to be home.

HUNT #2
FALL OF 2002

9

HERE WE GO AGAIN

It was that time of year to wake up unusually early and catch the why-is-it-still-dark-outside flight to Salt Lake City, Utah. I was looking forward to my second big-game hunt with Jon and another highly questionable group of deviates. And this time, the trip would straddle the very end of the elk season and the beginning of the mule deer season.

I had packed the night before (and, yes, I still pack like a girl), though I did remember to properly alert the airlines that I was flying with a firearm. I was hopeful that I could avoid the debacle I'd suffered through the last time I'd taken a gun to the airport in St. Louis.

The outward plan was mostly similar to last year's as far as flying out alone and driving up to the cabin, though this year I flew through Denver and was to arrive in SLC later that evening, around six p.m. So nearly the entire day was to be wasted in airports and on airplanes and was certain to set me in a foul mood.

Jon was already up at the cabin with a couple of guys who'd met him several days before I was to arrive, so I would not have the pleasure of his company (or his navigation skills) on the way up from civilization to the ranch. I would, however, have Boy Wonder as my copilot, so I just had to find my way from the airport to his house by myself. While that made me moderately uncomfortable, it seemed completely doable.

I checked my bag and rifle case through for the flight without incident, and apparently cleared security while I was sleep walking, as I don't remember a thing about it.

I waited patiently (sound asleep) at my gate until someone from the airline was kind enough to announce my name over the public address system to let me know that I was about to miss my flight. I stumbled to the podium, where an attendant greeted me with one of those smiles that allowed me to count every single tooth in her head. She was so bubbly and profoundly blissful and chipper that when I heard her say, "Thank you and enjoy your flight," in that high-pitched, cheerful, and overly perky voice one normally reserves for greeting a pet Chihuahua, I just wanted to flick her in the eyeball. (I have a hard time processing excessively happy people early in the morning.)

I glared at her through the one eye that was focusing, thanked her, and walked down the jetway. I arrived at the door to the plane, where I met a flight attendant who was none too pleased that I had kept the plane waiting. She grunted a hollow greeting at me and told me to find my seat. I walked to the first open window seat I could find (conveniently located in row 27), crawled over the two people who were already seated but not kind enough to stand up to let me in, and parked my somewhat negative attitude in the chair.

Just as I was putting my headphones in the seatback pouch in front of me, another flight attendant snapped at me to fasten my seatbelt.

Out of courtesy to others, I intentionally said nothing for fear that if I opened my mouth, I might say something that would cause me to be seen in a negative light by the other passengers. In fact, I didn't even look up to acknowledge her, figuring she was just doing the required flyby through the cabin. I reached for both ends of the seatbelt and located only one.

Now, mind you, only seconds had passed (like three or four) since I was told to secure myself in the safety restraint. So imagine my surprise when I looked down to locate the other half of the belt and heard, "You're sitting on it, sir," in a tone dripping with impatience. "Do you need assistance?"

Let's just say she was lucky that I refrained from commenting the first time. I can be a bit of a handful early in the morning, and I was aware that maybe the people around me, rude flight attendants included, deserved a little latitude when it came to my annoyance threshold. But this was twice in a matter of moments, and I just couldn't stop myself from engaging.

"Assistance? I'll pass, but thank you," I responded with sarcasm. "I'm fully capable of finding it myself," I snapped with a certain amount of contempt.

It was certainly not one of my prouder moments, but I think the two of us came to a mutual understanding in that brief exchange, which was essentially this: don't be condescending and instigative, and I won't be a pugnacious malcontent.

She briefly glared at me before continuing down the aisle, checking overhead bin latches and telling people to turn off their cell phones.

I considered for a moment that maybe I had more in common with her than I cared to admit. It was quite possible she was not a morning person either, or perhaps she had gotten a ticket for double parking her broom that morning. There was really no way to know for sure.

Suddenly, as I was lost in amusing thoughts, I was interrupted with, "Are you quite ready now?" as if I, alone, had been holding up the plane's departure because I simply couldn't buckle fast enough.

I looked up at guess-who, and she was staring at me with a pained look on her face, begging a response. I took the high road and simply said, "Ready when you are," in a somewhat dismissive tone and settled into my seat.

After taking off and reaching the appropriate altitude for headphones and general inattention, the announcement was made regarding the drink cart. Granted it was like six-fifteen and I was still groggy at best, but I started to think about how excited I was to see my favorite flight attendant again. Within minutes, there she stood, fangs at the ready, backlit from the morning light coming through the windows on the other side of the aircraft. She tossed two foil pouches of Planter's finest at me and asked with censure, "May I get you something, sir?"

I looked straight at her, managed a grin, and said energetically, "I dunno. Whatcha got?"

It was an attempt at levity, albeit a weak one, to lighten the sour mood.

I got zero response from her—not even a raising of one of her heavily painted-on eyebrows. I earned a snicker from the young woman and her husband sitting in my row, but nothing from Witch Hazel manning the mobile bar.

Clearly my efforts to change the course of our doomed friendship had failed, so I simply offered her a short, "Never mind."

I pulled out my headphones and decided that giving up this war was the smartest thing I could do. She was clearly not a fan of mine, and the feeling was quite mutual. I got as comfortable as one could in that small seat, leaned against the wall, and listened to my music until I fell asleep roughly halfway through Pink Floyd's "Comfortably Numb." I slept until our descent into Denver began.

When I came to, I immediately made sure to be organized with raised tray tables and stowed headphones. I was not about to test my boundaries for fear of incurring the wrath of the most unfriendly flight attendant in North America . . . again. We touched down and taxied to the gate, at which time the crew announced our arrival. Those of us deplaning in Denver did so, leaving behind the poor passengers who still had to endure the maladjusted trolley troll for yet another leg. I was relieved but surely felt sorry for those souls who couldn't yet escape her bitter demeanor.

I exited the jetway and embarked on my own new adventure — an eight-hour layover.

It was about eight-thirty a.m. by the time I found myself roaming around the airport. I had been off the plane for three minutes and I was already bored.

I wandered through one of the souvenir shops and read some T-shirts before crossing the concourse to stroll through a bookstore and peruse everything I had no intention of buying there either.

I looked at my watch to discover that I had managed to kill only ten minutes. It was time to deploy an old-yet-reliable strategy that had served me well for years. I went off in search of a bar with plans to warm a seat there for the foreseeable future.

It wasn't even nine o'clock, but what the heck else was there to do? Besides, I had been up since four that morning and, with the time change, it seemed like it was almost lunchtime anyway.

I found a restaurant with what looked like decent food and personable staff. After a brief period of observation from the entrance, during which I gleaned that they even appeared to possess a sense of humor — unlike the dragon lady from the airplane — I parked myself at a table and requested a menu and a large, ice-cold Coke. Much to my delight, they were only too happy to oblige.

The request was granted swiftly, my soda's mug was crusted with ice, and the server who delivered it was in absolute contrast to the gargoyle from the plane, in both mood and attitude. The two couldn't have been more polar opposite. Her genuine smile was pleasant, disarming, and seemed to say to each person she addressed, "If I could pick only one customer to serve today, I would surely choose you." Admittedly, it was refreshing. She clearly understood how to make one feel he was being well looked after.

As my flight was hours away, I ordered some wings and settled in for the wait.

The long and short of it was that I ended up telling jokes, something I have a propensity to do, almost all of which she thought were hilarious.

Granted, she likely assumed that her tip depended on it, but she laughed with the other patrons, and that's really the result I had wanted. In fact, I was doing a bit of a standup set for that end of the restaurant, and everyone, which is to say all four people, seemed to be amused. Apparently, I was the entertainment, which was really quite fun.

By the end of it all, I must have ordered five baskets of wings and had countless sodas over the six hours I spent role-playing as a comedian. The time flew by, I had entertained an audience, I'd made new friends (and spent over a hundred bucks) . . . and knew that I was lucky to have enjoyed what would have otherwise been a long and agonizing layover.

I parted ways with my new favorite restaurant in Denver's airport and walked to the gate to await the boarding announcement. Shortly after I had been seated in the gate area, a broadcast was made.

"Ladies and gentlemen, this is the boarding announcement for flight #1277 with service to Detroit, Michigan, and Washington, DC."

As the announcement droned on, I became somewhat alarmed.

I thought *uh-oh* and scrambled to pull out my boarding pass to check the flight number and gate assignment. I then ran to an electronic board to see what had happened, and I found my flight's gate had been switched.

Not to worry though. It turned out that the new gate assignment was just around the corner — and all the way at the other end of the airport. Just a hop, skip, and a seven-minute sprint down the concourse.

I took off running for my "on-time" flight and arrived at the gate just as I heard my name over the public address system for the second time on the same day at consecutive airports. I collected myself, tried to ignore the tidal wave of soda sloshing around in my now-aching stomach, and calmly approached the gate attendant.

She looked at me and said, "You just made it."

And after having just run what, for me, was the equivalent of the Boston Marathon, I was lucky not to get sick when I opened my mouth to thank her.

I boarded the plane, quickly found a seat to occupy, and prayed I'd feel better when we landed in SLC.

Thankfully I slept the entire flight.

When the plane touched down in Utah, I awoke relieved to find no ill effects from my poorly chosen gastronomic experience at Denver International Airport.

After claiming my bag and gun case — something I handled like a seasoned pro this time — I headed off to pick up my rental car. I presented my paperwork to the agent, who, after looking it over, asked me if I had any special requests.

"Yes, I do," I said. "Please be absolutely certain that it has a tow hitch."

He got me all checked into an SUV and directed me out to one of the porters who would bring the vehicle around.

The vehicle arrived, and it was another Tahoe — this time in silver with a light-beige interior, a roof rack, and a shiny steel tow hitch.

I pulled out of the airport on time and followed precise directions to my first destination: Boy Wonder's house.

For the sake of reference, directions have always been a challenge for me. I don't do well with north, south, east, and west. What I can follow are instructions like, "Get on the big highway and exit at Essex Street, exit 41. Turn right at the top of the ramp, go one mile, and turn left at the big rock onto Bourne, then left at the gas station, right after the second yellow mailbox, and it's the fourth house on the left with the paisley front door."

Jon was painfully aware of this, so my directions were thirteen pages long instead of six lines. The pamphlet was not only challenging to juggle while driving, but it also made the journey somewhat dangerous as well.

I arrived at the house after only a modest amount of difficulty and was relieved to have achieved step one.

It was great to see my young friend again. He hadn't changed much, but I could tell he had grown up a bit since last year. His attitude was better, he was calmer, and, overall, he seemed a bit more comfortable with himself.

We left his house and he told me that we had one stop to make before heading up to the ranch.

When I inquired about it, he said, "Jon wants us to stop by the store and get a few things for the cabin."

With that, he reached into his backpack and revealed a grocery list that looked more like the pre-flight checklist for NASA's space shuttle Endeavor.

We pulled into the grocery store lot, parked the car, and rearranged our gear to maximize the space for the groceries. Knowing Jon, I was certain we were going to need every square inch we could find.

We walked into the store, and I was already tired from traveling all day and consuming enough soda in Denver to float a battleship. I looked at this five-page list and thought, *This is going to take all night.* Even Boy Wonder asked how we were going to be able to tackle this in a reasonable amount of time.

I said, "Watch the pro at work," and engaged three baggers, gave them each one sheet, and told them we were in a huge hurry and needed their help. "First guy to complete his list gets twenty bucks."

Those guys each grabbed a cart and disappeared into the shelves. The race was on. I gave Boy Wonder a sheet and took the last one myself. Within thirty minutes we had eight shopping carts overflowing with groceries, including fourteen pounds of bacon, half the contents of the meat case, and every last Cinnamon Bear in the store. We checked off items on the list as they landed on the cashier's conveyor belt and were thrilled (and a bit surprised) to conclude that we had successfully acquired everything on the list.

The tab was a whopping $1,200, which I put on a card. We then proceeded to the car with a parade of carts behind us and loaded the Tahoe to its limit.

I tipped the guys each twenty bucks for helping (they were all winners, truly), and we drove off to the cabin with an ETA of eleven p.m.

The two of us spent the time in the car catching up and telling horrible jokes. We talked about our year, families, the fear of Jon's chili, you name it. And within moments, it was as if it had only been a week or two since we had last seen each other. It was great to know that we were still close and could easily relate to one another.

We arrived at the cabin having survived the trek up the mountain and the three gate obstacles. There we had expected to meet our entire group—all of whom were new to the insanity except for Jon, Wonder, and me. To our surprise, however, we were one man short. We got all the gear and groceries inside, then sat down to meet new friends and find out why our one little camper had not yet arrived.

The man in question lived in St. Louis, Missouri,

and worked with Jon. He was an exceptional gunsmith and had wanted for years to come out to Utah and be part of this infamous annual hunt. The only problem was that due to his weight (three-hundred-forty-plus pounds on a five-foot-six-inch frame), the altitude and physical exertion for a hunt of this magnitude would have put him in grave danger — literally.

In a healthy and well-meaning compromise, Jon had made a deal with him after returning from last year's hunt. It stipulated that if he lost sixty-five pounds by the following first of September, he could go on the trip that year.

To his credit, the guy busted his tail on a diet and daily exercise regimen that he'd stuck to for ten months without fail. And to everyone's shock, including his own, he achieved his goal by the deadline.

Because he had been successful, he and Jon sat down and talked about what he was to bring for the trip.

Jon was very specific and told him precisely what rifle to bring (a .30-06 that he already had and was deadly accurate with), what cartridges, what scope, etc. Jon also told him to fly, despite this guy's insistence that he drive so he could tow his ATV out there. Jon explained that that would be a terrible idea because he'd spend two days driving, possibly more with the trailer behind him, and once he got there, his ATV (which was older and not fuel-injected) wouldn't be calibrated for the altitude, making the effort completely worthless.

We sat fireside, enjoying another world-class inferno at the cabin, and asked where this man was. Jon shook his head and explained that the nimrod had decided to drive anyway and tow his trailer and

ATV along, in spite of what he had been specifically told not to do. Jon said the guy had been on the road for three days and ought to get in the next morning around seven. We hadn't planned on hunting the next day due to all the work we had to do in preparation for the week to follow, so he wasn't going to miss anything except a good card game, a head start on getting to know this year's group, and getting his fair shot at a truckload of Cinnamon Bears.

Before we knew it, the raging fire had turned to embers and it was time to call it a night. We headed into the dorm beneath the staircase, the one we had called home for a week the season before, and crawled into our respective bunks. Jon hit the lights, welcomed everyone again, and then made one last announcement. "The water system for the house has not yet been repaired, so there are no showers and no toilets."

I had heard this song before and found it even more insufferable this time around. I reflexively recoiled inside my sleeping bag and silently dreaded another season of outdoor latrine experiences.

"The outhouse is out the side door about thirty paces across the ridge," he continued. "Make sure you check for unfriendlies before you enter. See you Neanderthals in the morning."

10

AT HOME, WE JUST HAVE IT DELIVERED

We were all treated to a rare morning of sleeping in. Jon didn't dynamite us all out of bed until six, which to us, well, still seemed entirely too early. Okay, so it wasn't that big of a treat, but at least the sun was rising and it was better than nothing.

Jon invited any and all who wanted to ride down into Coalville with him to meet our friend who couldn't follow instructions. While we all began to get dressed, Jon headed into the bitter cold. He walked out to the meadow behind the cabin in an attempt to get cell reception so he could call our errant colleague. There he called his ATV-dragging acquaintance for an ETA and returned to us with astonishing (not really) news.

"I know those of you who know him will be shocked to hear that he is still three hours out. He took the wrong highway somewhere and added a couple hundred miles to his drive."

Jon told us not to worry, though, as he had plenty to keep us busy until it was time to drive into town. We all finished dressing and immediately started badgering our host for one of his now-famous breakfasts. After all, we figured that if he was going to put us to work, we would procrastinate for as long as we could.

Once we put the first two pounds of bacon through a rigorous taste test and had consumed as many pancakes as we dared, we figured it was time to take a nap. Jon, however, had a different outlook on things, so we all headed into the frosty world outside and awaited further direction from the boss.

He let us know that despite his efforts during the summer, when he'd cut down a tree, sectioned the entire thing, then split it all into logs before stacking and stockpiling the wood for our current weekend's comfort, there was not enough wood to get us through the week. He continued to explain that the shortage was due to the fact that the Village Idiot had been to the cabin and used it all with his group of followers, users, and rapacious egomaniacs. It was therefore our task for the day to fell a dead tree and turn it into kindling and firewood so we could stay warm in the cabin.

Naturally, I offered a much easier solution. I suggested that he simply call someone and order a few cords of wood. After all, that's the way it works at home, right?

The others laughed until they realized that I was being completely serious. Then they really got a roar out of it.

Of course, Jon was ready to beat me to death, but I just couldn't seem to appreciate that besides being inordinately expensive and the easy way out, it was entirely unrealistic to expect someone to drive hours on end to deliver a truckload of firewood to a cabin surrounded by woods. Clearly, one camper's obvious solution is not necessarily another's.

One of the guys grabbed a chainsaw and a pair of gloves, and we all walked down the road from the cabin looking for the right tree to cut down. We got down the hill a bit from the cabin, around the first two turns on the switchbacks, and Jon declared that the dead tree directly in front of him was the one. Without hesitation, the man armed with the chainsaw walked into the underbrush and said, "We can't get at the base safely, so we're going to have to keep searching, or I could cut it off higher on the trunk and we'll be okay."

Jon gave the order and we all looked on in disbelief as the lumberjack clipped the saw to a line off his belt and free-climbed about eight feet up this hundred-plus-foot tree. Then, as if to tempt fate, he secured himself with a strap around the trunk and cut the thing down.

It fell perfectly alongside the road to a modest collection of cheers and whistles. The lumberjack (from then on referred to as the Monkey with a Chainsaw, so-called for his adept climbing ability and prowess with the saw) then dismounted the tree and marched over for the segmentation portion of the project. This was our cue to get to work.

We were in charge of standing the newly cut short sections of the main body of the tree upright so they would not roll down the embankment. Once we finished sectioning the tree, it was time for the real labor to start. We made a stable base with a perfectly flat-topped log from the base of the tree and pulled out the axes. It was time to split wood.

This would clearly go on for hours, and we would all be called upon to take our turns. As it ended up, it really wasn't too bad — it was great as far as keeping warm and had its element of destruction too, which guys always appreciate.

About an hour into the latest segment of the chore, Grizzly declared that it was time to go into Coalville to collect the "last man outstanding," who was often maligned and rarely undeserving of it.

All seven of us suspended the wood-cutting exercise, piled into the Suburban and made the ninety-minute drive into town.

We pulled into a short-order restaurant's parking lot and impatiently sat waiting — frequently getting out of the car to stretch briefly before again needing the warmth of the vehicle to thaw. This went on for an hour.

Jon called again and, low and behold, Pinhead was, according to his map, five minutes away. Knowing better, Jon corrected him and suggested that he was at least thirty minutes away.

And then it started, "Of course, you'd have been here days ago if you'd listened to me," Jon scolded. "But no — you had to bring your ATV, which I guarantee is going to sit motionless on that trailer for the entire week."

The conversation ended abruptly, and we all continued to sit and wait. As we grew more impatient and annoyed, a couple of the boys decided that they were hungry and strolled into the restaurant to order some onion rings, burgers, and sodas. They came out raving about the food, and suddenly we all had to pile in and see what all the accolades were about. So, of course, the remaining members of the clown patrol (myself included) walked into the restaurant to order and consume stacks of food that none of us really needed.

After stuffing our faces with double cheeseburgers, fries, onion rings, burritos, enchiladas, and, believe it or not, hot fudge sundaes, we gingerly waddled out to the parking lot, groaning and holding our bellies.

We were just in time to see Jon emphatically yelling into his cell phone and jumping up and down in frustration at our tardy friend. We all just looked at one another as if to say, "This ought to be good."

"Well, where is he?" I asked after Grizzly hung up.

He replied, "He's finally on the correct road and should be coming from that direction," as he pointed behind him and down the road, "in *another* fifteen minutes! I'm gonna lose my mind."

Sure enough, after another fifteen-minute wait, here came Speed Glacier around the curve, over the bridge, and into the parking lot. We all cheered as though he had just arrived at the finish line of the Dakar Rally and mobbed him as he got out of the car. Of course, he had no idea why we were doing this. In fact, he didn't even know half of the guys yet. He thanked us reservedly for the welcome, and the introductions followed right there in the lot as we were all freezing.

He already knew Jon and me from back home, as well as another gentleman from St. Louis who worked as a superintendent for TWA. The airline guy was given the name Santa Claus because of his prominent white beard. Santa was a great guy who was beyond considerate of others and who, like Jon, would've given you the shirt off his back if you asked for it. He was a patient man approaching his fifties, with gray and silvering hair, the aforementioned beard, and a perpetual smile that was his signature. Having hunted all his life, he was extremely knowledgeable and quite a welcome resource, particularly for those of us who were new to the lifestyle.

Also from Missouri was a superintendent for Jon's business. BB, as he was called, was about thirty years old, approached six feet tall, had dark hair, and hailed from Birch Tree, Missouri, population 276. (I'm serious.) He was a funny guy with a lot of comedic energy and adapted to our ill-mannered brand of humor as though there were no adjustment needed to begin with. In other words, he was just as warped as we were.

As for the others, he had never met Boy Wonder or the Monkey with the Chainsaw, who, incidentally, was one of the last people you would ever want to insult or make fun of. He was one of only three people on the trip that had a physique that served his hunting proficiency in a positive manner. He was a big man and, under the right circumstances, could have come off as extremely intimidating. Suffice it to say, I think we were all relieved to be on his good side. Even though his outward appearance was rugged and menacing, he was actually the most reserved, approachable, and even-keeled person on the hunt. He was really a gentle giant at six-foot-three and two hundred forty pounds with a muscular build.

The other guy, with the do-not-disturb appearance, was Harry. He was a former collegiate football standout who had been considered by multiple professional football organizations until he was badly injured in his second-to-last game as an amateur. He was also well over six feet tall and chiseled and looked to be a building cleverly disguised as a man. Harry (so nicknamed as a shortened version of his last name) was one of the nicest guys you'd ever want to meet and had the gift of being able to roll with the punches, provided that he got the last one. That was usually a deal-breaker, so most of us were smart enough to endear ourselves to him rather than make an adversary of him.

Finally, there was the new arrival—the big guy. (And I mean horizontally, not vertically.) After all the introductions were complete, Jon just couldn't wait to sink his teeth into him about the trailer, the ATV, the need to drive, etc. Jon lit him up like a Christmas tree. Once Grizzly got his pound of flesh, he sent the new guy into the establishment to get a soda before we headed up to the ranch.

After a few minutes, a couple of us wandered into the restaurant to see what was taking so long, and here we found our new buddy chatting up the girl behind the counter as though he had all the time in the world.

"C'mon, bud, we've got to make our way back up to the cabin," I said in an effort to pry him away from the siren.

Once I was able to extricate him from the restaurant and turn his focus from dating back to hunting, we all climbed back into the vehicles and started our journey back up into the mountains, where it became very clear, at just the second gate, that the trailer was, at least at this altitude, way too much for the big guy's car to pull.

The solution was that we had to switch the trailer onto Jon's Suburban, which, as you can imagine, made Jon all sorts of cheery. It also reintroduced the monologue about the trailer and its useless presence.

As we got on our way again, we passed through the second gate and then, eventually, the third. We locked up behind ourselves and drove up to the cabin, where we promptly disengaged the trailer from Jon's

Suburban, parked it on the corner of the gravel driveway, and forgot about it.

"Welcome to the cabin," Jon said to our newcomer. "The tour is later. For now, grab your coat and follow us. We've got logs to split."

We all wandered down the road and returned to the project we had started earlier in the day. With the newfound energy from the food and sodas we consumed in town, as well as the hilarity of Jon's ongoing monologue showcasing his frustrations with the trailer and four-wheeler, it was back to work on the tree.

After we had amassed a fairly significant pile of split wood, it became my job to bring the Suburban down and, with Boy Wonder's help, neatly load the firewood into the back. We were then to transport it to the side of the cabin and stack it for later use. The two of us must have moved a hundred fifty pieces of wood per load and completed eight or nine trips before the last of the wood was carefully stacked in its proper place — no doubt, a job well done.

For the record, I still maintain that it would have been easier to buy it and have it delivered. But I have to admit that there was a sense of pride and accomplishment after we finished, which I hadn't ever really experienced. To be fair, there was a backache the magnitude of which I had never experienced either. So there was definitely a tradeoff, but one that Jon and my therapist are convinced was worthwhile in the end.

When we finished cutting the wood, Jon decided to take the group on an introductory tour of the grounds. He took a group in his car and I took the rest in mine.

As we had done the previous year, we pulled away from the cabin and drove down the hill, through the opening in the band of trees and into the open where we arrived at the intersection of the three roads. We turned right onto the East Road, my favorite, and headed off toward the Bear Claw and all other points north and northeast. It all came flooding back to me just how magnificent a property this entire ranch really was. It was truly one of the most scenic and majestic places, filled with raw natural beauty, that I had ever seen. And judging by the comments from the others in the car, they were in agreement.

We drove across the wide-open meadows and wound through and around all the swaths of timber as we started getting closer to the forests. Before I knew it, we were riding along the top of a familiar ridge without a lot of room for error but beautiful country vistas in the balance.

We then proceeded through another mass of trees and arrived at one of the most peaceful spots on the entire property—the shallow waterscape where Stunt Mouse and Beanpole had had to clear our passage the year before.

As we slowly pushed across the hard-to-navigate path to the other side, we even saw the very rock and tree trunk that had been moved by the guys that day. Everything seemed as though no one had touched a thing since we'd left, and I felt as rejuvenated as I had the last time I was here—although back then I didn't quite yet know why.

We continued past the serene setting and across the ridgetop with the Bear Claw to the right and Deep Canyon beyond the open fields giving way to sagebrush and evergreen stands to the left. Then, as we emerged from a thicket of aspens, I could see ahead the place where I'd embarked on my adventure to the fence line the previous season.

The scenery was amazing as usual, but what really got the guys wound up was the abundance of wildlife we all saw standing around grazing and mindlessly wandering about. The deer were everywhere, and we were even treated to a cow-moose sighting. That, of course, prompted Jon to rib me about my previous encounters when we all got out to stretch our legs and listen to him describe the property and tell some stories.

The tour continued down the open hillside, past the Jackrabbit Stage, and back into the woods. Eventually the road led to the switchbacks, where I quickly rediscovered the anxiety they'd generated the first time I'd approached them.

Jon got out of his car and walked back to mine to make sure I was comfortable with tackling the road ahead. Now here I was in quite the predicament. I had ridden with Jon down the Switchbacks of Death several times the year before, each time being a bit less terrifying than the last, but I had never been in the driver's seat before. Here I was being handed a great deal of responsibility and trust — a tremendous compliment that I didn't want to squander.

On the other hand, this was no joke. Not only was this a treacherous stretch of road that called for some serious driving ability, but I had the very real responsibility of the safety of others in my hands, to say nothing of the accountability I had regarding the return of the rental car in its original form.

Jon asked me if I was up to it and, not wanting to let him down, I said that I was. I rolled up the window and tried to conceal the fact that I was shaking like a possum passing a peach pit.

"Why are you so scared? What's the big deal?" asked Santa Claus from the passenger seat.

Boy Wonder sounded off from the back seat, "Oh, just wait. You'll understand soon enough."

Within thirty yards, the road fell away to the steep angle that initiates the descent into Deep Canyon. It was the first stretch that led to switchback curve number one. Santa immediately leaned forward and peered over the hood as he saw the roof of Jon's Sub-urban literally disappear before his very eyes. I slowed to a crawl and inched over the crest of the hill. I was alarmed at the steepness of the grade, which seemed twice as severe from the driver's seat as it ever had from where Santa currently resided. At that point, Jon was past the first turn and immediately under us on the second straightaway, some sixty feet below and facing the opposite direction. I approached the first turn with great caution, trying to remember the line Jon had used in his approach a year ago. I success-fully navigated the first turn and then the second, all at the blazing speed of about four miles per hour. The third turn was the tightest of them all and offered zero wiggle room. There was no way to reverse from a bad angle and try again. The road was so narrow and the turn so tight that any attempt to improve your position by reversing would likely make it worse by putting at least one tire dangerously close to the edge of the road, which fell away sharply.

I was doing fine until I ended up taking a poor line into the turn. I had driven us into a remarkably poor sit-uation. Both Boy Wonder and Santa had to get out and watch, with meticulous scrutiny, every inch I covered in trying to right my wrong. It took five minutes, but we finally cleared the turn and were on our way again down the next cliff-hugging straightaway and into turn number four. Ultimately, it took a good twenty minutes to descend to the base of Deep Canyon, but I had done it. (Thanks to some greatly needed help from my team.)

We drove across the shallow waters flowing on the canyon floor and exited the vehicles for a well-earned deep breath. (I was a nervous wreck!)

After everyone's nerves had returned to their normal baseline, we headed through the far reaches of the property's northeast corner and back to the Middle Road. Turning north, we then explored the lower end of the ranch before returning to the cabin via the West Road. It all looked just as amazing as I remembered it, only now I had the experiences to go along with the landscape and scenery. My excitement began to build again, and the next day couldn't arrive fast enough.

In fact, we were all excited to begin our hunt that next morning. It was easy to look past the evening's festivities, but we didn't dare. We were equally excited for dinner, cards, a warm fire, humorous stories, copious amounts of abuse, and the beginning of new friendships. We just hoped that Boy Wonder was smart enough not to pick a fight with the chainsaw-wielding Monkey Man.

As we sat in front of the fire back at the cabin, we got to know one another. As usual, the barbs flew around the room like a flock of seagulls over a fishing trawler. There were obviously some easier targets in the group, particularly the latecomer with the must-have-ATV debacle and his shameless advances toward the girl in town.

After enduring Jon's continuing rant about the four-wheeler and its trailer, our chubby friend excused himself to unpack. Shortly after leaving the room, he was heard making some odd remarks from the dorm.

"What the? Oh, c'mon! What is *this*?" he was heard saying in an agitated tone.

He reappeared and asked for some paper towels after having discovered that his shampoo bottle had leaked. There he stood, obviously annoyed and flustered, holding his camo hat, which now had a pool of neon green shampoo in it. Leading to even more of his displeasure was the discovery of his other hand—the gooey strings of sticky slime that stretched from each finger to another from having grabbed the soap-covered bottle.

Being the decidedly compassionate friends we all endeavored to be, we directed him to the closest roll of paper towels. However, what I may be glossing over was the intense laughter at the latest arrival's expense.

I could sense a nickname coming from this event, and it wasn't long before someone made a reference to the green ooze from their children's favorite animated movies about a team of shelled reptiles wielding Samurai swords.

It was clear at this moment that he was not taking the harassment in stride. In fact, he was rapidly becoming highly defensive and more aggressive than seemed appropriate or normal by most standards. Apparently, we had really rattled his cage.

Now, anyone who knows anything about a bunch of guys knows that if you let something like that get under your skin, the last thing that's going to happen is that the group will let it go. It's a cruel fact of nature and human interaction, specifically among adults acting like children. So, naturally, the more visibly angry he got, the more we rode him. Within minutes and much to his dismay, his nickname was cemented in the annals of lore at the ranch. Forever, from that day forward, he would be known as "Turtle." (Likely it had more to do with the common bond he shared with them — the inability to right themselves when on their backs — than any relation to the green goo that was now all over the contents of his suitcase.)

It was unmistakable. He was at his threshold for tolerating our shameless and ever-escalating behavior and finally disappeared up the stairs with a stern, "Yeah? Well, you guys are jerks!" which predictably set us off all over again.

By the time he returned from the kitchen sink and was devoid of shampoo, we had managed to calm ourselves and were almost slightly ashamed for jumping this guy over something so silly. In fact, it had prompted us all to agree that we owed him an apology upon his return, which we were entirely prepared to extend, until he showed up and immediately began to laugh from the bottom of his soul.

"Yeah, that was really funny," he admitted. "I do have a hard time getting up from being on my back."

We all recognized that it must have taken a pretty strong backbone to tolerate all of that abuse (particularly after having lost a significant amount of weight) and then laugh at yourself.

We all apologized anyway, and he was instantly assimilated into the twisted group that made up the season's hunt. Unfortunately for him, the name Turtle was now official and well beyond retraction.

The baptism of fire complete, it was time for Jon to get started on dinner and the rest of us to continue to mold the couch cushions and chairs into the shape of our backsides. (For the record, we were all really good at that right off. It was practically instinctual.)

As we all talked, we heard about Turtle's agreement that he had made with Jon, how he'd achieved his goal, and how thrilled he was to have ended up on the hunt. It was a remarkable story for which we all applauded him.

However, the part that we were starting to dread for him was sitting at the dinner table for Jon's phenomenal dinners every night and watching us gorge ourselves. We wondered whether he was planning on sticking to a healthy diet or a specific calorie count, or perhaps he had met his goal and would drop the diet altogether for the trip.

I finally just asked him, and he pointed out that he understood exactly what was about to happen at the table and assured us that he was fine with it. He mentioned that he was going to have reduced portions and try to eat multiple small and healthy snacks throughout the day instead of one or two colossal meals as had been his habit in the past.

"Go ahead," he said. "Eat until you pop."

The dinner bell sounded with a pleasant, "Come and get it if you want it. If you don't want it, get up here and pretend."

We all filed upstairs to discover the feast du jour was home-smoked (right on the deck) baby-back ribs and pork loin, mashed potatoes and gravy, corn, biscuits, and homemade preserves.

At this point, Boy Wonder and I knew what was coming and were simply giddy. We looked around the table and saw these other guys absolutely drooling. They thought they had won the lottery. (And in a lot of ways, they really had.) The dinner was outstanding as usual, and after all the talk throughout the day and over dinner, it was quite apparent that we had another great group for our hunt.

By the time dinner was over and we were all sated, we were dead tired. Boy Wonder and I had our kitchen duties to perform (after retrieving the water with the coolers from the spring) and the rest of the guys spoke of one or two rounds of Ninety-nine before bed. The lone standout was Turtle, who declared that he was going to adjourn to the bathroom for a spell and then promptly apologized in advance.

We all laughed a bit as we knew exactly what was coming. Jon repeated his announcement about the bathrooms and showers and then declared those destinations entirely off limits. He then spoke of the outhouse and described its location while our reptilian friend (in name only) stared at him in disbelief.

"You have got to be joking," he stammered with a puzzled look on his face.

"Have a nice stroll," Jon said as we all laughed again.

Turtle looked frustrated as he turned to walk down the steps and out to the scenic pooper. But when he returned, the guys said he seemed quite invigorated.

"Wow, it's cold!" he said when he walked through the door ten minutes later and rushed over to the fire.

I guess it wasn't so much that he was relieved as it was that he'd frozen his shell off out there and was now overly alert.

Boy Wonder and I arrived downstairs just in time for the last hand of Ninety-nine for the night and a well-deserved handful of the precious Cinnamon Bear stash.

We recounted stories from the past season for the new group and laughed until our sides were sore. It was certainly shaping up to be a fun time.

At this point, though, I started to wonder if I would get to shoot my gun this time, let alone if I would actually kill something with it. Only time would tell, but oh, was I anxious to find out.

The world's most annoying (and threatening) alarm clock was merely hours away from sounding, so we all decided it was time to call it a night and head to our racks. Within twenty minutes, we were all comfortable in our bunks. Jon cut the lights and, with an ever-so-soothing voice, invited each one of us not to utter another syllable lest he be shot and thrown to the mountain lions.

11

THERE'S BLOOD ON THEM THAR HILLS

Another morning arrived, and I mean Jon's version of morning, not everyone else's, which would include some portion of the sun being visible.

He thundered, "Everybody up. It's time to go play outside. It's going to be a beautiful day . . . for an arctic fox! Breakfast in ten."

A member of the group stirred slightly and muttered out of his semiconscious haze, "Morning? It's still dark."

Jon shouted back over his shoulder as he walked out of the room, "That's right! Now get up! And somebody explain it to him while I start cooking."

Off to another spirited start, I thought, snickering a bit as I got out of bed. I had conveniently forgotten how difficult it was to get up "Grizzly Style" at the cabin.

The dressing process was a bit rough since I hadn't organized my clothes particularly well. So while everyone else was properly clad and leaving to go upstairs, I was fumbling around looking for fundamental elements of my daily wardrobe. I searched urgently for socks and long underwear, let alone the vital components I hadn't yet even gotten to yet, like thermal camo pants and my heavy coat.

"You coming, Fred?" asked Jon's friend BB.

"Be there in a minute," I responded. "I can't find my pants."

A collective chuckle made its way throughout the room as those of us lagging behind struggled to catch up to the others. Finally managing to assemble ourselves, we stumbled upstairs to the breakfast festivities.

The day's first meal turned out to be quite an enlightening event. We were told, first and foremost, that it was still lip-splittingly cold outside and no change in that feature was likely to happen during our stay. Additionally, we found out that the food pantry to whom we'd donate our harvested animals was running especially short on food this year, and that they were very concerned heading into the colder months. (Thank you for the extra pressure.) Finally, we were informed that, halfway through the trip, we would have a crowded cabin again; the Village Idiot was bringing another "couple of friends" up for a hunt.

Naturally, we interpreted that to mean the equivalent of Rhode Island's entire population. That was a fair guess, but we would find out in a few days for sure.

In his infinite wisdom, Jon got down to business for the day and began pairing hunters and letting them know where they would be spending their morning. It was my assignment to drop off Harry and Boy Wonder all the way down the Middle Road at the Weather Station. I was then to turn around and drive halfway back to hunt Bluebell Flats with the Monkey. I was told that I was responsible for him, which technically meant that I was his guide, given that he had never been on the property. This left Jon and Santa hunting together.

Bluebell Flats was a pretty easy walk in the woods, and I knew where I was going, so I felt comfortable with that part of the task. But how I was going to set up, taking into account the wind and other details, was a mystery that had me entirely perplexed. I just didn't have the experience yet to make those kinds of decisions with any degree of expertise.

Looking at the big picture, this was a comedy in the making: the inexperienced hunter who couldn't locate north if he were holding a compass (and whose preference would be to have professional staff bring him cocktails out in the field), leading an experienced hunter who was tall enough to pinpoint a direction by simply looking over the trees.

I asked Jon, "So, essentially, I'm the carpool driver because I know the road and have the Tahoe, and I'm the activity leader for the hike to the hunting spot because I've been there before. All other responsibilities fall to Monkey Man. Does that about cover it?"

We all laughed (because the truth is often funny), and Jon said, "Couldn't have put it any better myself."

Monkey then inquired, "So, in plain English, I'm babysitting Peach Fuzz this morning?"

Another round of laughter circulated and Jon replied, "Exactly."

The others decided on their hunting destinations as we all consumed traditional sausage-and-egg biscuits and hot chocolate. The sun's advent was becoming imminent, so we left the table and ambled downstairs to collect our coats and guns. Only a short time later (but a bit tardy by Jon's standards), we were all piling into the cars to head out for the morning hunt. Indeed, we were late, but the sun was rising and we were able to see — so that was a plus in my opinion.

Before we left, Jon declared that there would be a detour before everyone was free to go to their assigned spots. "Follow me," he said. "We are going to drive down the East Road. I have a feeling about something."

Now, just to be absolutely clear, this was not a road-hunting expedition — something that, while legal, is not how I was taught to hunt. Jon told us on the way down from the cabin that before the shooting got started on the ranch, often there were elk in a clearing toward the end of East Road and a couple hundred yards into the woods. This is what we were setting out to investigate. However, before we got that far down the road, we were surprised with an opportunity of a lifetime.

Jon was driving the lead car, occupied by Turtle in the front seat and Santa and me in the back. Boy Wonder was driving my Tahoe and had Chainsaw, Harry, and BB with him. We drove down the East Road and slowed to a crawl as we approached the wide-open rolling hills between Deep Canyon and the south end of the Bear Claw.

We were in the midst of a perfectly normal conversation (at least, normal by our standards) when Jon brought the vehicle to a stop just over a rise in the road between Deep Canyon and the south end of the Bear Claw. He quietly addressed us all with the universally understood utterance requesting silence, and in a manner indicating some sense of importance: "Hey, everybody shut up!" Then, under his breath, "Turtle, get out of the car slowly and shoot it."

Our conversations ceased immediately and we all looked directly out the windshield. Standing exactly one hundred three yards (according to a rangefinder) from the hood ornament, was a bull elk for the record books. Our jaws all dropped as we watched this majestic beast posing in the morning mist on the very spot where I had begun my hike toward the fence line the season before.

This animal was truly massive and left us all speechless. It had to weigh well north of one thousand pounds, and he towered over a rock feature next to him, which used to look significant. His neck was a dark chestnut color, his body a light caramel, and he stood there as if he ruled all he surveyed. Our eyes were all the size of dinner plates. The antlers were gigantic in mass as well as in length and height — they stretched out beyond the animal's hindquarters when he lifted his head up into the wind. This was, without question, the trophy of a lifetime for any hunter, in any state, and was declared by our host to easily be a top-two Boone and Crockett elk.

Now Jon was keenly aware that if there was anyone in the group that needed a shot in the arm, it was Turtle. Here was a solid guy, a great person by any criteria, who was simply down in the mouth and had a lot on his shoulders. Here was a chance for him to experience one of those life-altering moments, and Jon didn't hesitate for a moment in assigning that opportunity when he saw the bull.

Turtle carefully and quietly opened the truck's door and stretched his foot toward the ground. He stood out of the vehicle, pushed his rifle through the open window, and rested his barrel on the sill. Carefully, he took aim, then lowered the stock from his shoulder and climbed back into the car.

"What are you doing? Get out and shoot it!" Jon said anxiously.

Turtle again crawled out of the car. This time he walked slowly around the door, placed his elbow on the hood, and extended the barrel right over the corner of the engine cover.

"You're going to destroy my hood! Stand up!" Jon whispered.

Turtle slowly came back around the door to use the sill again.

Jon, now about ready to wet his pants, exclaimed urgently, yet quietly, "Not from the road! Duh! And you'd better hurry up, he's going to go into the woods. Shoot!"

Meanwhile, Boy Wonder had approached from the other car and appeared at Jon's window asking if he could shoot it.

This was taking forever, and we are all dying with anticipation.

Finally, Turtle deftly stepped off the road without alarming the animal and raised his gun for the shot. The elk now presented a full-on broad side and was just standing there waiting to die.

The suspense ratcheted up beyond all reasonable levels, and we were holding our collective breath awaiting a gunshot. And then, to our horror, the elk threw his head back and began to take a step. It was now or never for Turtle, and we thought he was going to drop the ball.

Finally, the gun discharged, and the report echoed in the silence. We all saw the elk wince as it absorbed the bullet, then watched as he ran off the plateau. It circled back around behind the hillside and entered the trees.

We were certain that the elk had been mortally wounded. Our cheers rang out immediately and high-fives became the order of the morning. We had just watched our friend blast the biggest elk any of us had ever seen, which was really saying something when we considered that Jon had been hunting them for thirty years. This elk was the granddaddy of them all, and none of us could've been more excited for our buddy.

Jon announced that we needed to give the bull time to expire, and we should all clear out to head for our spots. The plan was to return in a few hours and track the blood trail to the harvest. Once again, congrats were offered as we regrouped and jumped into the appropriate vehicles to drive to our preassigned locations.

As I had been instructed, I dropped Boy Wonder and Harry off down near the tower. I then drove back to Bluebell Flats with the Monkey, ditched the car beside the road, and began the short walk to the scenic field, which we would be glassing in thirty short minutes.

It was all about to start again, and I was so excited to be back. Unlike last time, however, the weather was a bit unstable; the sky was gray and the landscape looked a bit drab without the benefit of the bright sun showcasing all the brilliant colors of the aspen trees and the diverse ground cover. It was also bone-chillingly cold, with no electric blanket in sight.

Walking kept us warm, but I was concerned. It was only a twenty-minute hike to our destination, followed by a brief setup. After that, we would be taking cover in the tree line and staying put for a few hours while the breeze intensified the biting cold.

We reached the fields and needed only to shift about a hundred yards to maximize our position related to the wind. We found a collection of huge trees that we used to our advantage for physical comfort as well as for indirect shelter from the wind. Once we were settled, the rifles were at the ready, the binos were out, and the glassing began.

While we hadn't seen anything yet since we'd separated from the guys, there was evidence of activity all around us. We had noticed fresh tracks crossing the creek back by the car, we had observed multiple sets of tracks and fresh sign on a trail in the woods, and we were encouraged having already heard a gunshot from east of our position, likely in the woods descending into the top of Deep Canyon. There was also the excitement of Turtle's monster elk, which had already set a positive tone for the day.

Directly behind us, the morning mist was retreating into the woods and the field was primed for action. We watched intently for any movement and eventually saw a younger bull, due south of our position, wandering slowly down the hill to the clearing. He was well out of range for any reasonable or responsible shot, so we just watched and hoped that he would eventually get close enough to present us with a practical opportunity.

Meanwhile, there was some movement on the southwest corner of the Flats: two does were bravely testing the open. We kept an eye on them as well, hoping that they wouldn't spook our boy strolling down to the meadow. I glanced over at the Buzz Saw Primate and pointed directly west to make him aware of another doe that had wandered out into the field. We were in the thick of it that morning, and I was getting really excited. I was thinking that this could be the day.

I was reluctant to take any of the does. While I had the proper tags, they were all quite small—oh, and out of season, as I was reminded. (Sometimes it's tough to make sure your excitement doesn't override your situational awareness. Had I shot a deer, it would have been an honest mistake, but I'd still have broken the law.) But both of us had our eyes on that bull coming down the hill, and we both knew he was a shooter.

As we continued to watch him, he went behind one of only two tree clusters on the hillside. This one was out in the middle of the landscape, while the other was at the base of the hill and closer to the corner of the opening. It was our hope that he would continue to walk down into the Flats, rather than follow a path toward the other bunch of trees that would lead him to the woods. Had he followed that path, we would have had only one long-range opportunity just before he stepped into the timber. Neither one of us wanted that shot.

All the while, the does were multiplying in the corner. They now stood as a group of five, and the doe to our west had a new friend as well: a spike (a young deer with unbranched antlers) had joined her to graze for a moment.

The entire situation was mesmerizing. It was hard to imagine that we would want to startle them and run them off with a gunshot — until we got a really good look at the bull on the hill. He had gotten closer, and he looked to be a three-year-old. He was a smaller four-by-four but would still mean hundreds of pounds of meat for those benefiting from our harvest. At that moment, it was still a two-hundred-fifty-yard shot.

While both of us were certainly comfortable at that range, we also realized that the closer he got, the less distance we would have to carry the spoils. We were, therefore, obliged to give him a bit more time. Admittedly, though, I was becoming keenly impatient.

In the minutes that followed, the bull changed course a bit and was now angling toward the collection of does gathered on the corner of the field.

In other news, the little spike had walked clear across to the middle of the Flats and seemed entirely oblivious to any activity going on around him.

It had been ninety minutes since we first sat down, and we were enjoying every minute of the show.

As the bull cautiously ambled ever closer, we both slowly reached for our rifles. I slowly rocked forward and got into a prone position, raised the stock to my shoulder, and looked through my scope. I then looked back at Monkey Man, who was seated with his back against the tree and looking through his scope. We waited, motionless, for another ten minutes and ranged the elk again.

The bull was at one hundred ninety yards and stood partially behind an outcropping of rock, shielding all but his head from view. He seemed apprehensive as he simply stared ahead. I glanced to the corner where there were only three deer left. They too appeared pensive and began to step closer to the woods. I couldn't help but wonder if there was something going on off-stage that would jeopardize the opportunity. I looked back at my partner and whispered, "Do you have a shot?"

He nodded and pointed back at me. "You?" he mouthed.

I shook my head and motioned to him to take it.

I watched though my scope and remained ready to back him up.

After what seemed like an eternity, a shot rang out like the crack of thunder. The bull charged across the hillside with an impressive burst of speed, covering forty yards in just seconds. It then slowed to a walk as it appeared suddenly yet decisively disoriented. It stopped, stumbled to its left, and then crumbled to the ground.

The hillside was still again. The deer in the field had all scattered into the trees, and Chainsaw and I exhaled and looked at each other with big smiles and gestured to each other with a thumbs-up. We watched for another couple of minutes before confirming what we had already suspected: the bull was hit, and hit hard. The animal was dead.

As we approached, it was clear that its death had been swift. It was a textbook shot, placed immediately behind the shoulder through both lungs. It looked peaceful lying there in the grass — quite the contrast from the violence of only moments ago. But this was a triumph, an event to be grateful for, because we knew that this meant food for people who could otherwise not afford it for themselves.

Chainsaw set his rifle down as he knelt behind the beast, removed his hat, and said a few personal words of thanks. After a short moment of silence, he donned his hat and picked up the elk's head by the antlers. It was a beautiful specimen with eight symmetrical points (the way normal people count them) and looked to have a lot of meat on his bones. There were a couple energetic high-fives before the knife came out to notch the tag, but then he quickly and quietly got to the task at hand.

The extent of my assistance was holding the bull's legs out of Chainsaw's way. Beyond that, I explained to him, he was on his own. He asked, "Well, what's going to happen when you kill one?"

I said that based on my performance last year, we may not have to worry about it. Then I told him that if, in fact, I was able to put one on the ground, my hope was that I would be with someone who was sympathetic to my aversion to butchering animals and do most of the dirty work, if not all of it, for me.

"What does Jon think of that plan?" he asked as if he didn't already know the answer.

I responded, "Well, Jon and I have a unique understanding on this subject. I understand that on the ethical side of things, I have a responsibility as a hunter, to perform this out of respect for the sport and the animal. He understands that I have a very weak constitution when it comes to that sort of thing, and that while I respect these animals and this sport deeply, I dislike throwing up a great deal as well."

He smiled and said, "So who's going to win that battle?"

I simply replied, "I suppose that depends on who I'm hunting with that day, doesn't it?"

He finished dressing the elk, stood, and wiped his blade. We secured all our gear, each grabbed an antler, and started to pull the carcass toward the road. All it took was three steps for us to realize that the likelihood of us reaching the car before dying of exhaustion was negligible.

We then decided to go with plan B: make Jon come down with the four-wheeler and drag it out to the road after lunch. We were quite pleased with our new approach of dropping the problem in someone else's lap, and we returned to the SUV at a relaxed pace while we debated how long the weather would hold out. The skies were still gray and had become somewhat daunting, but our moods had greatly improved knowing we had contributed to an important cause.

The two of us headed off to retrieve Harry and Boy Wonder, fulfilling our assigned duties before heading back up to the cabin to give Jon another chore to manage. We spent the entire ride back telling them about our adventurous morning hunt, and they were impressed and eager to see the spoils.

Back at the cabin, it turned out that we weren't the only ones who had scored that first morning. BB was also on the board with an atypical six-by-four, which had a unique drop tine that gave him some serious points for character. He shot the elk on his hunt with Jon as it stepped out from behind a cluster of evergreens. It was also a hefty bull, so we were off to a good start for the food pantry and the people that it served. That was something of which we were particularly proud.

Lunch was fun for sure—at least that's what I had heard. Jon, Turtle, and I had headed back to the scene of the early morning opportunity to find Turtle's bull. I drove Jon's SUV while he trailed with the four-wheeler. When we arrived, we parked right where the elk had been standing when Turtle pulled the trigger. We looked around carefully until Jon noticed a droplet of blood and a tuft of fur. We marked the spot and started scrutinizing every blade of grass and every fallen leaf in line with the direction the bull had run. We found another drop of blood, and then another and another and another. They were about fifteen feet apart, consistent with an elk on the run. Again, the excitement was building. But as we worked around the hill and got to the brush line and then into the trees, the animal was getting harder to track as the blood trail was diminishing, not growing. We were concentrating so hard that we were silent, except when noting the discovery of another drop of blood, a displaced leaf, or any evidence of a large wounded animal running through the forest. As the droplets of blood were getting smaller and farther apart from each other, Jon started to speculate that this may not have the ending we were all hoping for.

We tracked the animal for a solid quarter mile over a three-hour period, turning over every conceivable leaf on hands and knees, continuing to search well after running out of blood to follow. The trail had gone cold and the elk was nowhere to be found. It had escaped into the deepest recesses of the Bear Claw without a trace. Jon and I were disappointed, but Turtle was devastated.

Jon asked him to explain the shot to the best of his recollection, and Turtle said that he had the crosshairs on the elk and was just about to pull the trigger when the bull started to move forward.

"So I led him a bit and pulled the trigger." he lamented.

"You led him?" Jon asked? "At a hundred yards? What gun were you shooting?"

Turtle quietly replied, "The 300 Weatherby magnum you told me not to buy last week."

Jon just hung his head and said, "Other than the few shots at the range, that was your first time shooting that gun, wasn't it?"

Turtle affirmed his guess.

"You're one of the best shots I know," Jon offered. "Had you brought the gun you've been familiar with for years, the one that I told you to bring, you'd be sitting on the elk of a lifetime right now."

Turtle just shook his head, and we all moped back to the vehicles.

We then drove to Bluebell Flats, where Jon was going to help retrieve Chainsaw's bull. Once we parked the Suburban, Turtle and I jumped on the back of the quad, and we all rode to the hillside just south of the open field.

The mood was pretty somber, and Turtle was clearly down. We felt bad for him, so Jon tried to cheer him up a bit.

"See, Turtle? This is what it looks like when you actually hit what you're aiming at with a gun you're used to shooting."

He responded with a disconsolate, "Yeah, I know. Can we just drop it?"

"Drop what?" Jon mused. "The ball or the subject?"

Silence persisted from Turtle but came with a nonverbal and very recognizable expression that said, "Back off, Jon!"

We wrapped a strap around the bull's antlers and mounted the quad again. As we dragged the field-dressed elk out toward the SUV, the weather turned markedly colder and the wind picked up. It was clear that a front was approaching, although with what, we weren't sure.

When we got to Jon's Suburban, Turtle and I retreated to the comfort of the enclosed interior and followed Jon back to the cabin with the sad news that there was not a Boone and Crockett elk to celebrate.

"It appears to have been nothing more than a brisket shot with very little blood," Jon reported. The cabin fell quiet, and we all tried to take Turtle's mind off the disappointment.

As we sat down to talk, we had a lot of stories to tell that featured action beyond the drive to and from the places we hunted that morning. Of course, I took a conversational beating over my stance of not wanting blood in my rental car, but I had expected that. Jon got everyone refocused and took a bit off Turtle's shoulders with a little pep talk on what we had accomplished so far and what we anticipated for the rest of our time on the ranch. Despite our setback, we were off to a tremendous start and enthusiastically optimistic about what was to come.

As a result, we were all anxious to get back out into the field and keep the streak going, and it wasn't much more than an hour before we were getting ready to head back out.

This time, Santa and I headed down the East Road, past the water feature and the Jackrabbit's Stage, to a thick stand of trees just above the walls of Deep Canyon. It was a dark and eerie place on the property — only a mile up the road from the switchbacks. We carefully walked in some five hundred yards and set up near the convergence of two game trails.

The paths formed a "Y," and after sitting for a few minutes, Santa had me walk into the trails' intersection and walk upwind (south) until I had a clear shooting path to both trails and optimal visibility. He stayed behind me and planned on calling a bit. He said the idea was to entice the elk to walk toward the call and focus on something farther in the distance. This, he explained, would offer a distraction and possibly give me a better opportunity.

I stalked through the trees as I moved up into position. I found a perfect spot where I could sit against a tree, had great shooting lanes to both trails, and could see relatively far up the paths into the woods. I sat patiently for an hour and didn't hear a thing, other than my heart beating in my chest.

As I sat against the tree, scouring the woods for any movement or shape that was out of place, I couldn't see anything. The rustle of leaves in a short breeze refocused my attention on the woods—both the tranquility of the moment and the potential excitement.

It's amazing what was going through my head as I sat and watched—all the scenarios like, *What if a bull comes from this side or that? What if Santa gets one behind me? If the wind shifts, what direction am I vulnerable from?*

It was actually quite interesting to notice where my mind was this year compared to where it had been last year, when I had been distracted by the clouds, the mountains or a certain squirrel as I sat on the fence line. It was almost as if I was picking up hunters' habits and beginning to think like one. Certainly, that couldn't happen to a city boy like me, who is generally more interested in hunting for a tee time on a sunny day at the country club rather than an animal in the woods when the temperatures outside were approaching freezing. Surely the divergence was a poser.

Even though I may have been transforming ever so slightly, each little noise I heard still put me on full alert. I would think, *Is it game? Is it a mountain lion or bear coming to attack me? Or is it death itself stalking and preparing to collect me?* It was frightening and exhilarating all at the same time.

Occasionally, Santa would call a bit—just a couple mews to see if he could stir anything. But it was not to be. There just wasn't anything moving right then. However, it was only about three-thirty, so we still had a good chance to see some animals toward day's end as they moved around between watering holes and their bedding areas. We just held our ground and played the waiting game, something that was still a difficult test for me. After all, patience had never been my strong suit.

This became much more about discipline as it was about anything else. While I may have been doing all right outwardly, there was a huge part of me that just wanted to wander back to Santa and start telling jokes.

Then around four o'clock, I heard a twig snap, and I became acutely aware of my surroundings. I slowly turned my head to the right and peered through the tree trunks and bars of light streaming through the thick awning of leaves overhead. Santa must have heard it too as he offered a soft mew through his call.

I got chills (and not just because the temperature was falling) and looked for any movement at all through the trees. I was never able to see anything, but it was as though I could almost feel a presence just beyond my sight line. Nothing ever appeared, the adrenaline took thirty minutes to subside again, and I continued my watch.

A couple hours passed without any excitement, and as the daylight dwindled, we met up and decided to head for the car. Naturally, as we exited the forest, there were two does and a yearling buck standing in a clearing about sixty yards from us — no doubt the lookouts for the elk we were hunting. There was nothing we could do but laugh as we climbed into the Tahoe to go back to the cabin.

It turned out that the afternoon hunt was a bust for everybody that day, but we had all enjoyed great experiences and looked forward to chatting around the fire before dinner. We were anticipating a big meal as well, but we allowed the chef to take a short break, seeing as how he was our host and all. The cards came out, the candy wagers poured into the center of the table, and the game ensued — not that anyone was paying particular attention to it; they were more interested in the stories about the hunts of the day.

There was one in particular that had Boy Wonder fired up. He could barely catch his breath to tell the story, and we could barely catch ours trying to listen to it.

To hear him tell it, he was walking up the hill below the Weather Station and startled a fifteen- to twenty-pound raccoon. It turned, locked eyes with him, and started charging.

"With fire in its eyes, it bounded toward me, baring all its teeth and snarling. It was ferocious, and I felt like I had to defend myself. I reached for my handgun (a Glock 9mm) and started shooting. He was thirty feet away and closing fast, so I emptied my magazine at him. That slowed him down, but he was still coming. By this point, I was running away from him and put another mag in my gun. I stopped, turned, and pulled the trigger until I was out of ammo again," he said, growing more and more frantic as he relayed the saga.

"Finally, I scared him off. But it was a close call. It must have had rabies or something."

Having reached the end of his story with the confrontational coon, the room was left littered with bodies laughing and holding their sides.

Boy Wonder just stared at us and said, "I'm serious. It was chaos out there."

He just couldn't grasp how ridiculous it sounded from where we sat.

Jon finally managed to say, "Thirty rounds in rapid succession from a semiautomatic handgun would've scared me off too!"

Then Turtle commented, "Thirty rounds and you didn't even hit it? You shouldn't be carrying that thing. It's just not safe."

The observation was delivered with a perfectly straight face, and we all believe, to this day, that Turtle was completely serious.

We erupted in laughter all over again and Boy Wonder, becoming defensive, decided to go cool off (pout) outside for a minute. It was then that Harry recounted the other version of the story — the one he referred to as "the accurate one," but only in bits and pieces as his laughter would allow.

"I was fifty feet across the hillside and in line with Boy Wonder, who clearly had no idea this thing was there. He must have disturbed it somehow, and I heard a hissing noise and something like a bark. Immediately, Boy Wonder burst out, cursing like a sailor. Before I could ask him what was happening, he grabbed a pistol and started tearing the landscape apart. He emptied his gun, screamed like a girl, and started running between the sagebrush while trying to reload. Meanwhile, I ran toward him trying to figure out what the heck was going on. I could see the terror on his face as I closed the distance. Then he racked his slide back, let it go, and started turning the hillside into Swiss cheese again. By the time I got close to him, he was out of ammo and had picked up a rock. I watched him throw it and hit a raccoon, which turned around and ran away. Then he just stood there, completely traumatized, and could barely speak to tell me that he was okay."

At this point none of us could breathe. We couldn't even decide which story was funnier. The fact that Wonder had shot thirty rounds at this poor, terrified raccoon, which was likely just trying to nap, and missed him entirely, was hilarious. But the coup de gras was that he'd had the wherewithal, and nerves of steel, to stand steady and throw a rock at it—accurately, mind you—to hit it and finally scare it off.

I looked at Jon and said, "I'm just grateful we didn't encounter that mountain lion last year. We'd both be dead."

Turtle then offered a very poignant query: "Who gave this freak show a gun, anyway?"

With that, Jon retreated upstairs to the kitchen to start on dinner. We all stayed by the fire antagonizing Boy Wonder and periodically all jumped on our respective chairs in unison, pointing frantically to various places in the room and screaming, "Raccoon! Raccoon! Shoot it!"

As you can well imagine, Boy Wonder didn't particularly appreciate that. The rest of us, however, sure did. And in this case, majority ruled. We went easy on him, though, and only did it, like, twice . . . each. What can I say? It was too funny to let go.

An hour later, we had not yet tired of riding Boy Wonder about his encounter with the now-infamous raccoon, who, by the way, was entirely healthy after the firefight with our buddy—with the possible exception of a black eye, a bruised rib, and/or persistent ringing in his ears.

Finally, the dinner command was given from the top of the stairs. We all charged up to the table to find large quantities of meat and potatoes—a sight that I have always appreciated and revered. We sat down to eat, and the only word I can think of to describe our actions at the table is *carnage*. Naturally, the destruction was total. We were so ravenous that if one wasn't careful, he could very easily lose a finger reaching for something on the table.

Cleanup looked daunting, but not as daunting as the soup pot that had been pulled out of the storage closet, wiped clean, and set upon the burner. Boy Wonder and I knew exactly what that meant for tomorrow or the next day, and we couldn't help but start to laugh, having survived the torture last season.

"Tomorrow night is going to be a train wreck, you watch," I said. "And we only have one outhouse. Somebody better introduce a time limit in there, or there's gonna be a serious problem."

We finished in the kitchen and joined the others downstairs in front of the fire. We looked at Jon and said, "You're an evil man."

He said nothing and just grinned . . . he knew exactly what we were talking about.

That sparked a conversation all its own as everyone started asking what that little exchange had been about. We didn't say anything for fear of Jon's wrath, and Jon elected not to enlighten the group just then either. The nonanswer went over as well as you'd expect from a now-paranoid group of guests. But the secret remained and the chatter lasted well into the ten o'clock hour before we all realized that morning (Jon's version of it, anyway) was rapidly approaching.

We all walked into the dorm and lay in our bunks. Jon turned the lights off, the talk died down quickly, and all was peaceful for a full minute before Harry started screaming, "Raccoon! Raccoon! Ahhhhh! Shoot it!"

We laughed ourselves to sleep that night . . . at least, most of us did. While I couldn't help but smile a bit, I was no longer in a laughing mood. All I could think about was having to wait another year for my bull . . . my first elk season had ended with the setting sun.

12

WE GOT UP
JUST IN TIME...
FOR WHAT, I HAVE NO IDEA

As we were all diligently examining the backs of our eyelids and resting soundly and comfortably in the bosom of night's gentle embrace, a most unpleasant event was getting ready to occur. The wake-up routine was about to begin, and we were all as unsuspecting as any other normal people would be at four a.m.

"Okay! What does four o'clock mean?" Jon bellowed at a volume loud enough to be heard by the neighbors . . . in Wyoming!

"It means your watch had better be slow by three hours or you're going to die a slow, painful death when I get out of this bed," mumbled Harry.

We would've laughed if we weren't still mostly asleep and secretly hoping Harry wasn't joking.

"No," Jon replied, "it means get your worthless bodies out of bed! We're hunters, and hunters get up early. It's officially early, so get up!"

The complaining began almost immediately as we all dragged ourselves to the edges of our beds and tried to push the sleep out of our bodies. I thought to myself, straining to comprehend why we were getting up so early, that there had better be bacon in my immediate future or somebody was going to get hurt today.

As the group started to become a bit animated, Santa suggested that we should get excited about the day of hunting ahead. That idea seemed to make a small difference in our attitudes, but we were just plain tired. Jon left the room (a healthy choice, I thought) and embarked up the stairs in the direction of the kitchen, leaving us all to attempt to find enough energy to get dressed and somehow make our way to the breakfast table.

By the time we managed to arrive upstairs (with at least one eye open), Jon was diligently frying bacon and making a wicked batch of pancakes. The hot chocolate was ready and waiting at each of our places, and I was brought back to a time when this was my routine before leaving for grade school on a cold day. I could feel a rash breaking out as I thought about the horror of having to go to school after breakfast, but I quickly recovered when I realized that immediately following this first meal of the day, I would be roaming the forests and countryside hunting game.

Right about then, the first platter of hotcakes hit the table. Thankfully, no one was injured, but I can tell you that it sparked a frenzy. They didn't last long. The platter was empty within moments and only managed to provide short stacks for half of us. Jon dutifully scrambled to prepare the next wave as we all started talking about where we might hunt that day. We entered into a couple discussions about where we thought the animals would be and whether or not we'd pushed them as a result of our wanderings the day before.

With that, the next platter full of pancakes arrived, along with a plate weighed down with two pounds of bacon. (It was nirvana! I could barely contain myself.) The hunting discussion continued, although without me, as I had pig strips to concentrate on.

When Jon arrived at the table and sat down with the third platter of pancakes, the "other shoe" dropped with a resounding thud.

"There will be no hunting today," he said calmly while he cut a bite from a stack of syrup-coated pancakes.

A momentary hush fell over the table while we all processed those words. A few seconds later, the silence was broken with a quizzical, but otherwise aggravated, "What? Why?" from Boy Wonder.

"Because," Jon enlightened us further, "deer won't be in season until tomorrow, and elk season ended yesterday. Therefore, since nothing is in season, there will be no hunting today. That's the law."

"Well, pardon my candor," said an obviously disgruntled Harry, who raised his voice slightly for effect, "but why, then, in the name of your pasty white butt, did we all get up before the crack of frickin' dawn?"

Jon responded with a smirk, "Like I said, because we are hunters, and hunters get up early."

Jon instantly received one high-velocity pancake to his face. After he carefully peeled it from his forehead, he announced, "Today, we will explore. So there will be no long guns leaving the cabin."

We were all unquestionably disappointed, but clearly hunting out of season was not something we condoned nor considered to be responsible practice. It didn't take long to come to grips with that. However, getting up at o-dark-thirty for no good reason is something we are all still, to this day, a bit sore about on some level. Wasted was a perfectly good opportunity to sleep late, and that was a travesty.

On the bright side, though, breakfast wasn't rushed, and we all had plenty of time to savor our sugar-laden carbohydrate disks with strips of grease-sizzled pig while we explored new and more creative ways to insult and degrade one another.

After Abuse-a-Palooza came to a close, Boy Wonder and I cleared the table and began our traditional morning cleanup in the kitchen. The rest of the squad wandered back downstairs, presumably to get dressed and ready for the day of adventure without firearms.

Boy Wonder and I had a slower-than-normal pace on that morning, being that we were busy continuing the barbed attacks against everyone from the breakfast table. It was much easier to mistreat them in their absence and eliminated their interruptions and efforts to defend themselves. It was simply a better use of our time. Mocking them behind their backs without fear of reprisal made for a much easier format through which to slander them.

When we finally finished our cleanup, we headed to the dorm to finish getting dressed for the day and await our instructions. Jon was eager to get going — though, given the circumstances of the day, I have no idea what his particular hurry was.

We piled into two vehicles and drove down the Middle Road to explore some of the more obscure destinations on the property.

As the sun rose, we pulled over several times to wander across fields, discover creek beds and foothills, and see parts of the ranch that would have otherwise gone unnoticed. The place was truly magnificent—not that that was unexpected, but, somehow, I kept wondering if I had managed to build it up in my mind such that it would never meet my soaring expectations. However, every square inch of the ranch was simply spectacular, and I was repeatedly amazed by the scenery around every corner.

After a few sorties into the woods and adventures down previously unexplored paths (by us, anyway), we found ourselves at the gate on the property boundary. We passed through that as well as the other two and pulled alongside each other just before the pavement began.

Here, Jon filled us in on part of the day's plan. We were headed into Coalville to meet a friend of his.

Our thirty-minute drive on paved roads was both smooth and soothing.

Our drive complete, we arrived at one of the small businesses in town—a very successful and highly respected taxidermy outfit. Jon explained that if anyone were to want a special mount, from this trip or anywhere else around the world, this was where to get it.

We all walked into the shop and were immediately surrounded by artistic mounts that looked so realistic, I was notably cautious, more than once, trying to make sure I was approaching something that wasn't actually still alive. There were game animals in

the workshop from all over the globe and in various
stages of completion. There were elk, deer, bear, ante-
lope, sheep, greater kudu, and several cats, including
a jaguar, a leopard, and a mountain lion. (That's the
short list.)

The cats were what really caught my eye. They
were so realistic that I was genuinely afraid for a
moment to approach one of the full body mounts. In
fact, I distinctly remember walking into a room with
a workbench and seeing a cat's head that was in process at the time. There it sat on the countertop, with
long pins through the face holding the hide's various
wrinkles and muscle definition in place, while the
glue beneath set properly. The rest of the skin was
carefully set in a pile behind the head, clearly indicating that the cat was not even remotely intact and
therefore extremely not alive — as if being there in the
taxidermist's workshop hadn't been a big enough clue
on its own. The detail in the face of this cat was so dra-
matic and freakishly realistic that it was sincerely and
markedly terrifying, despite having literally forty or
more six-inch needles sticking out of the pelt to hold
the expression in place. It affected me to the point
that I dreamed about this specific unfinished mount
more than once and, in fact, over several years after
the encounter.

It was then that we had the privilege of meeting
the owner and artist behind these glorious mounts.
He was kind enough not only to let us wander around
his entire business, but he must have spent an hour
with us answering questions and telling us stories.
The man was a remarkable person and, according to
Jon, the single most talented taxidermist he had ever
met. (I could see why.) He was simply extraordinary

at capturing and shaping the expressions on the faces of his mounts. He managed to bring them to life while stopping just short of actually restoring their breath and heartbeats—although one would swear they could see the living soul in the animal's eyes.

The talent was unrivaled and indisputable, and to this day he remains the only taxidermist who has impressed me to that level.

The morning was fascinating, and we were all completely gobsmacked walking out of that store. We all swore that someday we would do business there.

After leaving the taxidermist's, Jon threatened to stop by the infamous restaurant to visit with Turtle's new love interest, but ultimately he decided to head back to the cabin for lunch and a relaxing day around the fire while we all secretly fantasized about taking naps.

Once we arrived back on the mountain, Jon retired to the kitchen to work on a late lunch while the rest of us concentrated on restocking the wood next to the hearth and getting a fire raging. Shortly thereafter, lunch was ready and we headed upstairs to dine on tomato soup and grilled cheese sandwiches. We ate until we were almost uncomfortable, and while some of us began discussing out loud the desire for a siesta, Jon suggested instead that we ought to go fishing on one of the property's many ponds.

While I will give him credit for being creative, the idea was met with a staggering lack of enthusiasm and acceptance. Frankly, there was such a dearth of interest in engaging in that pastime, it was as if Jon had just asked a group of committed vegans if they'd consider experimenting with cannibalism. It was a valiant attempt but, tragically, an epic failure. In the end, it was the nap that won out as the preferred activity of the afternoon, and we all began to retreat to our couches of choice or to our bunks.

Naturally, Jon was emphatically against the idea but allowed us our wish on the condition that any one of us must beat him in a game of Ninety-nine.

We all filed down the stairs, added two or three logs to the fire, and dealt the cards.

As irony would have it, before the first player was even out of the game, guess who was dozing off in his cards? Our fearless leader succumbed to a food coma as he basked in the warmth of the flames. The rest of us quietly continued the game for a few minutes, just to make sure he was fast asleep. We then slipped off to the dorm and climbed into our bunks to address the morning's unfinished business.

My guess is that we slept for about four hours. I was the first to awaken and wandered out into the commons.

There I found Jon, right where we had left him hours before. Only now he was contorted into a most awkward and uncomfortable-looking position on the couch, and sawing logs vociferously and without any rhythm or shame whatsoever. After I chuckled a bit to myself and carefully weighed the old adage about sleeping bears, I decided to wake him—though from a safe distance. I walked outside, shut the door, and began banging on the wooden window sill with both fists in rapid succession. Jon was immediately startled awake.

Initially, he was disoriented but quickly retained his bearings, wiped the drool from the corner of his mouth, and composed himself briefly before threatening me with great bodily harm. By now, the rest of the group was awake, although I'm uncertain as to whether it was due to my woodpecker imitation on the window or because of Jon's yelling at me through it. In any case, it was time to start dinner as the sun was taking its final credits for the day and exiting stage west.

Once I deemed it safe to come back inside (translation: when there were witnesses in the room), I assisted the crew with restoring what remained of the fire to a respectable blaze. Jon had a few choice words for me and finally departed for the kitchen. After chatting with the boys for about fifteen minutes, I followed to offer my culinary assistance.

When I walked into the kitchen, Jon was busy preparing a huge pot of pasta and making his famous marinara sauce. I was put in charge of the garlic cheese bread, which had been prepared on freshly baked French bread loaves (store-bought raw dough in canisters) and an Italian salad with freshly sliced tomato, onion, salami, pimento, parmesan cheese, and Italian dressing.

Prep time was about an hour and, needless to say, the meal went over quite well with the group. That is, until Turtle wiped his mouth with his napkin after a third helping and announced that even the slightest bit of garlic gives him spectacular abdominal gas.

We all looked on in horror as we tried to even imagine what that must be like. A prideful smile crossed his face and suggested that we were all officially on notice and in danger.

By the time the table was cleared and Boy Wonder and I had put the kitchen back in working order, we arrived downstairs to the cries for mercy from Jon, Santa, Chainsaw, Harry, and BB. Turtle sat opposite the group in a wooden chair, apparently a quivering mass of intestinal wind, torturing the guys and finding endless satisfaction in it.

Jon finally gave in and walked to the dorm, stripped Turtle's bunk of the sheets and blanket, and transported them across the commons into the other dorm. He then emerged empty-handed and declared that Turtle had a new home for the night.

Jon had officially banished Turtle to the other end of the cabin for the greater good of humanity as we knew it. There was much jubilation, replete with applause in the form of a collective, yet polite, golf clap.

So ended the evening as our usual bewitching hour approached. We adjourned to our appropriate dorms, crawled into bed, and got comfortable.

After the lights went out and the comments and laughter died down, a silence that was both peaceful and inviting settled into the room. As we all contemplated a deep sleep, our reverie was disrupted by a bodily discharge that was clearly audible through the wall between the dorms.

We were astonished and horrified. We wouldn't have believed it except that we next heard the unmistakable sound of Turtle laughing. It was a sour note to go to sleep on, but at least we were protected by a common wall and some distance.

BB commented simply, "Wow. There's something very wrong with that man."

The room remained silent, apparently indicating that nobody disagreed with the recent assessment.

13

How to Kill Your Host and Make It Look Like an Accident

The day was off to a glorious start (in the middle of the night) as Jon rousted us all out of bed at the traditional four o'clock mark. At this point I wasn't sure why it came as such a shock every time, but my body was entirely intolerant of getting up when it was still dark outside. (It occurred to me that it was a good thing I didn't live in Alaska.) I cleared the sleep from my eyes but couldn't even think through the fog in my head. I got out of bed saying to myself, *If I can just find my feet, I'll be okay.*

On the other hand, Santa was an early riser. He was already dressed and prepared to assist Jon with breakfast (brown-noser). They exited the room together and as we heard Jon walking up the stairs, we heard Santa express a rather innocuous utterance from the other room: he stood at the doorway leading to the outhouse from the cabin, and, looking out the glass into the ray of light provided by the flood lamp, said, "Hey guys, what's this white stuff?"

The dressing ritual that was taking place came to a screeching halt as we all processed what we had just heard without the benefit of being able to see what Santa was really looking at. The cognitive wheels turned slowly, and, to make matters worse, the gears must not have been entirely engaged.

I pulled some pants on, much to everyone's approval, and walked out into the great room. There stood Santa at the windows looking out over a blanket of snow that had accumulated while we slept.

We all gathered by the windows and looked out upon a small area illuminated by the single porch light. Based on the impression Turtle had made when he slipped and fell on his can en route to the outhouse, we guessed that the snow was only about two inches deep.

We all managed to make appearances at the table for a bite, and, looking ahead, only Boy Wonder and I knew what was in store for dinner. The two of us, therefore, knew to eat as much as we could at breakfast and lunch.

Between the two of us, we must have blown through sixteen pancakes and a pound of bacon. We packed down the hash browns and even managed to scarf a couple pieces of toast. The rest of the group looked on in amazement as arguably the two smallest guys, and certainly the youngest guy, devoured a significant percentage of the food that had been presented.

Not wanting to rob the group of one of the basic experiences that helps shape the entire trip or incur

Jon's fury for spoiling the surprise, we said nothing other than that we were just hungry. Feeling almost guilty, we left out any mention of the chili and the ramification associated with eating it.

The assignments were handed out and the pairings were made. It was time to go hunting again. We all headed downstairs to get our gear and meet at the cars.

On this morning, I was dropped off alone to wander into the woods east of the West Road, about a mile from Box Canyon. I remember feeling, as the car drove off, particularly intimidated as things looked much different now with snow on the ground. Walking into the trees, I felt overly alert—almost certainly an effect of being completely terrified. Not only was this an area I had never explored, but I had no one to rely on as I navigated my way to the place Jon had directed me.

I was aware that he carefully placed everyone so that there would never be a safety issue with hunters shooting in the general direction of other hunters, but it didn't allay the discomfort I felt being on my own. The pressure intensified knowing that because safety hung in the balance, it was imperative I interpret my instructions correctly and execute them precisely.

In this case, I was to walk due east exactly three hundred fifty yards, then turn south and walk two hundred yards, where I was supposed to find the edge of a small rock ledge immediately to my right. I was to sit so that I could not only watch the woods, but also see over the ledge to the forest floor some distance below. Jon had said that it was a unique place on the property but one that, due to deadfall, was tricky to navigate to and often not visited.

Without any markers or paths to follow, I was to count on my ability to accurately judge how far I was walking and find the location based on Jon's approximations and memory.

My hike was made infinitely more uncomfortable when I looked down to see a very well-defined set of mountain lion tracks in the fresh snow. They crossed right in front of me.

I proceeded with extreme caution, so wrapped up in fear for my safety and anxiety about potentially getting lost (or eaten) that I didn't notice the buck directly ahead of me until he went bounding through the trees and disappeared. I persevered and, surprisingly, found my way to the spot Jon had described.

I set up on the outcropping and, as I looked around, discovered that I had a truly magnificent view of two levels of the forest. I figured that, in addition to my advantage of being able to watch two elevations, I would also benefit from the wind, given that any deer down below would not be able to smell me if the wind shifted. However, I felt vulnerable when I realized I was not shielded from any side, so I was constantly looking over my shoulder in case something was coming up behind me.

From the scenery perspective, I was in awe. The new snow changed my view of this entire property. Everything looked so peaceful and serene, and the bright yellow leaves that had yet to fall from the aspens offered an amazing contrast to the new white landscape. The trees were quiet, the air was still, and I managed to find some intermittent peace in the beauty around me. That is until I realized, again, that I was in the sticks by myself and miles away from anyone.

Below, the rocks presented a whole different world. The trees were not nearly as dense, offering a much more open environment, better visibility, and unobstructed shooting lanes. I was all set. All I needed now were the animals.

I knew they were around me. I faintly heard an animal slide on some rock well behind me and another grunt somewhere off to my right. In fact, it was here that I first heard an elk bugle, and it was like nothing I had ever heard before. It sounded like a synthesized elephant trumpeting through a faulty set of bagpipes during a pelvic exam. For someone who's never heard it, it is marginally comical, seemingly unnatural, and spooky beyond explanation. Admittedly, it gave me the shivers.

The snow began again and I fell into a daze of sorts, contemplating life and trying to figure out just what I was doing in the woods again when I could be sitting on a beach, being catered to as though I were important.

I remembered having repeatedly struggled with this very thing the previous season. I had thought about it less this time around, but I was still thinking it on occasion—mostly the times when I found myself bored, cold, and worried about being disemboweled by predatory wildlife. I still longed for the warmth of the sun, the sand between my toes, and the familiar feeling of a colorful drink adorned with a slice of fruit between my fingers. However, I also began to wonder if, amid all the fun, fear, and adventure I was having, whether I was learning something about myself that I had never considered? Was I becoming an outdoorsman—or, at the very least, someone who liked the outdoors?

It was a perplexing thought, and I became very introspective in those quiet moments on the rock. I experienced an inner peace in those couple hours that I had never felt at any other point in my life, despite the contradictive notion that I was there on the pretense of shooting something and killing it.

The morning was becoming a dynamically complex and thought-provoking exercise in discovering the very definition of who I was — or who I was becoming. To be honest, I wasn't sure whether to be proud or disappointed in what I was discovering about myself that day.

While it wasn't part of the plan I had walked into the woods with, I set my rifle down and looked into the vast reaches of the forest, both across the elevation I was on and through the clearing beneath me. I watched not for the animals, but for the sheer beauty and grace that the moment offered. I marveled at the expansive view before me, highlighted by the bars of light breaking through the canopy above and revealing patches of the woods — as if to explicitly draw my attention to the solitude of each precisely illuminated point.

It was then that the silence was transformed into a symphony overflowing with the sounds of existence. I heard water dripping onto rocks below, the ice-clad branches clicking together at the whim of the wind, woodpeckers trying to knock their fillings loose, and a bird of prey crying out in the skies above. To live that moment in the state of awareness I was blessed with was an extraordinary and awe-inspiring gift. It nearly took my breath away as I sat in genuine wonder of it all.

I considered it a breakthrough, one that represented an evolutionary step into the world of a real hunter and what it must be like to recognize and appreciate the hunt for everything it is — and for everything it is not.

It was then I understood that bloodshed was a distant priority, and that the real magic occurred on a much more transcendent plane.

At that point, I knew my hunt for the morning had ended. It was obvious to me that nothing that might happen in the hour ahead could eclipse the epiphany I just experienced. Even if a world-class mule deer presented himself and surrendered to one of my rounds, it wouldn't have come close to the internal revelation by which I had just been irreversibly changed.

I stood up feeling content and profoundly enriched, put the rifle strap over my shoulder, and walked out the way I had entered. I followed my footprints, only slightly less visible now due to the flurries, and made my way back out to the road.

Jon was already waiting for me and, as I got into the Suburban, asked me how my hunt had been.

I said, "I really don't know how to answer that. Walking in, I didn't see much other than one buck and a set of lion tracks. Once I got to my spot, I saw nothing, yet everything at the same time. I'm not entirely sure how to put it into words, but it was somehow the most thrilling hunt I may ever have. All I know for sure is that I will remember it for the rest of my life."

I'm certain he knew exactly what I was talking about, though I wasn't entirely sure that I did.

We picked up the others and headed back up to the cabin, adding another deer to the collection under the deck. Congrats rang out to Harry for dropping a nice eight-point with broad shoulders and a great inside spread.

We put lunch together and gathered at the table to eat and talk about the morning. I didn't say much about my adventure; I was still processing everything and trying to analyze my experience and make sense of it all. (Guys with psych degrees—we're all a bit peculiar.)

We finished lunch and cleaned up the kitchen. Boy Wonder and I were still quietly laughing about the soup pot, which sat ominously atop the stove burner while we finished our chore. As we had predicted, it was apparent that Jon had been busy brewing his stomach-debilitating concoction while we had been freezing our posteriors off in the snow that morning. Again we kept our mouths shut, leaving the mystery intact for everyone until later that evening.

We all relaxed for an hour or two while we waited for the right time to head out for the afternoon hunt. The adventure had me paired with my friend Grizzly, and we were headed to Box Canyon for the first hunt of the year inside the topographic anomaly.

When the time came, everyone got into the appropriate vehicles and drove out.

Upon arriving in Box Canyon, Jon and I grabbed our gear, walked to a good vantage point, and glassed the entire hillside. We spotted three mule deer up the steep grade at four hundred fifty yards. They were separated from each other by about fifty or sixty yards, and Jon designated the deer on the right as the one we were going to target. It was a big buck, although I didn't spend too much time evaluating it; I was more interested in getting it on the ground than anything else.

Knowing my experience and proficiency with rifles, and having often referred to my marksmanship as "surgically accurate," Jon told me to get set up and that we'd take the shot from where we stood. I started to prepare for the shot and immediately began to overthink it. I became a bit nervous, all things considered. Here was a moment two years in the making, and I was in front of my friend who had been responsible for getting me into hunting again. Let's also not forget that this is the man who had taught me essentially everything I know about the subject. And here I was about to get my first real opportunity at a big buck, with him looking on right beside me.

He told me not to worry and to remember to breathe. I was set up in a seated position, with my elbow balanced atop my bent knee to provide the angle I needed for the hill in front of me.

I peered intensely through the scope at the deer, which, not unlike the other two, had no idea we were present. I then attempted to collect myself and concentrate enough to make the nerves subside.

I slowed my breathing down to measured, deep, and deliberate breaths and gradually created a uniform pace and settled in for the shot. I reached up with my right hand and pulled the bolt up and back, then slid it gently forward again, pushing a shell into the breech before locking it in place. I centered the crosshairs on the deer again, then reached up with my thumb and disengaged the safety. Now it was all about the concentration and the breathing. I knew I had this. I slid my finger inside the guard, placed it gently on the face of the trigger, and slowly squeezed it.

Crack!

The gun went off, the shot echoing around the canyon walls.

The deer was hit. It recoiled from the energy of the bullet slamming into its shoulder. But to our surprise, the buck didn't fall. He turned and retreated up the hillside on three legs while Jon said, "Quick . . . another round in the chamber! Shoot again!"

I racked another shell, but it was too late. The buck hobbled into the tree line and vanished.

"Well, this is all part of it," Jon said, tucking his binoculars into his coat and zipping it up. "C'mon. Let's go find him."

I flipped the safety on again, put the rifle strap over my shoulder, and followed Jon and his historically bad knee directly up the side of this daunting hill. We made our way to the right, where we could benefit from cover and an easier grade to climb. It took us the better part of an hour to get to the elevation where we had last seen the deer. The tree line's edge was just sixty yards from us, and Jon could see the half-fallen tree where he'd marked the deer's entry point.

We were both out of breath, but I was in far worse shape than Jon from years of dedicated indifference to fitness. The only thing hindering him was his knee, which was disintegrating below him with each step and had become roughly the size of a basketball.

Despite the pain, he pushed on, insisting we continue after the deer. "It's the ethically responsible thing to do," he taught.

Time, though, was not on our side. The sun was going down, we were losing our light, and we figured we had just over an hour left to get down the hill and back to the car.

Jon was confident that he had accurately marked the deer's entrance into the trees and motioned me to walk in front of him.

Slowly we stalked toward the tree and the surrounding underbrush. Jon was to my seven o'clock as I held with my rifle in both hands out in front of me, ready to throw it to my shoulder and finish what I had started.

We got to within twenty yards and, in just the blink of an eye, the buck sprang up from the brush in front of us and bolted deep into the trees up the hill. He was out of sight in a flash.

I was definitely excited and could no longer whine about not having had an opportunity, but I was still batting .000, and that had me pretty upset.

Worse was that I should've had that one. Now it was crippled and we had to face the fact that we were not going to be able to recover it, a scenario no hunter ever wants to have on his conscience. I felt terrible.

And now we had another problem. We had to figure out how to get down the mountainside, and Jon was in real pain. This left me, the one with minimal experience and even less brute strength, to help get him to the car.

I tried to come up with some sort of solution to our situation but failed . . . predictably. The priority became getting Jon off the hillside before dark, and the pain-mitigation factor took a back seat. The reality was that, barring a helicopter, he was going to have to walk — agony be darned.

It took us the entire hour to get down, with Jon trying to walk as gingerly as he possibly could. When we finally reached the bottom, Jon hobbled to the car and carefully climbed in. I then rushed him back to the cabin so we could get some ice on his knee, telling him all the while how grateful I was that he had helped me go after the deer, even to his own detriment.

I felt awful about the whole situation. I'd wounded the deer, caused Jon to climb the mountain with me, and failed to recover the animal in spite of it all. And then for him to come down empty-handed and in such pain was even worse. It was just a poor set of circumstances all the way around.

Back at the cabin, the guys all helped Jon get into the house and become one with the couch. We got ice on his knee, which now resembled a medicine ball more than a human joint, and then sat down to talk with everyone about how it had happened.

I became the target of their comments, my marksmanship now officially suspect. It was all in fun, but I will admit that my ego was bruised. Jon let everyone know that I, in fact, did hit the deer. He just clarified that I didn't hit it well enough to bring it down. In my opinion, this only served to make it worse. But it was my turn, I suppose, and I'm sure Boy Wonder was happy that he wasn't wearing the bullseye for once.

We had struck up a card game in front of a raging fire when Boy Wonder said, "The good news is that you've already made dinner, Jon. You won't have to be on your knee at all."

The three of us smiled knowingly at each other, and I said, "Let's go get everything, and we'll just eat down here."

Boy Wonder and I headed upstairs with a couple other helpers in tow. We sent down all the necessary accoutrements for chili, including freshly chopped white onion, shredded cheese, hot sauce, crackers, (a blowtorch to cauterize everyone's raw rear-facing orifice later in the evening,) and water for all. The last trip downstairs was with the paint-peeling product itself, and seven steaming portions of Chili con Flash Point were served.

Just as those of us who'd enjoyed (endured) it the season before remembered, it was really quite tasty. The rookies all complimented the chef as well and wolfed down their helpings with a frightening and reckless lack of restraint. It wasn't long before the first-year guys were going for seconds and, in some cases, thirds. Boy Wonder and I knew better but looked forward to the show that was sure to come later.

Jon, Wonder, and I placed a bet. I simply looked at Jon and said, "Ninety minutes."

Wonder knew what I was referring to and countered, "Sixty."

Jon chimed in with, "Two hours, even."

The rest of the group was clueless, and the three of us simply sat back and waited for the massacre to begin.

Everything was carried back upstairs and the kitchen was put back together in record time. We straightened the cabin, as we knew that the other group was arriving the next day, and returned to the hearth to harass Jon, who was still immobilized on the couch. The cards came out again, as did the sharp-witted barbs and unflattering critiques of my shooting prowess. It was all good though, because in only a matter of minutes, I would no longer be anywhere on their mental radars.

We all played cards and talked as the three of us inconspicuously watched the time. Wonder's prediction went by uneventfully, as did mine thirty minutes later. But as the two-hour mark approached, the group was starting to belch and become noticeably unable to sit still. Then, in a moment of silence, as the conversations had come to a natural lull, Turtle's eyes got markedly larger and the expression on his face turned to one of absolute panic.

"Ohmygosh!" he exclaimed, as if it were all one word.

He sat straight up and froze, clearly afraid to move. (Heaven forbid he had to cough or sneeze!) We all looked on as he sat perfectly motionless, obviously cycling through the various emergency protocols flooding his head.

Suddenly he jumped up, sending his cards to the floor. He reached around with his left hand and grabbed his backside, presumably in an attempt to hold it all in, and hobbled to the door as fast as his short legs could carry him. Once outside, Turtle staggered along the snow-covered ridge toward the outhouse and disappeared behind the door.

We had never laughed so hard. Somebody commented that he looked like a penguin after too many sardines. BB laughed so hard that he gave himself a nosebleed, and the rest of us were simply beyond help. The laughter finally subsided but resumed again with just as much intensity when Turtle finally returned, drained and exhausted from his experience "down the hall."

He walked through the door and declared with the utmost sincerity, "I feel like I've literally passed fire."

We all hit the ceiling—it was like pressing the replay button. We dissolved into hysterics that only strengthened when the next soldier fell.

Chainsaw left abruptly and sprinted toward the door. And when we saw the whites of his eyes again, Santa bolted toward the sandbox. They were dropping like flies.

We couldn't stand it. It brought back so many unpleasant memories from the year before, and we were so glad we had known better than to go back for seconds and thirds this time. To our amazement (and his relief), it never bothered Harry a bit. We decided that his stomach must have been forged from iron, but we cautioned him that the night was long and likely not so lonely in the outhouse.

For the next several hours, even after we had long since gone to bed, there was a revolving parade of people walking out and back from the funhouse all night—each of which seemed to convey some malicious comment toward Jon upon his return.

Due to all the activity and the doors continuously opening and closing, none of us got much sleep that night. However, there was one silver lining that benefitted all of us: we no longer had to check for animals in the outhouse before we entered. We were all quite certain that if they had been in there in the first place, they would either be long gone and miles away by now, or simply dead from the noxious fumes.

14

AFTERMATH VS. AFTERGLOW: A STUDY IN DICHOTOMY

Our wake-up alarm sounded quite different this day, as it was Turtle, not Jon, who woke us all. His announcement sent us from peaceful slumber into immediate fits of hysterics: a door slammed closed, followed by, "Thanks a lot, Jon. I just ruined my second pair of shorts tonight!"

Turtle was clearly frustrated by the multiple trips he'd made to the relief shed throughout the wee hours.

"And what's with the corn?" he begged.

It was a miracle no one fell out of their bed.

Jon, after fits of laughter, finally stammered, "NASA has asked me to let them test the chili as an alternative fuel source for their solid-fuel booster rockets. What do you think I should do?"

"I think your chili is going to kill me!" Turtle retorted indignantly.

As if there hadn't been enough gasoline poured on the fire already, I continued, "From the newsroom, Sherwin-Williams Paint Company has released a new formula of paint thinner with a special ingredient, which they claim can take the paint off the side of a barn from fifty feet away. Meanwhile, the surgeon general has issued a new warning regarding a certain chili out of Utah which will read: 'Do not consume this product unless your stomach is lined with iron, your appointment calendar is open for at least thirty-six hours, and you remain within ten steps of a toilet.' And finally, this just in: Mr. Turtle's Fruit-of-the-Loom guys have resigned their post, citing unrealistic expectations."

Turtle stormed off again without a word, which just incited us further. I remember noting that laughing this much, this hard, and this often couldn't be healthy, but that I was really, really enjoying it.

Upon arriving at the table upstairs some twenty minutes later, everyone had calmed and breakfast went off largely without incident. And while most of us were ready on time, it should be noted that there were a couple or three that were lagging behind and cited the indicator as their reason for needing a bit longer to get into the field. Naturally, that didn't stop Jon from heckling them.

"Turtle! C'mon. Santa, you too. Where are you clowns? Let's go!" he shouted from the doorway.

Turtle's patience was wearing very thin. He started baiting Jon with sarcasm and little fits of insolence— like a ten-year-old throwing a tantrum. (That always goes over big with Grizzly.)

A couple of the boys stayed back to clear their systems a bit more thoroughly while the rest of us headed out armed with water and a couple sandwiches. The day's plan was to skip lunch at the cabin and stay in the field.

Santa and I were headed to the sagebrush-covered hillside sloping into Deep Canyon, just west of the East Road. Santa offered to drive Jon's Suburban, so I gladly rode along in the passenger's seat. As we pulled away from the cabin, Jon barked, "Be careful . . . and get Freddie a deer! Just don't put any of those smelly dead things in my car. I'm serious!"

We drove off and I thought, *I would love to have the opportunity to think about putting one in the car, but clearly I'd have to actually kill one first.*

Santa and I drove out to our spot and parked across the road from the lower side of the Bear Claw. He and I got our gear together and walked across the field to set up on the hillside as it poured over into the gorge. We had a spectacular view of the entire slope, which became pretty steep and very rocky toward the bottom, where we could see an enormous, flat slab of stone that was slightly tilted back toward us. There was a small, narrow, rocky ravine between the slab and the bottom edge of the hill, which likely carried the runoff from the upper part of the canyon as it drained off to the south. Beyond that was the forest, which ran from the base of the canyon all the way back up the other side and over the ridge. We had acres and acres that we could glass and about seven hours to find at least one deer to remove from the gene pool.

The morning went on and on without an animal in sight. Don't get me wrong, I was thrilled to be out with Santa. However, from an action perspective, the morning was distinctly boring by anyone's measure. It seemed that the morning was a dud all around the property. Not a single gunshot had been heard, and we began to wonder when would be a respectable time to give up and grab a sandwich back in the warmth of the car.

As the day progressed, the weather grew warmer, and the snow melted off at a quicker pace than expected. Santa and I finally pulled the pin on the morning hunt around eleven a.m., giving up in favor of a couple bologna double-deckers and some bottled water.

About an hour later, and so as not to be bested by an uneventful morning, we returned to the hillside to start glassing again. Right away, Santa noticed a trio of does standing at the base of the canyon.

While we were hunting for meat, we couldn't help but wonder if there were any majestic bucks lurking within the tree line, so we elected to wait awhile.

We sat on that hill for nearly four more hours anticipating the arrival of their antlered boyfriends, yet we failed to spy anything else in the area.

At this point, my nerves were frayed, my patience level was at the low end of the spectrum and my immaturity had gotten the best of me. Those does were beginning to look pretty good. I finally mentioned to Santa that I wanted to take a shot at one of them.

"You do realize," he said, "that if you hit one, we have to go down there and get it, right?"

I said that I understood and continued, "I really think I can hit it. She's 570 yards away, says the rangefinder, and there is an elevation difference of approximately 450 feet."

While he considered it, I recognized another challenge. Due to the slope of the hill in front of me, which started falling away gradually before turning steep, I would have to stand and shoot free-handed. If I were to lie down, I'd gain stability but wouldn't be able to see the target. Success became unlikely as the plan unfolded, but I figured that it made for an all-or-nothing shot. Either I would kill it or miss it cleanly. I said, "I really believe I can make the shot. And if you back me up, our odds will increase."

He agreed to back me up but remarked that it was a long shot.

"Besides," I reasoned, "I want to shoot my gun, and I really want to do my part for the food pantry."

"All right, let's take a poke at her," he said.

I stood, chambered a round, and took a few deep breaths. I raised the gun to my shoulder and flipped the safety off with my thumb. I then looked through the scope, placed the crosshairs on her neck at the base of her skull, and drew in a big relaxing breath. I steadied the rifle, started to slowly exhale, paused, and squeezed the trigger. I let the rest of my breath out and took the rifle off my shoulder, hoping I didn't have to concede that the shot was too ambitious for me and exceeded my ability. The deer had scattered like cockroaches. And to be honest, regardless of the outcome, I was thrilled to have made so much noise.

I looked at Santa, who had been watching through his scope. He had been ready to back me up, but I never heard a second shot. He lowered his rifle as he turned to look at me and just said, "Impossible . . . she's down."

I was speechless. I raised my rifle again and looked through the scope. There she lay between a pair of rocks not three feet from where she took her last breath.

I was ecstatic—I had my first kill! It was a highly technical shot (for me anyway), and she hadn't suffered at all. I got a tremendous round of congratulations from Santa, and we were both impressed that I had made such a shot.

But after a moment or two, reality crept back into our heads when Mr. Rain Cloud reminded me that we had to hike down and retrieve her.

That was fine with me. I eagerly threw the gun strap on my shoulder and began walking a game trail down into the valley, talking about the shot the whole way.

Santa was genuinely happy for me, despite the walk we were now both regretting. Truth be told, the hike was a lot harder than the shot, as the rocks on the "trail" we chose kept falling away under our feet. It was a treacherous ramble through the bramble, but we took our time and managed to get there in one piece. We stood over the kill and looked back to where we had been standing when I'd fired the shot. Santa shook his head in disbelief, reached into his pocket, and pulled out a knife. He then locked the blade and handed it to me.

"You're probably not going to be very happy with me, but I can't do it," I said.

"Do what?" he asked, still holding the knife in his outstretched hand. "Dress the deer. I'll get sick," I admitted. "Will you please do it for me? I will help as much as I can; I just can't do blood."

He smirked as though he'd just been conned and said, "You tag it, and I'll take care of the rest. But," he demanded, "you have to watch and listen to me explain what I'm doing. One day you're going to have to learn to do this. It's all part of being a hunter."

He made sure I notched my tag properly and then kindly attached it to the deer's hind leg through a slit between its tendon and bone. He then knelt down and began the unpleasant task of gutting my deer while I held the legs at his request.

As I mentioned earlier, Santa was a tremendous guy. He and I had known one another for several years, and he understood that I wasn't being disrespectful of the sport or the animals I hunted, but still, he wasn't about ready to let me off scot-free either. Apparently, the trade-off was a bit of guilt and some manual labor.

"You will help me get this deer up the hill, right?" he asked.

I nodded in accord, and within ten minutes we had a dressed deer.

He and I both took a leg and started to drag the deer back to the loose trail. We climbed back to the path through the thick sagebrush and then began the trek up what, from this perspective, was now an imposing hill.

We must have been walking for fifteen minutes and were no more than a quarter of the way to the top when poor timing and inconvenience struck me pretty hard. I felt an asthma attack coming on and I started to panic.

Now, my asthma is exercise-induced, and I was clearly overtaxing my body's threshold for exertion. I sat for a few minutes, trying to stay calm and let my inhaler do its job, but Santa correctly pointed out that daylight was fading fast and we needed to be at the top of the hill before dark. Otherwise, he explained, we were going to have a real challenge trying to navigate the perilous trail without light.

"You walk at your own pace and just breathe normally. I will handle getting the deer out," he said.

Before I could debate his offer (not that there was really a better alternative), he slung the doe over his shoulders and we were again marching up the hill. We arrived at the top, he before I, and continued our individual paces all the way to the Suburban.

When I reached the truck, Santa was already out of his gear and loading it into the back seat. I dropped the tailgate to put my gear up, and Santa hoisted the mulie and put her inside Jon's vehicle.

I stood there with my jaw wide open and reminded Santa what Jon had said upon leaving the cabin.

"Well," Santa responded, "I'm not carrying it back to the cabin on my shoulders, nor am I coming back out here to get it with someone else's car. So, since we're not leaving it here to waste, the only alternative is this."

That being settled, I returned to the task at hand — removing the rest of my gear and putting it in the vehicle. Just as he lifted the tailgate to shut it, Santa froze and whispered, "Freddie! One o'clock, right at the shadow line. Get your gun up."

I looked up, and there were two deer: a small eight-point and a doe. They stood near each other about one hundred twenty yards off. We both carefully picked up our guns, and Santa said, "On the count of three, you take the buck on the right and I'll take the doe on the left."

We both stood there, guns on our shoulders, and I heard, "Are you ready?"

I was so excited that I had trouble focusing on the timing, my aim, and the fact that I was half in and half out of camo all at once. When I had finally collected myself, I nodded and he began to count.

"One . . . two . . . three!"

Bang!

The shots were in perfect unison, and the two deer jumped and bolted for the trees. The buck ran for twenty steps before piling up in the sagebrush; the doe made it almost to the tree line before stopping, trying to maintain her balance and then falling on her side in the grass. It was an amazing moment that would have only been better had Jon been there to see it.

We jumped into the car to drive up and collect our pair of deer. We each tagged our kill, and then Santa really stepped up for me. He gutted both of them without saying a word. I held the legs as I had done before, trying to be as much of a help as I was able.

We carried them to the back of Jon's Suburban and put them inside with the other doe, then loaded up the gear and headed back to camp.

When we arrived, it looked as though we'd been invaded. There were fifteen new vehicles scattered about, turning the area around the cabin into something that looked like a used-car lot. The Village Idiot had arrived with his three or four friends, and apparently all of their friends, to hunt for the weekend.

The place was jumping with social activity, which made our group a bit nervous given the antics from last year. A social environment is a good thing, but not when it comes at the expense of everybody's safety.

We backed the truck up on the grass in front of the cabin to make it easier to hang the deer on the beam under the deck. And while Santa started to unload the Suburban, I ran inside to grab some help before Jon saw that we had put the animals in his car.

As soon as I walked in, I motioned to Boy Wonder and BB to come help us. Naturally, BB got excited for me and piped up with, "Did ya' get one? I knew you'd get on the board tonight!"

Just as I was motioning for him to keep it down, I heard Jon: "If you did, I hope you didn't put one of those smelly dead things in my car!"

I yelled upstairs, "I didn't. Don't worry."

Then I heard, "Swear it's true?"

I thought, 'Well, now I'm in trouble.'

I quickly sorted through my limited options and replied specifically, "*I* did not put one of those smelly dead things in your car. I swear it's true."

We all scrambled to get the deer out of the truck and hung on the beam so we could return Jon's car to the driveway. Hopefully, we could manage to accomplish this before he could take a break from fixing dinner and see what was really going on.

We had the deer out and up in no time flat, and I drove the car back to the driveway. We then began to celebrate our success a bit with the other guys who had killed that night.

Jon suddenly appeared out of the blue. He took one look at the beam and knew that Santa and I had added substantially to the total. He glared at me and argued, "You swore it was true!"

I quickly responded, "I swore it was true that *I* didn't put one of those smelly dead things in your car — and I didn't lie. *We* actually put *three* of those smelly dead things in your car. But just three . . . I swear it's true."

Jon stared at Santa and me for a moment before conceding with a sinister look on his face.

I knew I had gotten off on a technicality, and I was certain he'd never fall for that again. But the bottom line was that I hadn't lied, and that was the biggest issue I'd faced.

Jon came over and congratulated me on the kills and gave me a bear hug so tight that I lost all feeling in my lower extremities. He was thrilled for me, as was everyone else in the cabin. Even the new group was out admiring the harvest and seemed sincerely happy for me and the rest of the guys.

After having waited a season and a half, I'd finally gotten to shoot my gun, savor success, and fill both my tags in a matter of minutes.

BB and Harry both had does down that day to go along with a buck for Boy Wonder. His wasn't anything particularly special for a six-point, but the height on the rack was notable, and the brow tines looked more like jousting lances. So far, we were tearing it up for the food pantry.

Over dinner I seemed to be the celebrity of the hour — I'm sure by design. Jon went out of his way to stir everyone up when I told my stories. Clearly, he was trying to boost my confidence, and it worked. I have no idea what we had that night for dinner; I was too excited to take note. But I can tell you, I felt like a million dollars. What a day!

After our meal, we sat downstairs and told all our stories again over cards and candy by the fire. We were all relieved to hear that Turtle was no longer seeing corn, but of course we did have to point out to him that he had managed to cut a trail from the cabin to the outhouse in a single day.

Literally, there was no grass on the ridge heading out to the shed. The path was suddenly and completely devoid of all evidence of snow or vegetation, and it looked like a horse trail that had been ridden every day for a decade. The unrelenting back-and-forth expeditions at all hours of the day and night had formed an actual depression in the ridge that is likely still there to this day.

Members of the new group, who seemed much more pleasant than the people from the season before had been, were mingling and participating in our conversation. We even managed to deal them in for a couple hands of Ninety-nine.

One gentleman had actually brought his daughter to the cabin for the weekend. That was something no one had expected, but it seemed like an event the guys were all willing to tolerate once they met her. She happened to be one of the dancers from the Utah Jazz cheerleading squad. She was twenty, friendly, and drop-dead gorgeous. To her credit, she also had a spectacular sense of humor. She was ready to put up with all the wisecracks that came her way and dish out some of her own—something else that was unexpected.

Not surprisingly, Jon, who never misses an opportunity to put someone on the spot, grabbed Turtle and dragged him across the room to meet her. He parked Turtle right in front of her and introduced him.

The setup was cruel and uncomfortable for Turtle, while she took it in stride and made the best of it. Within moments Jon was wielding the camera, and suddenly Turtle became Mr. Red Carpet. He threw his arm around her and mugged for the camera just like the shameless nut we all knew him to be. From then on, he seemed to really come out of his shell when she was around. Then again, we probably all had a bit of extra personality when she was around; she was a lot to compete with, and we all tried to rise to the occasion and out-charm the rest of the group.

Meanwhile, the Village Idiot was busy trying to prove how important he was so he could have a share of the spotlight. He could be found upstairs by the fireplace, holding court and talking down to those of his entourage who felt as though they needed his approval.

Except for those upstairs, we were all having a great time after such a successful afternoon. Even Turtle was upbeat, given that he had finally been liberated from the indicator and had gotten to meet a blonde goddess, all in the same day. There was even photographic proof.

Eventually, we all became tired and succumbed to our fatigue.

The evening ended on a pleasant note, and we all turned in knowing that we had knocked it out of the park on this day. We wandered into our bunks and settled in while the party raged on upstairs.

Goodnights echoed around the room until it was quiet. But as we laid there inviting sleep into our tired bodies, there was nothing that could curb my excitement about having filled my first-ever tags. I bet I slept with a smile on my face clear through to the next morning.

15

STAY ON YOUR SIDE

I just thought I'd offer some friendly advice for those who are either too obtuse to understand one of the more basic principles of being a guest or who simply fail to grasp rudimentary common sense and the minimal threshold for proper behavior and safe hunting protocol.

As a guest, you hunt where you are told you're allowed to hunt, both as a matter of safety and courtesy.

Now, it's possible, I suppose, that some people just don't comprehend simple hunting etiquette. However, in this case, I (the guy new to hunting) was the only one who could claim not to know this uncomplicated principal — yet I knew. It just made sense to me. However there was at least one person who didn't catch on, and it almost resulted in a serious accident.

The day at the ranch started like the rest of them. Jon screamed, and we all jumped out of bed in a stupor and fumbled around while trying to get dressed and eventually wandered upstairs for breakfast. Today had a slightly different element to it, which only some of us were used to: there were other people in the cabin to consider.

We all attempted to be quiet while we got ourselves together, and in spite of being a bunch of big dumb guys, I thought we had managed to do a fairly decent job of it . . . until Grizzly dropped a pan that came to rest with a resounding crash. The good news was that it only woke up the Village Idiot, who was sleeping in one of the more private bedrooms upstairs next to the kitchen. He came trolling out in his shorts and a robe that was almost closed to see what had happened. After being assured that it was nothing to worry about, a conversation ensued about planning for the day and where to send each group's hunters with regard to safety.

"Oh, just send 'em out. They'll find a place on their own," said the Village Idiot.

"Well, as safe and responsible as that sounds," Jon sarcastically responded, "we should really plan this a bit better. Tell you what. I will send my guys down the East Road and keep them all to the east of Deep Canyon. You can have all your guys scatter over the rest of the ranch. Any location off the Middle or West Roads is yours. That gives your group over seventy-five hundred acres and keeps it simple. We will maintain those boundaries until you guys leave, day after tomorrow."

The plan was set and there was hunting to be done. Jon was very explicit in his instructions to confine our group's hunting to the East Road and all points east of Deep Canyon. We suited up and were off before sunrise, as was our usual practice. We thought it odd that nobody from the other group had bothered to get up, except for the guy and his Jazz-dancer daughter.

Maybe the group was just sleeping in or only planning on the afternoon outing. But dad and daughter were out even before we were, and it was nice to see at least one pair of hunters from the other group taking their weekend hunt seriously.

I drove out with Turtle, and we headed to the Beaver Hut, a destination just east of the Jackrabbit's Stage. It was an old structure that often flooded when the rains were heavy and looked much like a duck blind. There was water nearby, so the game trails through this area, back and forth from the woods, were abundant.

The drive down the East Road was relatively uneventful, save for the doe we almost hit when she leapt directly in front of the Tahoe from the cover of the trees. The result of the brake check was successful both in saving the deer's life and scaring the living daylights out of Turtle. (Two birds with one stone! I love it when a plan comes together.)

While he was trying to get his heart started again and put his eyeballs back into their sockets, I continued to drive almost all the way to the treacherous switchbacks. We parked the SUV in a wooded nook just off the road and began to gear up.

This early in the morning with the sun just getting ready to rise, I often felt eyes watching me as I was getting myself together. It was a sixth-sense kind of feeling that really unnerved me. Though, on this day, when I heard a stick snap loudly behind me, you can imagine how quickly I turned around and how many things I dropped in the process.

There I found my hunting buddy with a stick that he had broken over his knee. He seemed extremely happy with himself knowing that he had caused me to jump nearly out of my skin.

"You're not the only one who knows how to break," he said.

"Nice pun — touché," I retorted.

"Toosh what?" he asked.

I just shook my head and mumbled, "Never mind."

We walked the tree line and eased into our spot as we got close to the Beaver Hut. We set up downwind from the intersecting trails where we had a clear shooting lane to the water at our ten o'clock, and into the woods at our two o'clock.

The sun was on its way up and the haze was starting to clear. We could already hear the woodpeckers clocking in to work and the squirrels barking and chasing each other through the leaves.

Turtle was somewhat of an experienced hunter and was taking a bit of time to explain to me, at a whisper, the direction from which the deer would approach this morning, if they did at all. He based his opinion on where they most likely slept and their need for water, etc.

As he was detailing his expertise, I happened to casually look around a bit and saw a doe thirty yards from us (which had approached from an entirely different direction than what Turtle had predicted) that was staring at the two of us as though she were more interested in hearing what Turtle was shoveling than I was. I calmly interrupted him as he was imparting all this knowledge to me and told him to look five degrees to the right over my shoulder.

"I'm going to just slowly lie back on the ground and roll out of harm's way. You shoot her," I directed.

Twenty seconds later he had fired a shot, stood up, and racked another round into the chamber. "Go down. Go down!" I heard him say. Moments later, he was ecstatic about the harvest he had just made for the food pantry.

We walked over to her; he cut and attached his tag and then started doing his happy dance. (Note: Turtle doing a happy dance is something no one should ever be subjected to, even if there's money involved. It's a frightening sight that simply cannot be unseen. Ever.)

He then proceeded to gut the doe. When he had finished, Captain Fantastic stood from bended knee with an arrogant glow about himself and proclaimed, "That's how it's done."

I said, "I thought they were supposed to come from over there," pointing into the woods in the direction from which he had originally anticipated her arrival. (I couldn't resist, really. Being a pain in the butt just comes naturally to me.)

We dragged the doe back toward the truck and walked across the road to the tree line to set up again, this time looking deep into the woods across two game trails with decent shooting lanes to both. And there we sat for three long hours, finally resorting to jokes as there was absolutely no action. Even the squirrels must have gone back to bed — they hadn't been heard from in at least an hour.

We decided that we were cold and bored enough to call an end to the morning hunt. We put the deer on the roof of the Tahoe (against my wishes and better judgment) and drove back to the cabin. Upon our arrival, we offloaded Turtle's doe and suspended her from the beam, proudly displaying another win against hunger in SLC.

As we walked inside, we heard a real commotion going on upstairs. Being the nosy pair, we headed up to see what the fuss was about. We discovered the rest of our group and the new assembly (who were finally awake) oohing and ahhing as they all sat around listening to the Jazz dancer recount the story of her morning hunt.

According to her account, she and her father, along with one other gentleman from their group, had gone out to an area off the West Road. They found a rock outcropping hanging over the aspens with a great view of about four hundred acres. The three of them sat and glassed for an hour or two and saw plenty of animals beyond range, but nothing close enough to get excited about—that is until they heard something directly beneath the overhang they were sitting on.

The girl then recalled how she had gotten on her stomach, belly-crawled to the ledge, and peered over.

"I slowly pulled back," she continued, "and whispered to my dad that there was a buck directly under the ledge."

She explained that they hadn't seen the deer approach from any angle in front of them and that there was no way it could have walked in from behind as it was all a rock face. She then surmised that the deer had been beneath them all morning.

It was then explained that they all tried to come up with a plan for a shot, but that it was complicated because she couldn't just walk up to the edge and shoot down. The deer was actually standing under the overhang. In the end, though, some out-of-the-box thinking won the day.

She described how she removed her coat and directed her dad to stand behind her. She then told him to get a firm grasp of the belt and waistband of her camo pants and follow her as she carefully approached the very edge of the rock.

"I told him to hold onto my pants so I wouldn't fall," she said, "and then I slid down into the splits."

At this moment, naturally, everyone was riveted. Me, I sat wincing in pain at the notion of such a pose. I can't, however, speak to where the minds of the others wandered, despite what their facial expressions suggested.

The Jazz dancer then explained how she cleared the safety, put the gun to her shoulder, rocked forward, and, while hanging over the edge of the rock, shot slightly back underneath herself and killed the eight-point buck.

Everyone burst into cheers and applause, all the while thinking that, despite being a good story, it was almost certainly not true.

Jon was one of the biggest skeptics, although he had enjoyed her story immensely. He grabbed me and the rest of our group and we went downstairs to look at her deer.

"Well, I'll be," Jon said as he examined the bullet hole in the top of the deer's neck. The bullet had traveled through and out directly below the entrance wound at an almost perfect ninety-degree angle.

Jon went and spoke to her dad and asked, "Can you take me out there? I want you to show me how it all played out."

While everybody else ate, several of us went to the site of the circus shot of the year. We walked out onto the ledge, and the girl's father explained again how it all transpired. Then he pointed to the ledge where she did the splits and leaned over for the shot.

Jon stepped to the edge and peered over, and sure as we were all standing there, blood could be seen inside the sheltered space. It was drying in the shadow of the overhang some thirty feet below us.

We walked around through the woods to get to the kill site, and there, on a slab of rock where the pool of blood was concentrated, was a ricochet mark from where the bullet hit the rock after passing through the deer. Jon looked up, and the angle was greater than ninety degrees, indicating that she would have had to be hanging over the edge to get the shot. Detective Grizzly was satisfied and completely amazed. We reported back to the cabin to confirm the story as fact for those who still might not believe, and the young girl was commended for a remarkable shot — and deservedly so. (For the record, I would no sooner hang upside down while doing the splits with someone's hand in my waistband than hang fresh meat around my neck and play with the tigers at the zoo.)

The cabin was buzzing that day with all the talk about the shot. I had to concede that while her shot was only thirty feet, her degree of difficulty and style points completely outshined all my efforts. Suddenly, my shot seemed somewhat pedestrian in comparison. Moreover, she was a lot better looking than I, so I lost on all counts.

After a later-than-usual lunch (thanks to Detective Jon), we headed back out. We drove down the East Road and then walked out to another grassy point overlooking the aspens.

In the meantime, Jon had told Wonder and me that after he hunted down the road a bit with BB, he was going to set up immediately to our right on the next point over. He said that he would head out onto the other point and set up just inside the tree line.

For safety reasons, we looked over to the adjacent point and took note of where he would be sitting. Only then did we set up ourselves and start glassing the landscape.

Boy Wonder and I immediately saw some activity. Several does and a button buck were walking through the trees a hundred yards off, and there was a cow moose approaching the small watering hole at slightly more than two hundred.

We watched these animals for forty-five minutes before hearing a faint gunshot echo from down the road. We figured BB had shot a deer and that we would be seeing Jon in the next hour or so.

Time went by, the moose walked off, and the does with the button buck had managed to walk almost a mile in a big circle, only to end up right where we had first noticed them.

With only about ninety minutes left in the hunt, we heard Grizzly walk into his spot on the next point. We assumed that he had set up right where he had planned to and didn't really give it another thought.

Then, about thirty minutes later, we noticed a man, clearly not Jon, walking out onto that point. We looked at each other with puzzled expressions and turned our heads back at this guy, who proceeded to set up his gear and park himself at the edge of the point. It took away a portion of our shooting lane, which had us a bit irritated, but we noticed that if Jon was still where he said he would be, this guy was sitting not even a hundred feet directly in front of him and eliminating any shooting opportunity for Jon whatsoever.

Certainly, he had to know Jon was there because nobody misses a big guy like Jon—especially when he's wearing a hunter-orange hat and vest.

The rest of the daylight went to waste and we walked back to the car, leaving the mystery man behind. When we arrived at our vehicle, Jon was already there. And he was hot!

A bit confused, I asked, "Was that you on the point?"

"Did I say I would be on the point or in the tree line?" he replied, obviously frustrated.

"Okay," I said. "Then who was it?"

I was not given an answer and decided to drop it. Clearly Jon was in no mood to talk about it. He didn't say much on the drive back to the cabin—a sound indication that someone was about to get chewed out.

When we reached home base, and without so much as a word to Boy Wonder or me, Jon immediately jumped out of the truck and went for a walk behind the cabin.

We went into the cabin, found BB, and asked him about his kill. Oddly enough, BB was angry as well. (Geez . . . you leave these guys on their own for one afternoon . . .) We asked him what had happened to put Jon in such an epic mood, and he explained that while he and Jon were set up on a clearing down the East Road (Jon concealed in a tree line and BB behind a short berm in a clearing), a huge ten-pointer had walked out into the middle of the field.

"All I had to do was wait for the animal to walk ten steps across the meadow and clear the berm so I'd have a clear shot at him at thirty-five yards. I slowly gripped the rifle, waited about three minutes, and just as I put the crosshairs on him, someone else shot it! The deer jumped and started running to the woods but crashed to the ground within thirty yards. I stayed put for a minute, and up walks this guy from the woods. He's all excited that he shot this deer."

BB was already getting irritated describing the event.

"I waited until he got closer," he continued, "and then stood up and asked him just what the heck he thought he was doing."

I interrupted and asked BB if it was one of our guys, and BB said that it was a member of the other group, adding that this was likely what Jon was so angry about.

Then he explained how Jon came marching out of the woods and started yelling at the guy, demanding to know why he was east of Deep Canyon.

BB then recited the guy's response and Jon's reaction: "Well, this is my favorite place to hunt on the property; I hunt here every year. I didn't think it would be that big of a deal."

"That big of a deal? Are you serious?" Jon raged. "We assign people to areas for safety reasons. If you'd have missed that deer, you could well have killed my friend, who was, incidentally, lined up to shoot it himself. And you don't decide where you hunt here. You are a guest, not a landowner."

BB said Jon had sent the guy packing to the cabin after he had cleaned and tagged his deer. He added that they stood there while he dressed it and didn't say a word except to chide the guy for being completely irresponsible and reckless.

At that point, BB just shook his head, then continued, "I could've gotten shot today! I was pretty upset, so Jon drove me back here and then said he was going to hunt near you guys."

I then explained to BB that the hunt near us had been a train wreck as well. I told him about the guy that sat in front of Jon.

About then, Jon came bursting in the door, and it brought both groups' conversations to a screeching halt.

"I want to know who was hunting off the East Road point today with an hour of light left?" he said as he stared at the groups with resolve. "I also want to see the man who shot the deer off the East Road today. I will be outside waiting for five minutes. I expect to see you both by then."

He turned and walked outside, and everyone started looking around. The genius who'd nearly shot BB walked timidly out the door after Jon. Little was said and the tension was obvious.

Jon then walked back in after the five-minute deadline he had imposed and started walking up to people and asking them eye to eye if they had been on the point. Finally, with nobody coming forward, Jon asked for everyone's attention.

"I will make this as painless as possible, and I apologize to all that this may affect. If no one comes forward, I will declare an end to this hunting season, and no one will be allowed to hunt this property, effective immediately. This is a very serious safety issue that needs to be cleared up, and I will not allow hunting to continue without addressing it. Whoever you are, you have five more minutes to meet me outside, or this season is officially over—for everyone. You can all head off the mountain tonight."

Jon disappeared out the door again and waited in the falling temperatures on the deck above the harvested deer.

Finally, one of the guys from the other group walked outside, along with the Village Idiot, and words were exchanged for a few minutes. According to what we could all hear through the glass, which, given the volume of the conversation, was everything (and as clearly as we would have heard them had they spoken to each other inside), Jon first addressed the guy who had knowingly been on the wrong side of the property and described how he had nearly shot one of our guys.

The next item he addressed was that someone had sat in front of him for the last hour of light and completely ruined his hunt, all because he hadn't been courteous enough to follow the simple boundaries that had been provided, which also, and more importantly, had created another serious safety issue.

"This is the end of the road for your two guys," Jon advised the head of their group. "They are off this mountain in the next hour, or your whole group is leaving. It's your choice."

Jon walked back inside, headed downstairs, and sequestered himself in the dorm.

Well, that definitely put a damper on the evening. But it was clearly a necessary evil given that two wildly poor errors in judgment, along with a total lack of simple courtesy, had occurred that could've resulted in an incident far more costly than losing a shot at a nice deer or an hour of shooting time.

The two walked down to their dorm on the opposite side of the lower level, packed up, and headed down the mountain that night.

As the saga came to a close, it was well past time to start dinner, and Jon was in no mood.

The rest of us pitched in and tackled a steak-and-baked-potato dinner with the much-maligned bacon-and-canned-green-beans dish. Jon eventually joined us for dinner and, for the most part, had the respect and approval of all the remaining guests from the other group, along with some sincere apologies.

Around the fire that night were many conversations about responsibility, accountability, respect, hunters' ethics, and firearm safety. All things considered, the outcome was good. It actually brought people together to bond over critically important pieces of the hunter's code.

Naturally, not everybody shared in the positivity. Mr. Know-It-All disapproved of how Jon treated his guests, despite the clear and present danger they had visited upon other hunters that day. I suppose the old adage is true that you really can't please all of the people all of the time.

It was time to turn in, and nobody could resist the thought of a warm bed. The crowd dispersed and the lights were out within fifteen minutes. A moment later, the silence was broken as Jon explained, "For the record, if it had been any of you guys, you'd have been on your way off the mountain too. Safety has got to come first, and nobody's getting hurt on this mountain during my watch."

Everyone said goodnight as we all bundled up. It was getting cold in the cabin, which led us to wonder what weather was on tap for the next day. Unless I had to dash outside and get a preview while I used the facilities in the middle of the night, I was content to wait until tomorrow to find out.

16

YOU REALLY DON'T HAVE A CLUE, DO YOU?

You know what they say . . . another day, another holler. All around the room, bloodshot eyes opened and tired hunters mumbled about staging a violent coup against the alarm clock. We tried our best to get dressed in our semicomatose states, but were having trouble with the simplest of tasks . . . like standing. We then headed up the stairs at a pace slightly slower than tectonic plate subduction.

By the time we all made it to the breakfast table, Jon was still quite unpleased with yesterday's issue and made it crystal clear to everyone in the cabin that a deep internal review of basic hunter safety and respect was highly recommended. Oddly enough, the majority agreed and promised to be vigilant in their observation of both safety standards and general civility toward their fellow hunters.

Confident that we would be alone on the East Road after yesterday's debacle, Jon officially put it to bed and told everyone to go out and have a great hunt. The groups retreated to their respective dorms to get ready, and the hunt was on.

Our group piled into two SUVs and drove down the East Road, electing to choose our spots on the fly. The weather was bitterly cold and a new round of precipitation had just started rolling through. The snow was falling at a considerable pace, which accounted for the inch already on the ground, with more falling by the minute. The unrelenting, driving snow was nearly impossible to see through as we drove. Each time someone got out of the car, the open door created a new adventure in hypothermia and made us feel like we were trapped in a snow globe until all the blowing flakes inside the car came to rest.

We dropped Santa off next to a thick bunch of trees that were part of the same forest as the Bear Claw, but this area was south of the Claw's mouth and at a higher elevation. There was plenty of cover to the north, and things thinned out to the south, offering open spaces and plenty of shooting lanes.

As we drove off, we carefully navigated the tight section across the ridge I spoke of earlier, which was now that much more precarious, taking the snow into account.

The next stop was for Boy Wonder and me. I had already tagged out, but he still had his antlerless tag and invited me to accompany him while he tried to fill it. The rest of our set, Jon included, spread out across the lower end of the East Road.

We found our spot and started glassing, but with the snow constantly shifting from heavy to light and back, it was like trying to look through a bowl of popcorn. It wasn't much better without the binos, so the two of us spent the next several hours freezing to death, talking about all the action we weren't seeing and what we were going to do if we ever thawed. When there was about an hour to spare before pickup, our lips blue and our extremities numb, we heard a gunshot not too far away. We deduced (correctly, as it turns out) that Santa had taken a run at something.

When Jon finally picked us up in the Suburban, he told us that Santa had been taken back by our other guys and added, "I thought I'd get you guys a bit early. I figured you'd be cold."

During our drive back to our appointment with the fireplace, the snow now all but stopped, Jon mentioned that Santa had killed a spectacular buck that we would see on the way back. Wonder and I were happy for him and excited to see the harvest, but also a bit nervous while Jon turned the land yacht around in a snowdrift just off the road.

He had us backed into the woods and facing the road when we saw the Village Idiot drive past the front of Jon's car and proceed up the road.

"Well, that's interesting, given that he's not supposed to be over here at all," remarked Jon, sounding a bit annoyed. "I thought I already covered this subject pretty well."

Jon waited a minute before pulling back onto the road and saying that he wanted to find out what this guy was up to.

Meanwhile, he said, "Santa's buck is just up here a bit. He's already gutted it, hung it in a tree to cool and drain, and is planning on retrieving it on the way in tonight. It's a monster."

We cleared the crest of a small rise in the road and saw the car ahead of us stopped on the narrow ridge . . . with a rifle sticking out the driver's side window!

As if that weren't shocking enough, being against the law and all, he was aiming directly at Santa's deer, which, mind you, was very dead and had already been tagged and field dressed. Even the most inexperienced hunter in the world could surmise that this deer was no longer a viable hunting target based on the fact that it was hanging by its antlers from a tree branch that was nine feet off the ground, chest cavity splayed wide open with a large stick to keep the ribcage spread apart, a huge gut pile directly underneath it and hunter-orange ribbon streamers flying proudly from each antler tip. It stood out like a sore thumb and presumably was decorated as such to be easily spotted from the road in the driving snow. (And now that the snow had stopped, one would think the deer, and its condition, would become even more visible.)

Now, I didn't have more than two seasons' experience with big-game hunting at this point, but come on! Even I could recognize the situation. I simply looked on in disbelief.

Jon grabbed his camcorder, which was usually located in his center console, and filmed for a few seconds.

"I just want to get this on film for the record."

He then honked the horn, put the camera down, and yelled out the window, "What in the name of all that is holy are you doing? Besides breaking the law, do you really think you need to shoot that deer again? I'm pretty sure it's already dead."

He put the truck in park, stepped out into the bitter cold and approached the vehicle ahead. Just then we heard him start yelling again.

"First of all, you're not supposed to be over here, which I thought we addressed with clarity last night. Secondly, you were about to shoot a deer that is clearly already dead."

(There was a pause for his response, though we couldn't hear it from all the way back in the other car.)

"If that's true, you must be the dumbest person alive," Jon continued. "When was the last time you saw a live deer floating nearly three feet off the ground with orange tape on its antlers and a pile of intestines under it staining the snow bright red?"

(Another pause.)

"There's no way that even you could be that hopelessly misguided. You should work on your identification skills a bit harder. Don't worry about species or even male versus female. Stick to the basics, gumshoe: try to figure out first if it's alive and intact or dead, drawn, and quartered! And if I ever see you shooting out of your car again, I'll report you. You're supposed to know better!"

Jon came huffing back to the car as all of us attempted to melt into the seats. We had never seen Jon that incensed before.

He got back to the car, climbed in, and slammed the door.

"Judas Priest!" he uttered with disgust. "How brainless can a grown man be?"

Meanwhile, the recipient of the lecture in the car ahead of us had driven off toward the cabin.

"I can't believe I just saw what I saw," Jon continued, slowly pulling up alongside the dead deer, and asked us, "Does that deer look like anything that is alive and worthy of shooting in its current condition?"

We all just said no and started to laugh. It was comical. No reasonable person could ever look at this snapshot in time and suggest that this deer was alive.

It was going to be another awkward day at the cabin; we could all feel it coming on like a bad storm.

We drove back and went inside, and the Village Idiot was nowhere to be found. I guessed that he'd locked himself in his room to save himself the agony of having to face Jon. What he hadn't counted on was Jon using the opportunity to teach a valuable lesson to all the other hunters about identifying potential targets before you shoot them . . . from a place other than inside your car!

He showcased a clip of the scene that he had taken with his camcorder and explained the situation. The entire cabin was in total disbelief that anyone, even in heavy snow, would consider shooting this buck — dead, flagged, and tagged — again.

By the time our road-warrior hunter emerged from his room, everyone in the cabin was questioning his judgment, his expertise, and his ethics. Understand, however, that the intent here was not to discredit anyone. It was to try to get through to him, and all those present, that laws are to be followed by everyone and that safety has to be something of which every hunter is constantly aware.

After all, we were outside playing with firearms, and they are dangerous if handled irresponsibly — another lesson learned, but certain people just seem to feel they are above accountability. For a hunter, that is simply unacceptable.

"Sub sandwiches, anyone? I'm starving," seemed to signal the end of all the serious talk. Jon excused himself and made the now-infamous Who-Can-Eat-This-Without-Rupturing-Their-Stomach   sandwiches. He put everything but glass shards on these freakish belly-busters and turned us loose.

To my shock and awe, not one of us managed to eat an entire sandwich on our own. All of us managed merely half, leaving a stack of sandwich halves for the other group, whose members were looking on, salivating all over their plaid lumberjack shirts.

The piggish display was disconcerting at best, but the Jazz dancer thought it was funny. (And if she was okay with it, then none of us were about to stop just to be polite.) In fact, I think Turtle actually considered going for another half just to try to impress her with the loudest belch. (I'm not convinced that she was into him, but winning the loudest belch contest surely could've won her over and cinched it for him . . . *or not!*)

The mood of the cabin had returned to normal and the two groups, with the exception of their two hosts, were getting along famously. The mood was returning to that of the hunting experience it was supposed to be. In fact, eventually, even the hosts had a brief word with each other that didn't begin with an accusation, threat, or cross word. (Hey, progress is progress.)

Apparently, in an attempt to pass an olive branch, the Renegade Road Reprobate approached Jon mid-sandwich and asked for help tracking an elk that he thought he had shot that morning in the Bear Claw. To clarify, this would be before his run-in with the already-deceased floating deer, and presumably when he was hunting exactly where he was not supposed to be hunting . . . again. (Did I mention the fact that if he were, in fact, hunting elk, he would have been hunting them out of season?)

Of course, Jon agreed to help, but it was likely more on behalf of the allegedly wounded creature than anything else.

Jon asked me to come along so I could keep watch for the litany of predators that live in the Bear Claw. After the passage of a few hours, they would certainly have already smelled fresh blood.

I grabbed my rifle and the three of us headed down to evil's portal, leaving explicit instructions for everyone to stay away from that area.

Jon then reminded me that we may have a significant issue, as elk season had already ended. "If this guy shot an elk, we'll have a problem up here tonight. I won't stand for that."

We entered the Bear Claw just south of where I'd had my up-close-and-personal with the bull elk the season before. Jon and I followed closely as the Village Idiot led us to the place where he had pulled the trigger on the elk in question.

"I was standing right here behind this tree," he said, "and saw it on the game path fifty yards that way," then raised his arm and pointed off into the trees.

Now, it is worth pointing out that given the recent winter weather conditions, any imbecile could track an animal's footprints, especially if there was a trail of blood in the pristine, unblemished, and blinding-white snow. So as soon as Jon and I examined the place where the alleged bull had allegedly been standing when it had allegedly been shot, we were skeptical of any outcome worthy of reaction, as there was no evidence of blood.

"It was dark in color and looked really big to me," advised our tour director, who was too lazy to walk the woods himself to find the animal at which he'd shot.

To our surprise, however, there were tracks in the snow that not only appeared to be large, but also indicated that the animal that had made them had been startled and sprung to a hurried retreat from the area.

"Not all wounded animals bleed right away," Jon advised.

We all started following the tracks, and while Jon searched for any signs that would suggest that an animal had been injured, I watched the surrounding area to make sure we didn't end up as something's dinner. We followed the tracks in the snow for thirty-five minutes, and while I heard a couple creatures crashing through the forest's branches somewhere off in the distance, we were otherwise left alone.

As Jon did frequently along the trail, he paused and looked around, examining tree bark or leaves on plants for blood or places where the animal's stride was showing signs of imbalance. He looked ahead along the trail of hoofprints in the snow and interrupted his whisper with an uninhibited belly laugh.

"Come here," he said, motioning me over to his side. "Look up the trail."

I looked and didn't see anything.

He grabbed my coat sleeve, pulled me to his right side, and pointed around an evergreen.

I looked ahead again and was absolutely speechless at what I saw. I simply looked on for a moment in disbelief, then moved so that the self-proclaimed expert hunter could get a glimpse of his bull elk.

"I don't see anything," he said as he walked up to Jon.

"Just walk up the trail a few steps and look around that tree as the path fades to the left," Jon said.

Our hapless boob wandered ahead about six paces

in line with the hoof impressions in the snow and discovered his quarry: a jet-black Angus cow that had
escaped one of the pastures at the base of the mountain.

"We're all fortunate that your shooting prowess is
equivalent to your identification aptitude," Jon said as
he walked past the Village Idiot on his way to inspect
the cow for injury.

Of course, I was trying to be respectful, so I said
nothing. Besides, I was sure that Jon would have
plenty to talk about and that anything I would think
to say would most likely get covered in the car on the
way back to the cabin.

Thankfully, the cow had the same number of
orifices she had when she'd wandered into a certain someone's path earlier in the day. Not only did
the bovine look unharmed (thankfully), she seemed
equally as annoyed with the day's events as Jon was.

We hiked back to the road and I continued on,
alone, to retrieve the car that was parked up the way a
bit. I remember thinking it a bad idea to leave the two
of them together without a chaperone, but I considered
my absence plausible deniability in case there was an
"accident."

With that in mind, I quickly began to walk away
from them, keys in hand, and was mindful not to look
back over my shoulder for fear of seeing anything.

To Jon's credit, the Village Idiot (the accomplished
outdoorsman who couldn't distinguish living from
deceased, elk from Angus cow, or responsible hunting
practices and common sense from blind and comprehensive ignorance and selfish desire) was still alive
and well when I returned with the transportation.

The drive back was uncomfortably quiet as Jon
drove and I sat awkwardly in the back seat. I could

only imagine what had been discussed while I was getting the car. (I'm sure he brought up that bull elk have antlers at this time of year and cow elk do not — particularly when they are actually farm cows. Even I knew that one.)

Naturally, we had to pass where the Village Idiot had nearly re-killed the deer earlier in the day. It was twisting in the wind — its spine clearly visible through the empty abdominal cavity as it hovered inexplicably over its entrails. Nothing was said, although I briefly snickered involuntarily from the back seat. (There are just some things in this life that are irrepressibly funny. I simply couldn't help myself.)

As we pulled up to the cabin, several people rallied around the Suburban to see what we had come up with. I climbed out of the truck and just went inside. I wasn't about to stir the pot, at least not until later when all the ingredients had been added and the story was at a full simmer.

Jon took another road, as if that comes as any great shock. He told the entire story to those who were curious and left the experience at a very sarcastic, "It was just simple mistaken identity. It could've happened to anybody: Stevie Wonder, Helen Keller, Ray Charles . . ."

He continued, "Elk and cows are, in fact, more similar than you may think; they're both mammals, have eyes, hooves, and fur; give live birth; and eat grass. They're almost identical."

It was obvious that this would provide fodder for defamation of character, what was left of the Village Idiot's anyway, all night. There came a point where one could almost feel bad for the target of these continuous assaults, but he was so dedicated to being a horse's patoot that it was hard to have any sympathy for him at all.

The rest of the huntsmen finally returned and there was more to celebrate.

Chainsaw had cut his doe tag with a nice-sized deer that had made what in hindsight was a horrible decision: to stroll across the open prairie thirty minutes before shooting time ended at not more than one hundred ten yards in front of his rifle barrel.

It took a few of the guys (not me, obviously) to hoist the carcass onto the beam under the deck. It was starting to look like quite the successful hunt. We were busy high-fiving each other and taking a few pictures when we learned that the other group was packed up and ready to drive off the mountain. Naturally, we were relieved that the mountain would again be safe to hunt on, and even more so since Captain Pompous Circumstance would be parting company with us as well.

He walked into the room to say goodbye to our group, which by all accounts was pretty magnanimous of him. I'll give him credit for that.

Unfortunately, Jon was ready for him.

As he appeared in the doorway, Jon cupped his hands over his mouth and let loose with a thundering, "Moooooooo!"

Not wanting to miss the proverbial lay-up, we all hit the deck shouting, "Don't shoot! Don't shoot!"

The joke's target was a good sport about it, and we all got one last giggle out of it before shaking hands and making a pleasant departure out of it after all.

While we were actually sad to see some of the guys go, especially the one with the Jazz-dancer daughter, our group seemed to get over it before they had driven out of sight on their way off the property.

Needless to say, the session that evening around the fire was vicious. Without any ears to be wary of, there was no mercy.

"Who can't tell the difference between an elk and a common farm cow?" Jon mused and actually snorted when he laughed. A barrage of tales and accounts of epic folly from years gone by had been triggered and seemed to flow unremittingly for a couple hours, yet there was no topping the dead-deer-hanging-in-the-tree story. That may live forever as the pinnacle of absurdity.

As the hour hand on our watches crept past eight, it was time for dinner.

Thankfully, tonight was an easy one. Jon was making pasta with homemade marinara and meatballs, along with two giant loaves of garlic cheese bread. (Naturally, we threatened Turtle with his life if he so much as glanced in the direction of the garlic bread or even considered taking a bite.)

As dinner progressed, the stories re-emerging about the antics of the Village Idiot and the fact that Boy Wonder screams like a girl when he's being chased by a raccoon were cemented in folklore that evening as we relived them over and over again. Even after our sides began to cramp, the stories persisted and seemed to become more savage by the minute.

When we got around to it, the cleanup was by now routine. Boy Wonder and I knocked it out in no time before rejoining the crew at fireside for a round of Ninety-nine and more ribbing.

Turtle brought up the Jazz dancer again and asked, "By the way, did anyone get her number? And if you did, can I have it?"

There was even more talk of the raccoon incident, and then the evening went entirely down the tubes when we brought up the chili stories, some of which were so detailed that it made at least one of us sprint for the outhouse just thinking about it. (Poor Turtle.)

When he returned, he fielded more grief over the tale and was getting tired of the attention again. Finally, he snapped back at us.

Jon returned fire. "Why are you so grumpy?" he begged, knowingly poking the proverbial bear.

Turtle shouted, "I am *not* grumpy! Now leave me alone!" and stomped off into another room to sulk.

Of course, once we all found out which buttons to push, things got fun for the group and we all just had to chime in and participate. After all, Turtle was being moody and defensive — not a sympathetic or particularly welcome attitude in this group.

After that, it turned out that any one of us could send Turtle into a tailspin simply by looking at him. Expletives and sarcasm would drip from his tongue at the slightest provocation, which was only fuel for the fire.

Admittedly, pushing someone's buttons to make them angry isn't very nice, but we managed to prove that, more often than not, it's really quite funny for most involved.

After the laughter died down, we decided that it was pretty much time to hit the sack. This having fun all the time was really starting to take its toll, and we were exhausted.

We were treated to a dialogue after lights out that showcased Jon provoking Turtle and his colorful retorts in kind, but the show was short-lived and we all passed out one by one, each of us praying that Jon would sleep in until eleven o'clock the next morning. We all knew we wouldn't be that lucky, but we still held out a glimmer of hope.

17

LAPSES IN GOOD JUDGMENT PERSIST

As I have mentioned, waking up at the cabin comes as an abrupt shock to the system every morning, and is as eagerly anticipated as a body cavity search before entering prison . . . so I've heard.

There we were, all resting comfortably in our warm sleeping bags, when Jon walked into the room and, having cut the corner a bit too sharply, stubbed his toe on the bed frame. Really, it would be more accurate to say that he place-kicked the metal leg of his bunk bed. A couple of us literally woke up to the sound of the collision when his bed moved across the carpeted floor due to the force of the impact. The rest of the group awoke to the bloodcurdling scream and the torrent of near obscenities that quickly followed. (How he managed to keep it PG, I will never know.)

Understand that it takes a lot to disrupt Jon; his pain threshold is higher than most mortals' tolerance levels. But this one had him crumpled up on the floor trying to decide whether to laugh or cry.

The toe in question was already turning lovely shades of gruesome and horrific, with an artistic touch of nauseating. The injury led to a brief panic over what to do.

"Are you all right?" Boy Wonder asked with genuine concern.

"What can I do for you?" I stammered while trying not to look at what was left of his foot's digit.

"Who's going to cook breakfast?" Turtle asked curiously.

At first, the inquiry seemed incongruous, insensitive, and terribly ill-timed. And after seeing Jon's toe, the idea of food was enough to make us all gag. But then, after reflecting on the topic for a moment and listening to our stomachs grumble, we decided that we may as well eat. Since it wasn't likely that Jon would be able to answer the bell, we had to get creative.

So in the shadow of Jon's mangled appendage, an idea for an inspired breakfast was born. A stand-in chef was dispatched to the kitchen while the rest of us further assisted the patient. (Isn't it amazing how guys can twist and point any situation toward food? Always look for the silver lining! In this case, the proverbial sunshine was that, despite Jon's clearly decimated hallux, we were going to have bacon within twenty minutes!)

We all helped Jon off the floor and back into bed, where he lay mumbling nonsensical words to distract himself from the pain until breakfast was ready. He then limped up the stairs and joined us for pork strips, scrambled eggs, and toast.

When we inquired about his mashed toe, he said he was sure that he had just jammed it and that now, after having "adjusted" it (which I suppose accounts for the hole we later found punched through the drywall next to his bed), declared himself ready for duty with a slight limp and some minor swelling. The good news was that we could hardly notice the swelling because his toes were fat to begin with. The bad news was that we could tell, instantaneously, which toe was injured due to the fact that it was purple (and blue, and green, and red).

After enjoying breakfast, restoring the kitchen, and returning the upstairs space to some semblance of normalcy, we headed down to get dressed. The process went smoothly for all of us except Santa, who couldn't seem to figure out what day it was, and Grizzly, who was having trouble with a particular sock. It was obvious he was still in pain, but nothing keeps Jon out of the action unless Jon wants to be out of the action.

With a little help from BB, Jon was ready to rock and roll with the rest of us, although how he managed to get his boot on, I will never know.

Meanwhile, I sarcastically advised Santa that it was Monday, that we were in Utah on a hunt, and then proceeded to remind him the names of all of us that were currently in the room. He looked at me with mild disdain for mocking him, and then grabbed his remaining gear and headed for the door with a smirk.

We all congregated on the driveway, where Jon told us to keep our eyes out for worsening weather. He added that we were all to be back at the cabin no later than eleven a.m. so he could reassess the plan for the afternoon hunt. With that, he told us to figure out amongst ourselves where we wanted to hunt and to be safe.

Turning then to Turtle, Jon declared that the two of them would be hunting together and commanded him to get on the back of the ATV.

"Why don't I just take my own? I'll get it off the trailer," Turtle said with a certain amount of excitement in his voice.

"Because," replied Jon, "it won't run at this altitude, and we'll waste twenty minutes messing around with it before you come to that same conclusion. Let's get on our way. Get on."

"But Jon," whined Turtle.

Jon became a bit exasperated and jumped off the ATV.

"Fine," he said. "Get the ties off yours and start it up. I'll wait."

So Turtle climbed up on the trailer in the dark and started to remove all the ties that secured the vehicle to it. When he had freed them all, he jumped on his ATV, turned the key, and pressed the start switch. To Turtle's delight, it fired right up. But as he tried to rev the engine to warm it up, it clearly didn't sound right. He let it run for a couple minutes, and then gingerly backed it down off the trailer. Meanwhile, we were all standing around turning blue.

"If you can drive it over to mine without it dying, you can ride it," Jon said.

Turtle popped it into gear and gave it a little gas. The thing sputtered and died without having moved more than a foot.

Jon looked on silently as Turtle started the ATV again. He revved the engine a few times and started across the gravel driveway, but it seized and died again.

"That's it," proclaimed Jon. "Leave that pile of bolts right there. We will load it back up after the hunt. Now get your butt on my ATV."

Jon merely pointed behind him as he sat with his hands on the handlebars, and Turtle reluctantly climbed aboard with his rifle slung over his shoulder.

"We're late now, so hold on," warned Jon. He took off like he'd been shot out of a cannon, and we could hear Turtle screaming in terror all the way down the hill and past the turn onto the West Road.

After the laughter died down, we started planning our destinations, and Santa asked, "What day is it? Does anyone know?"

I responded, "Are you suffering from some sort of memory short circuit, or does this brain cramp encompass the entire organ? It's Monday, you nut."

Now Santa is a razor-sharp guy, so to be honest, this had me worried. He and I paired off and headed toward Bluebell Flats. I figured if Santa really did have a problem, we wouldn't have to contend with a long or technically demanding hike back to the car. I made a mental note to watch for signs of weakness and slurred speech before I walked to the car, and I hoped with all my might that we wouldn't have any serious issues.

The rest of the group headed off for various points behind the cabin—a known target-rich environment that no one had bothered to investigate yet this season.

Santa and I drove down the Middle Road and pulled off into the grass below Bluebell. We exited the vehicle and tried to assess the weather as the light was just starting to filter through the trees. A plan would be forthcoming.

The sky was gray and the landscape had a menacing and blah tint to it—almost monochromatic. It was bitterly cold, and the wind was quiet until the occasional gust roared through and slapped me in the face, taking with it all of my skin's elasticity and leaving it stinging and sensitive to the touch.

We assembled our gear and made the twenty-minute walk to the Flats, where we tried to place ourselves in the tree line with enough protection from the wind to be able to stay warm for a few hours.

We positioned ourselves fifteen feet inside the woods, making sure that we had adequate shooting lanes through the timber and still better-than-average visibility of the open field.

Having glassed for about an hour with nothing to show for it except the glow of our red, wind-lashed noses, discomfort began to really set in. Even the rest of our bodies were cold despite being bundled inside some of the most technically advanced hunting gear available. It wasn't long after we had started discussing whether or not we wanted to stay out that I came to a brilliant conclusion.

"Santa," I said, "what are we doing out here in the first place? Neither of us has a deer tag left and both our elk tags are expired. Not only can we not shoot anything, we shouldn't even be out here with guns. Get your gear together—we're going in!"

We had to laugh at our futility as we trudged back to the warmth of the car, remarking to each other that we should've just slept in. Santa then reminded me, with textbook accuracy, that sleeping in had consequences far more dire than what we had suffered that morning in the cold. (Reference Chapter 8, first page.)

We headed back to the cabin and were the only ones there. Within moments, our gear was stowed, the logs were burning with a crackling rage, and a serenity rarely known at the cabin was ours to cherish.

Once we could feel our fingers again, we made ourselves some hot chocolate and then dozed off, enjoying an impromptu nap until the guys started to return from their hike behind the cabin.

Their report sounded much like ours in that, between the four of them, they had not seen a single animal nor fresh track the entire time they'd spent out there. They piled in next to the fire, and with the addition of a couple more logs, the flames were once again pumping out heat to thaw the next wave of Mensa candidates who thought a three-hour walk outside was a good idea.

We were all enjoying a very peaceful chat by the hearth, bathed in heat and slowly nursing our second batch of hot chocolate, when the calmness was pierced by an outburst of profanity emanating from our good pal Turtle.

The door flew open and we were treated to a chorus of, "I will never ride on an ATV with you again — you're NUTS! You scared the life out of me on purpose!"

Jon then passed through the door, responding only with an inadvertent snort from laughing while trying to catch his breath.

"You're a menace!" Turtle continued. "It's a miracle we're not dead!"

Now we were all laughing because we knew Jon to be not only responsible, but remarkably talented on an ATV. There's a reason we called him when we had to pack out a kill across a long distance of treacherous terrain . . . he's the only one who can get an ATV back into those tough spots. If he can't get it in there, nobody can.

We were all entertained by Turtle as his tantrum escalated — made even worse by Jon's continued amusement.

When he finally caught his breath, Jon removed his coat and pulled up his shirt. Exposed to all of us were five bruises on each side of his rib cage from where, Jon explained, Turtle had been holding on for dear life and screaming bloody murder the entire ride. Naturally, we exploded into laughter.

Turtle, who had previously stomped out of the room, popped back in and picked up his rant where he had left off.

"You could've slowed down, ya' know. I didn't come up here to be scared half to death," he scolded. His focus became derailed at the sight of the bruises on Jon's sides. He reacted with silence and a quizzical look on his face.

The moment he put two and two together and realized that he had caused the marks, his expression turned to shock, and then he too began to laugh. "Good!" he said. "You deserve every one of those!"

Once we had all settled down and order was somewhat restored, we turned our attention to lunch and the weather. We spent an hour talking about locations close to the cabin that were easy to return from, should the weather turn quickly during the afternoon hunt.

After lunch we all stepped onto the deck to look out over the property and compare the current weather to what we had experienced earlier.

It was a fascinating sight, but not one I will remember as making me feel particularly warm and fuzzy.

The decision was made to cancel the afternoon hunt based entirely upon the visual of a towering cloud bank pouring over the elevations and into the valley. Within minutes, the gray light under the already-overcast skies diminished by fifty percent, and we could see the front aggressively crawling up the mountain toward the cabin. It absorbed the trees and landscape as it approached, conquering acres and acres by the minute.

"Nobody's leaving the cabin today until further notice," Jon announced, then turned to Chainsaw and, in nearly the same breath, told him they were headed to Box Canyon to retrieve Turtle's deer.

This was odd for three reasons: we had no idea that Turtle had even shot a deer (because he was too busy whining and cursing Jon when they walked in); we had no idea that he could actually hit anything with the gun he'd brought; and Jon had just said that no one was to leave.

Then, before I could achieve any clarity, he and Chainsaw walked out the door, mounted an ATV, and sped off down the hill.

We all knew that this was among Jon's worst ideas ever—and all for a deer. (Not that the animal was insignificant, but safety had to come first.)

We all knew we were in store for a tense hour or two. The remaining crew stood wrapped in our coats on the deck watching this massive storm move in and wondering why anyone would go out as something like this approached. And then it happened: a thunder clap that rattled our fillings and rumbled on with intimidation after the initial blast—all of which reverberated off the valley's walls. The thunder continued and was shortly thereafter accompanied by lightning. That was our cue to go inside.

Meanwhile, the two lobotomy patients had been gone for roughly thirty minutes while thunder and lightning persisted all around us.

The clouds had marched up the closest visible hill and seized the cabin, enshrouding it in ice-cold mist and rendering visibility nonexistent. Trees that were fifteen feet from the windows were now completely imperceptible.

Suddenly, there was a very real concern. Two major questions had to be discussed urgently: 1) Should we disobey our orders to stay at the cabin in an effort to aid our friends in need? 2) If so, who should stay and who should go?

The answer to the first, which was decided by vote, was yes. And the answer to the second was terrifying.

I was elected driver since I knew the property well and had been driving almost all week. I knew the roads and was comfortable with their condition.

It was Boy Wonder's intimate knowledge of the terrain beyond the roads that put him in the mission, and Harry earned a spot due to his sheer size and strength. In case we needed to lift or drag one of these jokers to safety, he was our guy.

After the team was selected, we got ourselves ready to go help our friends.

The thunder was loud and daunting, while the lightning, though amazing, was creepy, unrelenting, and obviously dangerous. We scrambled to get dressed, grabbed four blankets off the beds from the other dorm, and ran toward where we remembered last parking the Tahoe. Once we found it, we climbed in, fastened our belts, turned on every exterior light we had, and started rolling slowly down the hill away from the cabin.

Due to the poor visibility, it took us twenty minutes to reach the intersection where we turned onto the West Road and continued to plod along. It occurred to me that with visibility as limited as it was — five to ten feet past the hood — we ought to open a window so we could potentially hear the ATV if it approached. The riders likely would not have time to stop if we suddenly appeared out of the cloud.

I also moved as far right as I could, trying to leave the majority of the smooth, snow-packed road for them. I'd say we got about halfway to Box Canyon after fifty grueling minutes. Thankfully, the lightning and thunder diminished, but our ability to see still was decidedly restricted. With windows down, heater blowing at maximum capacity, and silence within the vehicle, we pressed on.

Only a few tense minutes later, Boy Wonder pulled his head back inside the truck and announced, "I hear them!"

I pulled off the road as best I could and sat on the horn, flashing my lights continually. Shortly thereafter, they pulled up alongside the truck. Boy Wonder bundled up his coat, put his gloves on, and hopped out of the truck. He told Jon and Chainsaw to ride back in the SUV and that he'd take the ATV back up to the cabin.

Tweedledumb and Tweedledumber climbed into the Tahoe, blue and shivering, as Boy Wonder took off with the ATV that was newly adorned with Turtle's ten-point buck. I turned the SUV around and made my way slowly back up to the cabin, all the while listening to Jon and Chainsaw recount the details of the ill-advised excursion. I, however, elected to stay out of the discussion. The visibility was improving slightly, but the drive still required a lot of caution and concentration. Besides, this was not the time to offer my opinion, though it would come eventually.

Once safely back at the cabin, we all sat facing the windows in awe at the sight of the storm blowing through. I guess it was another hour or better before we realized that the storm was there to stay, which was right about the time that Santa returned from the outhouse to report that it was like Siberia outside.

By his estimation, we already had three additional inches of snow and counting. At this point all we could do was build up the fire, get the cards out, and start planning what we were going to have for dinner. It looked like we were in for the duration.

The next serious issues to address included how much snow we would have when the storm had run its course and whether we could still get off the mountain. We'd just have to wait to find out.

While we sat next to the fire, Jon and Chainsaw regaled us with the details of their highly unreasonable mission into the storm of storms, which still left us all a bit bewildered.

"Just to recap and make sure we're all on the same page," I said, to summarize the day's lunacy, "Jon and Chainsaw, who clearly ought to have known better, noted the ominous cloud rolling in at breakneck speed and jumped to the obvious conclusion that no one should leave the cabin . . . except the two of them, to retrieve a deer that was already dead." (And would presumably still be dead after the storm had passed.)

"Soon thereafter," I continued, "the storm overwhelmed the cabin, as those of us who were smart enough to stay inside of it noticed, while thunder and lightning engulfed the mountain. Cut back to aforementioned geniuses, who have now not only decided that this foray into the tempest of the decade may not have been the smartest course of action, realize that they are straddling a large hunk of metal which, mind you, is running and producing a static charge . . . in the middle of a lightning storm! Swiftly having come to their senses, which only minutes before had failed them so miserably, they decided to dismount said one-way ticket to the moon and seek shelter. Our whiz kids climbed off the bike and hid — now be sure to get this — under a tree! You know . . . those tall things that grow all over creation that act like lightning rods by attracting the electricity to them, funneling the charge straight to the bottom of the trunk, and then releasing enough energy in an explosion to rip even the strongest, thickest trees into roughly thirty billion splinters the size of your average whisker after a day's growth? And these are the wingnuts to whom we look for protection?"

I preached on, "Let me ask you two this: how many critical rules would we have broken if we'd made the decisions you made today?"

Neither of them said anything. Clearly, I was on point.

I was trying to bring everything into focus for them. While we were all glad they were back, the risk they had taken was ridiculous. I had to call them out because we had put ourselves at risk to help. Talk about compounding the problem. The fact that it had worked out meant we would all sleep well that night, but clearly there were lessons in that story for everyone.

Santa rejoined the group, after having gone upstairs to get a soda from the cooler outside, and said, "Anyone know what day it is?"

"Are you feeling all right?" I asked — this time with legitimate concern. I tried to play it off with humor in front of everyone else, but I started to get the impression that something was just a bit off.

"Santa, we've been through this two times already today," I said. "Let me try to teach you about this wonderfully convenient tool we on earth call a calendar. You see," as I pointed to one hanging on the wall, "each little square represents a day. So if you're supposed to be hunting for a week, then you shouldn't plan on going home before covering seven squares. Stick with it; you'll catch on eventually."

Of course, the look I got from him was priceless. Everyone else thought it was funny, yet somehow he was not amused. (It must be an age thing.) I laughed, but inside my head I was nervous that he might be showing signs of a stroke or something. This was highly out of character, so I mentioned something to Jon. The two of us decided to keep an eye on him just in case.

By then the dinner hour had rolled around, and Jon, along with his throbbing toe, excused himself to the kitchen.

The menu du jour included a spectacular roast with potatoes au gratin and broccoli. Not surprisingly, Jon had pulled it off beautifully, and we all sat down to eat. As was almost customary, we didn't stop until we felt ill. Of course, keep in mind that the belly laughs over Turtle screaming on the back of the ATV as though he had just had certain bits of his anatomy removed with quilting scissors didn't exactly help our stomachs feel better. It did, however, do wonders for our collective mood. Even I got tossed on the burning embers for calling out the two traveling nimrods. It was just another in a long line of great dinners with fantastic camaraderie. Neither the storm nor the cold could stand in the way of that.

After cleanup duties had been performed and our first round of Ninety-nine completed, we walked outside to see what the storm had left us. We found a total of seven inches of fresh snow for the day, with more likely as we were still in the cloud. In fact, nothing beyond six feet in any direction was visible. It didn't appear that the blizzard was over, only that it was taking a break.

I can vouch for the depth, having slipped on my way to the sand box a bit later and found myself almost completely under the snow. That was a chilly little adventure since, naturally, I slipped on the way there and not on the way back, meaning that the torture was compounded by snow down the back of my coat and in my boots—a gift I got to enjoy the whole time I was out in the bowel barn. Fate can often be so cruel.

Before we knew it, we had talked well into the ten o'clock hour, a time that usually finds us all in bed, if not asleep. We scattered the embers in the fireplace and headed off to change for bed, not knowing what to expect the next day other than a whole lot of snow.

The ritualistic parade to and from the outhouse ensued with all the usual suspects paying homage one last time to the cramped wooden hut with the intolerably cold toilet seat.

Once everyone was back safely inside the cabin, the lanterns went out and I quipped sarcastically, "Hey Jon, we have over thirty-eight inches of fresh snow and visibility is less than ten feet. We should go for a drive, huh?"

There were a few snickers before Jon retorted with, "Sounds good. It will be just you and me on the way out. That makes one less person I have to share the bacon with tomorrow at breakfast. Grab a shovel on the way to the truck and I'll meet you there."

18

CAMOUFLAGE, FIREARMS, AND SHOW TUNES

The reality of another early morning was upon us before we knew it, and we were awakened by a chipper and more traditional, "Everybody up! Some of us still have tags to fill!"

The moaning and groaning began, and Jon exited the dorm to fix breakfast.

The first thing most of us did was go to the door and look outside to see whether it was still snowing or if the storm had finally blown by us.

In fact, the storm was gone, the dark morning was clear, the weather was North Pole cold, and the total snow from the storm measured approximately twelve inches. The group was excited because when the animals get to moving in weather like this, they are easy to spot. We all dressed out for the morning feed and headed upstairs to the subtle sound of Jon's melodious voice floating gently on the air: "Breakfast is ready . . . right now!"

The morning briefing was very short. The weather report was quite obvious to us all: cold. The pairings were decided based on who had or had not tagged out (wish we'd thought of that the day before), so Grizzly went with BB, Boy Wonder with me, and Chainsaw with Harry. That left Santa and Turtle as floaters because they had both notched their last tags.

We finished breakfast and headed downstairs to get our gear with a renewed sense of determination.

We drove off in the Suburban, and Boy Wonder and I dropped Jon and BB off about halfway down the East Road in a stand of aspens and evergreens. They had to hike a hundred yards through the deep snow before cutting into the timber, and it was a rough go. Boy Wonder and I stayed for a bit to make sure they could get to the woods. We then headed to the Middle Road to hunt the trees above Deep Canyon from the dual-level vantage point with which I became so enamored just days before.

The hike into the woods was just plain grueling. I would have thought that the canopy would limit the amount of accumulation on the ground, but there was no such reprieve. Each step was difficult, and our legs became heavier with each stride as we picked up our feet above the snow and sank them back in. Imagine stepping over tall blocks with every stride, for what on this day seemed like miles, with the added weight of boots, gear, and the snow on your feet. You get the idea that this wasn't the most relaxing or entertaining walk we had ever had.

Not only was our progress slowed by the snow, but we had to take several breaks. I was reminded, repeatedly, just how out of shape I really was.

When we finally arrived at the spot, it looked much different from when last I had seen it. There was deep snow everywhere, which was mostly undisturbed. There was a new calmness to the setting, and I felt a bit safer knowing that I had an extra set of eyes with me — even though I knew that if we were challenged by a raccoon, we probably wouldn't make it out alive.

We set up twenty yards apart, giving us both a solid view of both game trails and the surrounding timber as well as views from different angles of the area below. We had the spot covered very well, and at that point it became a waiting game. The binos were out, and we were ready to punch Boy Wonder's last tag.

The forest was quiet that day and the wind was still, which made crashing branches more discernible and their direction obvious.

Off to the east and on the opposite rim of the upper landscape, we heard a commotion that was obviously a large animal powering through some brush. We both looked up and spotted a nice five-by-five bull elk as he surged out of the trees and began walking the edge. A moment later, he was followed by two cows. The situation presented the perfect opportunity for a kill shot, but elk season had already come to an end and our unused elk tags were useless.

It was still a beautiful scene as the three of them gracefully plowed through the snow, their dark bodies in contrast to it and their breath floating in the crisp morning air. We watched them for a minute or two before they turned back into the tree line and gracefully disappeared. They could be heard for a time as they pushed through the trees and heavy snow, but their sound soon turned again to silence.

When we looked back into the clearing below us, I could see two does, one decidedly larger than the other. There were two sets of tracks across the pristine field of snow, and the light that was able to filter through the trees created giant shadows on the snow's smooth surface.

They were standing in such a place that Boy Wonder couldn't see them, yet he was the one with the tag. I got his attention and slowly held up two fingers. I then pointed to the clearing below us.

He carefully stood and tried to reposition himself but couldn't do it quietly enough. He was stuck where he was. Our only option was to wait them out. If they continued walking, he would not get a shot. However, if we could turn them around, they would walk right through his shooting lane.

I slowly stood and backed out of my spot in the tracks I had made walking in. I then made a loop in the trees and walked toward the ledge right in front of where the deer had been standing. Again, I got Boy Wonder's attention and motioned to him to raise his gun. I then inched closer to the edge as carefully as I could, straining to see if I still had a visual on the deer.

As I pressed ever closer to the ledge and was only a foot from it, a portion of the snow cornice fell from the lip of the face and spooked the deer.

They darted back into my line of sight, and as they bounded across the opening below, the pair ran right into Wonder's sight line at thirty-five yards.

Taking a page from Jon's playbook, I made a quick sound: "Maaa."

The two deer both stopped on cue and turned their heads back, and Boy Wonder filled his last tag with one true shot just behind the shoulder.

The report ripped through the silence and dissipated far down the canyon. The smaller deer darted into the woods alone while the other scampered into the trees, leaving a brilliant red trail in the glaring white snow. We tried to listen as the deer staggered through the woods, but there was little sound due to the recent snowfall. I waited for a minute or two and then trudged over to my hunting partner to offer a congratulatory fist-bump.

He explained that we had to walk around through the woods and along the ridgeline until it sloped down to the lower elevation before picking up the blood trail.

It was to be a long walk around with the snow, but climbing down the thirty-foot wall over rocks was just not possible. We set off to follow the ridgeline, and it didn't take long for my legs to start burning again.

After a painful trek, we picked up the blood trail at the tree line across the clearing. It led us into the woods for no more than fifty steps and stopped at her side as she lay in the snow. I stood aside while Boy Wonder cut and attached his tag, and then I watched from afar as he proceeded to field dress her.

I then picked up his rifle and slung it over my shoulder as he threw the doe on his, and we lumbered toward the road without the benefit of a previously cut path through the drifts.

Once out of the trees, he put the deer down, and I set his gun against it. I then set off toward the truck about a quarter mile back up the road.

I returned with Jon's vehicle, and the two of us promptly placed the doe's carcass inside — something we were sure he'd appreciate when he found out.

We drove to the agreed-upon pickup spot to retrieve our host and company, and there sat Jon and BB on deadfall beside the road.

As we came to a stop, Boy Wonder rolled down the window and said, "Climb on in, boys. Try not to disturb the young lady in the back. She's sleeping."

Knowing exactly what the younger man was implying, Jon froze and glared at us with visible displeasure.

On the other hand, BB and the two of us thought it was quite amusing. I was sure to point out that it was Wonder's deer and that we had tried to get her to walk alongside the car, but she just wouldn't cooperate. "Ultimately," I explained, "we really had no choice but to let her ride along."

As we drove back to the cabin, we learned that Jon had shot a sizable buck. And since I had now been involved in stinking up his car twice, I was elected to take the two of them back down after lunch to retrieve it. (It was just then that the notion of taking a peaceful nap and having a relaxing afternoon quietly died.)

It was about three p.m. when we decided to go pull Jon's deer out of the woods. I drove his Suburban, Jon rode shotgun, and BB was in the back.

We were just pulling away from the cabin when I decided that we needed a little musical entertainment, and I started cycling through the CDs that were on hand in Jon's truck. By the time I got to the third disc in the changer, I knew we were onto something.

It turns out that Jon is an avid enthusiast of ABBA, the '70s band from Sweden. Admittedly, as luck would have it, I'm a huge fan as well.

"Do you like ABBA?" Jon asked BB.

"Never heard of 'em," came the reply.

Jon and I were surprised because, like it or not, almost everyone on the planet at least *knows* of ABBA.

Not wanting to deprive BB of an introduction to a culturally iconic band, Jon and I decided to acquaint him with the band by turning up the stereo and singing along to each and every tune on the *Gold* album, which, for those of you who, like BB, are without a clue, has nineteen songs on it.

The style is disco-meets-pop with very memorable lyrics and catchy, driving, upbeat tunes — which, if that's not your thing, can drive you completely bananas in a matter of moments, particularly when you're also getting it in stereo from two horrible singers.

Poor BB looked as though he were incarcerated and sitting on death row. We even went so far as to make sure there were no loaded guns in the car for fear he might rather take an early exit than listen to Twinkle Toes and me serenade him for another instant.

As for Jon and me, we had a captive audience for what would turn out to be the best (worst!) impromptu karaoke session of all time. We were bad and we knew it; in fact, we reveled in our tone-deaf mediocrity and were only further motivated by the look of desperation on BB's face. It seemingly begged us to spare him the torture of another song. However, one by one, they kept playing.

Of course, Jon and I were only too happy to continue singing, which surely sent any creature in the area scurrying for any shelter that would protect them from what undoubtedly must have sounded like a thousand cats being run tail first through a meat grinder.

What a performance! Jon and I were sweating so badly from our efforts that we had to crack the fogging windows.

Now BB was annoyed and cold as he sat with ringing ears, hoping to be struck by lightning before another song began.

At this point, I pulled over to maintain some semblance of safety. Besides, serenading someone properly requires a certain amount of eye contact, and as the driver, I felt it important to give the singing my full attention rather than risk wrecking the car and cutting short our energetic concert. Alas, I was directed to begin driving again due to concerns about losing daylight.

I would, however, like to point out that I still gave the performance my all, much to BB's dismay. Obviously, the drive took longer than any other time we had driven to that point on the East Road, but it was indeed the most fun . . . for Jon and me, anyway.

When we arrived at our spot, BB opened the door and literally dove out of the car, bleeding ears and all, just to get away from the recital.

Naturally, Jon and I were properly insulted. We vowed then and there to do better on the way back.

Hearing that pledge and interpreting it as a threat, BB glared at us with contempt and began to methodically load his gun.

Thoughts returned to the chore at hand, and I was advised to stay in the car and wait for them.

I reclined the seat and kicked the tunes back on while they went to look for Jon's deer. But after an hour or so, my mood wasn't as upbeat; it was still really cold out and these guys hadn't yet returned.

My thoughts shifted from dancing around in the car to wondering whether or not to get out and look for them. I figured I'd give them another twenty minutes before making that call. A decision like that could have its own bad repercussions, especially if they returned to find that I was gone. Then they would have to search for me in the cold and I would've put us all at risk. (Didn't we just cover this the night before?)

After the twenty minutes had gone by, the light was fading and my concern was mounting. I got out of the car, convinced I would have to take a risk I really wanted to avoid, and took my heavy coat out of the back. As I was putting it on, I looked up and saw the two of them walking toward me through the clearing . . . with no deer.

While I was only slightly curious about the deer's absence, I was very interested in hearing exactly what had taken so long.

Once back at the car, they explained that as they were dragging the deer out, it got hung up on a fallen tree. They explained that it was just too heavy to unwedge from the timber's grasp.

The plan moving forward was to return tomorrow with Chainsaw Monkey and his trusty hardware. I couldn't figure out if they were going to use the chainsaw on the tree or the deer, so I immediately voiced my intent to opt out of that errand before cranking the volume on the stereo. That catapulted us yet again into the thrilling universe of ABBA tunes, and I declared at the top of my voice, "Act two!"

Jon jumped right in while BB just stared in utter disbelief that it had all started again. He looked so defeated, the poor guy. I think we just about broke him.

Jon and I then did the only thing we felt was appropriate: we dialed it up and dug even deeper to give him the very best ABBA experience we could. We stripped our gears to cheer him up, but by the time we arrived back at the cabin, he was in a dark and dismal place.

We just shook our heads and were left wondering what could have possibly gotten this guy so down. It was very sad, clearly, but Jon and I didn't stop laughing for an hour. We had demoralized that poor man. We came to the conclusion that BB would most likely never listen to ABBA again and would certainly get a rash if ever he heard anyone even mention the band's name.

Meanwhile, Jon's colorful toe was in no condition for him to stand and cook, so the boys took over the final evening's dinner preparations — the last supper, so to speak.

With mounting disorganization in the kitchen and plenty of dissent in the ranks, it was clear that management was going to have to step in and delegate tasks before someone ended up with a paring knife in his spleen.

I sent Boy Wonder and Turtle to set the table while I tasked Santa with preparing the string beans: open can (times two), drain contents (times two), fry, and add two pounds of bacon . . . times two!

By the way, I was relieved to see that Santa's internal calendar was functioning properly again, as there had been no inquiries about what day it was since the night before. Apparently, his brain had only suffered an intermittent bout of conscious unconsciousness.

I took on baking the potatoes and seasoning the eighteen-ounce porterhouse steaks prior to their appointment with the grill. Chainsaw took the reins of the grill and delivered perfectly medium-rare steaks just as the potatoes came out of the oven.

It turned out that as soon as we stopped tripping over each other trying to perform the same duties at the same time, we made a pretty solid team and produced an outstanding dinner of which we could all be fat — I mean proud.

After we were all reunited downstairs in front of the blazing fire, it was time to take the day's inventory, which showed we still had tags to fill on the final morning hunt.

Other items of interest included the status review on various critical supplies. Of the fourteen pounds of bacon we'd brought, the remaining stock stood at zero. Regarding the roughly ten pounds of Cinnamon Bears, the stockpile was entirely depleted. Of the forty rolls of TP brought up the mountain, the residual supply numbered only six. (Of course, we all looked at Turtle.) Of the six dozen eggs, there were none left. And as for the countless bags of candy, chips, cookies, and pow-dered-sugar mini-doughnuts hauled up to the cabin, only half a bag of potato chips had survived, and that would soon be lost to someone grazing in front of the fire once the card games started.

Our last night there was an early one because we were all wiped out from trekking through the snow all day. There were two tags left for the last morning, and at least one deer retrieval had to be performed. It was decided that while the rest of us packed and cleaned up the cabin for our departure, BB and Chainsaw would go get Jon's deer and Jon and Harry would attempt to fill the last of their tags for the food bank.

One last round of Ninety-nine was dealt for brag-ging rights before our last fire was eventually scuttled in the name of bedtime. We dove into our beds one final time for the season, and I don't even remember the lights going out. While I'm certain there was some comment or another that I missed, I can assure you I was better off not being awake for it, as that won me at least another minute of sleep, for which I would be thankful come morning roll call.

19

THIS IS NOT HAPPENING

Once again, our wake-up "bell" was as subtle as a compound fracture—and almost as painful. We all started trying to clear the cobwebs and become partially coherent before the second alert signaling breakfast was ready.

This was one not to miss: Jon was preparing ham steaks with breakfast potatoes and toast, etc. While we were all looking quite forward to that, the rest of the day's chores seemed a bit overwhelming and tedious, not to mention disappointing. It was the day we had all dreaded: our last on the mountain for the season.

We scurried upstairs with all the energy, enthusiasm, and haste of someone going through the process of rigor mortis. We approached the table like a parade of zombies and discovered that not even coffee could reanimate our tired and aching bodies. And it seemed only barely feasible that ham steaks could break us out of our collective stupor, but we decided to give it the old college try just to appease the chef.

As it turned out, while delicious, the ham steaks failed to rally us into a conscious state. That said, Jon yelling at us and trying to motivate us with sheer volume seemed to do the trick just fine. We left the table slightly heavier and with a little less capacity for hearing than when we'd arrived.

Those who were hunting or collecting deceased deer got dressed and were dispatched to various areas around the ranch, while the rest of us had a list of things to do to clean the cabin.

These assignments included, but were not limited to, packing, vacuuming, sweeping, mopping, straightening, removing ash, doing the final kitchen cleaning, etc. You get the idea.

I divided the tasks among Santa, Boy Wonder, and myself, declared us all on cabin detail, and got to work. Thankfully, Boy Wonder was tasked with the basement, so the distractions were kept to a minimum.

By the time team number one returned with Jon's tagged deer and laid it in the snow outside, we were well on our way to being finished. I asked them to take down all the harvests from the beam so we'd be ready to load them just before leaving.

When team two returned (empty-handed), the cabin was relatively spotless. The cleanup team had only thirty more minutes of minor jobs to finish before receiving the Good Cabin-keeping Seal of Approval.

Satisfied with our progress, Jon then looked to establish and manage the loading crew. He selected (grabbed) the two closest people to him, and they handled packing the SUVs for the trip back down the mountain and into Salt Lake City. There we would stop to unload our harvest at the processing house and release it for distribution to the food pantry.

Within a half hour, all the gear had been loaded, as had all the harvested animals. Even Turtle's trailer was reunited with his vehicle for the journey back to the Midwest.

We were all sad to leave the cabin. We said one last farewell to it and walked outside to the trucks. It was then, to my horror, when I became aware that my Tahoe had been converted to a hearse, with a pile of deer carcasses within. (Ugh! Really, Jon?)

I seemed to be the only one in the group who failed to see the humor in the situation and immediately became anxious. I started to panic over how in the world I was going to return this rolling morgue with dirt and blood coating the interior to the rental company—to say nothing of tolerating the smell of death that consumed me as I climbed in to pilot the meat wagon down the hill.

Jon led the cavalcade, I was in second position, and Turtle followed me.

Jon's speed was slow but deliberate, and as the snow remained a factor, we were instructed to leave plenty of room between the vehicles while descending the mountain.

Jon's truck rounded a bend fifty yards ahead of me, and by the time I drove around the same turn a minute later, I found his truck stopped in the middle of the road, the driver's door open, and footprints through the snow leading off the road and into the trees.

Before I could process what might be happening, a gunshot rang out, and Boy Wonder leapt from the Suburban, knife in hand, and bounded into the woods.

I walked up to the Suburban to address Santa. "What the heck are these ding-dongs doing? Don't they know we have flights to catch?"

Santa explained, "Jon saw a doe and wanted to fill his tag."

Within ten minutes, Jon and the Wonder emerged from the trees with a fresh kill, complete with tag, and before I could stop them, they threw it in the back of my Tahoe to join more harvested deer — the remaining deer plus two elk were on Turtle's trailer.

They then returned to the Suburban, where Jon said, "Get back in your car, Freddie. Don't you know you have a flight to catch?"

At this point I was already on a slow burn; all I could envision was a thousand dollars in cleaning fees to the rental company for the comprehensive destruction of the vehicle's interior.

Despite being brand new and spotless when I'd picked it up, the truck now looked like a stage prop for a horror film.

Just after we got moving again and had managed another mile or so down the mountain, Jon stopped again. This time he and Chainsaw exited their vehicle, and Jon handed him a rifle and pointed up the hill. With that, Wonder hopped out and walked into the woods with the Monkey. I couldn't believe what I was witnessing. These guys were off the reservation.

After several minutes, a shot ripped through the valley, and Jon, who was staring intently through his binoculars, started dancing in the road.

By now I had lost all patience. We still had a long drive and the donation process to get through, and then there was the airport to deal with, not to mention what I was going to do with the blood-bathed death-and-dismemberment mobile.

After another twenty minutes had elapsed, the two pinheads emerged from the trees with a tagged and field-dressed buck which, to no one's surprise, was placed in my Tahoe with less care and consideration than one would expect from a baggage handler at Boston's Logan Airport after an eight-hour shift in the rain.

"Can we please get off the mountain so I have at least a fighting chance to make my flight?" I screamed out my window.

Everyone got back to their cars and we drove toward the gates and on to the highway.

Leaving definitely filled me with mixed emotions. On one hand, I was tired and needed a vacation from my vacation. On the other, though, the experiences over the last two seasons had been truly remarkable, and I couldn't remember ever having laughed so hard. I was happy I had finally gotten a buck but marginally disappointed that I still hadn't killed my bull. I was relieved that no one had gotten hurt (Jon's toe notwithstanding), but I was saddened by the fact that BB would never truly appreciate ABBA. There was a lot to process on the drive back to SLC, and the smell within my warming vehicle was not helping my concentration.

After a few long hours behind the wheel, we finally arrived at the processing station to donate the meat. I had kept a careful eye on the time, and we were cutting it close for the airport. We took all our paperwork into the little building and started sorting the tags and presenting our identification, making sure we had legal donations and proper transfers.

Meanwhile, the guys from the checking station unloaded the animals and verified the harvest tags.

After I finished checking in my donation, I walked outside to see what condition my poor Tahoe was in, and I was absolutely speechless at the sight of the interior. It looked like someone had fed spaghetti and meatballs to three-year-old twins during a high-speed police chase, and far worse than if multiple exploding antitheft dye packs had detonated inside the vehicle. There was even blood on the roof liner, not to mention the caked dirt and layer of dust that covered everything else. It was a disaster of epic proportions, regardless of perspective.

I was mad. All I could see was dollar signs.

I walked inside to ask Grizzly what we were going to do with the car, and while I was explaining to everyone else how bad it was, Jon was suddenly and conspicuously absent.

When I went back outside to look for him, I promptly noticed that the Tahoe was gone. I rounded the corner of the little shed and marched back toward the warehouse, where I spied the front end of the Tahoe barely sticking out from behind the building.

I approached and immediately wished I hadn't.

"What are you doing?" I screamed. "Do you realize I'm going to have to pay for this?"

"Relax," Jon said. "It's going to be fine. Besides, you've got the insurance, right?" (For the record, that didn't make me feel any better.)

There he was with all the doors and the rear tailgate open, holding the nozzle of a three-thousand-psi commercial power-washer and spraying out the interior of the SUV—from between the front seats. I looked on in horror as a river of red water poured from the payload section of the Tahoe while Jon blasted the interior from the front seats to the rear, including the roof liner!

I was at a complete loss for words. I simply turned around and walked back to the shed.

After ten more minutes, Jon pulled the truck around and jumped out.

"Just one last thing and you're good to go," he said, then hopped into the back of the truck. He lay with his back across the saturated carpet, put his feet on the ceiling, and pushed up until there was a loud *pop*. He climbed out of the car and said, reassuringly, "Someone dented the roof when they put the deer up there. I was just popping the dimple out. Other than it being a bit damp, you're all good."

Santa then announced that the process for turning in our donations was complete.

"We finished just short of our goal, but that's a successful hunt in anyone's book."

Congratulations went around the group as we were genuinely proud of what we had accomplished.

I looked back at my Tahoe and got angry all over again when I spied the roof liner dripping all over the back seats and cargo area.

"You'd better get going, Freddie," Jon said, pointing to the SUV and laughing. "You're gonna miss your plane after you explain all that to the rental agent."

It was a good thing I liked him so much, or I might have shot him where he stood and donated *him* to the food pantry.

I said my goodbyes, collected my gear, and placed it all in the car. I had to admit, it actually looked pretty good given what it had been through that week.

I headed to the airport, hoping upon hope that the good people at the Center for Wayward Tow Hitch Assemblies wouldn't notice that the car's interior had been roundly abused.

Thankfully, it was dark when I pulled into the return lot and drove the truck down the designated chute. I pulled up behind a gentleman returning his car and placed the vehicle in park, unloaded all my gear, and stood ready to run as soon as I had my receipt in hand.

The rental agency employee approached and asked me if everything had met my expectations. I told her that I had been very pleased with the Tahoe and would happily rent another.

She checked the mileage and the gas gauge and gave a cursory glance to the back seat to be sure I had gotten all of my belongings. She then walked around the SUV, printed my receipt, and sent me on my way.

I couldn't believe it, but wasn't about ready to stick around any longer for fear that, at some point, someone would get in the car and realize that something was just a bit off in the odor department.

I got to the ticket counter and was able to check my rifle and bag back to St. Louis without any challenges.

After then clearing security without issue, I walked down the concourse to my gate.

Shockingly, I managed to get to my plane with time to spare, and it looked like I wouldn't have to hear my name over the public-address system.

Determined to learn from last year's mistake, all I had to do was find a restroom to freshen up a little bit for the ride home.

After my wipe-down in the airport bathroom (another first for me), my flight's boarding call was announced, right on cue.

I boarded and sat in my preferred spot, toward the front of the plane by the window.

The flight was not crowded, so I had the row all to my pungent little self.

I settled in and watched out the window for a moment while all the preflight safety instructions were given, and then I casually reached for my seatbelt as the cabin lights dimmed and the plane started to push back from the gate.

"You're sitting on it again," said an oddly familiar voice with a distinctly rude tone.

I looked reluctantly toward the aisle and there she stood, Dracula's bride, in all her glory.

I couldn't believe my misfortune. I thought to myself, *Who did I anger in a previous life?*

I didn't say a word this time. I simply latched my belt and turned to look out the window.

This flight home was going to be a long one . . . I swear it's true.

HUNT #3
FALL OF 2003

20

ONCE MORE—WITH FEELING

Before my alarm even went off, I was awake, showered, and dressed for my flight. (As someone who regularly slept until noon, that alone was categorically amazing.) My bags were all packed and waiting by the door to the garage, and I just had a feeling that this was going to be my year. It had to be; I could feel it.

The experience I had had the year before had been remarkable, and I finally got a sense of the capabilities of my gun (in my own hands, at least). But I still hadn't managed even a single shot at my elusive bull elk—the top prize for many hunters.

From the first time I had seen one up close (and I mean *close*), I had known that a trophy bull elk was the big-game animal I wanted more than any other, and I was determined to get one.

Walking into St. Louis's main terminal that morning, I was still a bit uneasy with the whole hunting-rifle-in-an-airport scenario. Yes, I had done it before (twice even), but it was still awkward and went against all I had been taught about airports and general public safety. Besides, looking back at my experience from two years prior had made me even more paranoid that something unexpected and inconvenient was going to happen. I could feel that too.

As I walked up to the check-in counter, I greeted the airline agent (another morning person) and presented my tickets. I then put my blue duffel (body) bag with the obnoxious orange initials on the scale. True to form, I hit my seventy-eight-pound mark on the nose and could just picture traction in the poor agent's future after she lifted it onto the conveyor belt behind her.

I cautioned her to be careful lifting the bag, but she was smarter than the average bear. She called a big, burly colleague over to lift and transfer the bag. He heaved it onto the belt with an unintelligible grunt and retreated back to his station without so much as a smile. (Apparently, he was not much of a morning person. I could respect that.)

She then asked if I was checking the orange case.

"In fact, I am," I replied. "I spoke with the airline yesterday and printed out the form and waiver for traveling with a firearm. Here's the paperwork, and I will hand you the locked case whenever you are ready for it."

She immediately turned ashen and looked over to the big, burly guy again and said, with suddenly frayed nerves, "Henry, he's got a gun. What should I do?"

I thought, *Well, thank you for selling me out and throwing me to the wolves. I think the hair dye is beginning to seep into that void between your ears.*

As the big guy turned around and became fully engaged in palpable Serious Situation Mode, I left my hands where he could see them and emphatically said, "A hunting rifle, which is locked, per your airline's instructions, and accompanied by validated paperwork showing that it has been approved for travel and that you should be expecting it."

She was still a wreck—obviously she hadn't been through this drill before. In contrast, he calmed down right away and said, "Oh, well that's different. I got it." He stepped in front of her and started clicking away on her keyboard.

"There it is . . . yeah, it's okay. Checking through to Salt Lake City?"

There's nothing I enjoy more than going into full panic mode and experiencing the adrenaline dump that occurs right before you think your life is going to end, or at least before getting tackled by several large security officers and handcuffed at gunpoint. Of course, the next-best feeling is trying to fight back the sweat and impending nervous breakdown that occurs once the immediate threat has passed and all the epinephrine is coursing through your body, making it nearly impossible to simultaneously concentrate on speaking coherently and keeping your knees from buckling beneath you.

"You're all set," he said.

My attempt to thank him almost certainly sounded as though I was speaking with a mouth full of marbles, as my nerves were a trembling mess.

"Don't forget your ticket and boarding pass, sir," the agent said as he handed them over the counter. I turned again and took them from him with a nod.

I was shaking. As for the other agent, she must have taken six months off my life with that neurotic reaction of hers. I took my credentials and started to walk to security when I heard her pipe up with a cheerful, "Have a nice flight." I wanted to burn her fake eyelashes off with a dessert torch.

I ambled anxiously over to security and tried to compose myself. I hoped that all the fun for the morning had already been had, but, sadly, that was not the case.

As I passed through the metal detector without my shoes, keys, belt, etc., I was diverted into a holding chute of sorts for a "random" and more thorough examination. The security officer retrieved the bin holding my articles and asked, "Do these items belong to you?"

I respectfully responded that, yes, in fact, they did, and he placed them on a table just beyond my reach.

"Where are you going today?" he asked while holding my ticket.

"I'm headed to Utah on a hunting trip," I said.

Just about then I heard a gentleman in the next aisle address another security officer and say, in a rather arrogant tone, "What's wrong with me? How about what's wrong with you? Did you forget your pills this morning, dude?"

Call me old fashioned, but I always thought that being polite to people in general was a good idea. But I knew to always be particularly courteous and respectful to people in positions of authority, especially those who could cause you to miss your flight.

It appeared on this occasion that this gentleman was about to miss his travel reservation over nothing more than his sanctimonious predisposition.

Suddenly, I didn't feel entirely important as all the security guys descended on the wacko one aisle over.

The agent interviewing me simply gave me a nod and let me through, reminding me to collect my property.

As much as I wanted to stay and watch them tie this self-impressed clod into a pretzel, I collected my belongings as I was told, slipped into my shoes, and made my way to the concourse inconvenience store to buy a magazine and some chips for the flight.

While trying to get past all the "I Heart STL" T-shirts and shot glasses with images of the Arch on them, I managed to inadvertently brush an older woman while trying to squeeze by her overly padded frame as she stood in the center of the aisle. She offered a condescending, "Watch where you're going, young man."

Then, as I pulled a soda out of the cooler, I accidentally dropped it. Naturally, it ruptured all over a display of sweatshirts proclaiming undying love for the Midwest. As exciting a day as it was supposed to be, it was off to a rough start. I finally left the store with my (new) soda, some chips, and a *Robb Report* magazine so I could drool over the cool sports cars while winging my way westward to Utah.

As had become protocol, I boarded the plane and sat in my customary front-of-the-bus window seat, hoping for the row to remain open. It stayed unoccupied until the last moment, when a law-enforcement officer of some kind boarded the plane with his dog. The officer was dressed in a commanding black uniform, and his K-9 partner had a collar adorned with a gold police badge. I thought to myself that this was going to be pretty cool, as I respect law-enforcement officers and other first responders, and I absolutely love dogs. The officer sat in the aisle seat and his dog curled up on the floor between the two of us.

"Good morning, sir," I said and gestured to the well-behaved Belgian Malinois. "And who's this?"

I got a decidedly apathetic nod in return, and without even a look in my general direction, he said sternly, "Don't interact with the dog. He's on duty."

Then Officer Personality stared forward as if he were standing at attention in morning lineup. It was then that I knew I was in for a flight that was to be as exciting as root-canal surgery.

The plane left the gate on time, and my static, boring, uneventful, tedious, painfully quiet flight began and persisted without any interaction between me and the dog lying at my feet. I would almost rather have had the argumentative flight attendant from the year before.

As if it couldn't get any bleaker, I remembered the antics from the Denver layover and realized that I wouldn't be enjoying that interlude today either.

However, there was my elk to look forward to, and I knew that if I could just endure the flight, I'd be at peace on the mountain by day's end.

We finally landed in SLC, the plane slamming down onto the runway and literally bouncing twice. (Perhaps the pilot was in need of a new prescription for his glasses.) I exited the aircraft with a sense of relief and anticipation, making my way to baggage claim to retrieve my belongings.

I'm not sure why I was so surprised that my duffel bag was the very last one that appeared on the belt, but I was. And then when I walked over to the oversized baggage area to claim my rifle, I was told it wasn't up yet—despite the fact that I recognized a couple people from my flight picking up their guns and golf clubs, which seemed to have made their way up to baggage claim just fine.

I found a baggage manager watching over the carousels and asked him if he could check into the matter.

"Can you describe the case, sir?" he asked. "Maybe it's still on the ramp."

"Sure," I said. "It's neon-orange ballistic plastic. It's roughly the size of a living room couch and has the other half of this paperwork attached to it." I handed him all the documentation.

He disappeared to see what he could do to find it, which left me in a panic over the fact that my beautiful rifle was potentially missing. Thankfully, just moments later (or thirty-five minutes, but who's counting?), he returned with case in hand. He was very nice to offer an apology and let me know that the case had been sitting next to the conveyor belt down on the ramp, but that nobody had bothered to actually send it along.

I headed toward the car-rental desk, already nearly an hour behind schedule. I walked up to the desk, introduced myself, and handed them the reservation confirmation, along with my driver's license and proof of insurance.

Almost immediately, the agent excused herself and stepped through a door behind the counter—never a good sign. Not one minute later, another woman appeared through the same door, walked to the counter in front of me, and introduced herself as a manager. By now I knew that either my reservation had been lost, they didn't have the car I had been guaranteed, or I was their one-millionth customer and they wanted to award me free car rentals for life, take my picture, and pay me hundreds of thousands of dollars to be part of a new marketing campaign.

Well, they had my reservation and I was not a significant customer, so I cleverly deduced that they were going to shaft me on my car.

She was very apologetic as she let me know that they were unable to provide the Tahoe I had reserved. She did, however, try to make it up to me.

"Although we don't have a Tahoe, I can offer you a Honda Accord or a Ford Focus sedan, and I am authorized to discount the already-lower rental rate by fifteen percent for your inconvenience."

My day had already been problematic, so my patience was diminishing by the moment. I tried to remain as friendly and flexible as possible and replied, "I certainly appreciate the gesture, but I will be in the mountains, and I'm afraid those vehicles will not work for me. Let's focus on similar SUVs. What do you have?"

Her face remained the same: a huge smile that looked as though it had been spackled on and fixed with adhesive. She offered, "Once again, sir, I am terribly sorry, but we do not have any SUVs at this time."

More than a bit frustrated now, I said, "Well, I'm sorry too, but your alternatives are inadequate. I reserved and received confirmation for a Tahoe. The deposit has even been paid. You're going to have to find a solution unless you'd like me to return the Accord in a shoebox, which is exactly what will happen to it if I try to take it into the backwoods on top of a mountain — assuming it can even get me there in the first place."

"I see," she said, the smile remaining in place.

I could see the wheels in her head turning before she simply dropped the problem in someone else's lap.

"Why don't you take your paperwork to the lot, and the porters will show you what we have available. Have a nice day."

I was not pleased, but at least I could attempt to charm someone else because, clearly, she and I had gotten off on the wrong foot.

I walked to the lot carrying the oversize duffel on my shoulder and pulling the wheeled orange gun case behind me. Upon my arrival at the porter's office, I was the recipient of a very energetic and upbeat greeting from Al, who wished to know what he could do to assist me.

"Good morning, Al," I replied. "I'm Fred, and I just flew in from St. Louis. I have a reservation confirmation for a Tahoe here, and I need you to point out which one is mine."

I handed the papers to him for his reading pleasure and looked out at the lot, where I saw four Tahoes all parked next to one another in the first row of cars.

"I'm sorry, but we don't have a Tahoe today —"

"Except for the four that I'm staring at right in front of us," I interrupted. "It's already been a tough morning, Al. Please help me out. I have the confirmation for the vehicle and the deposit has been paid and received. One of those was mine and now has obviously been snatched from me and allocated to someone else. In any case, I'm here first, and I want the car I reserved and paid for, which is clearly available, as we both can plainly see."

"Go ahead and take your pick," Al said. "My shift ends in twenty minutes."

We both had a laugh, I tipped him a Jackson, and loaded my duffel bag and gun case into a charcoal-gray Tahoe with black leather interior. It was a new car with less than a hundred miles on it, and, more importantly, wouldn't show blood inside. I took off before Al changed his mind and was officially on the road headed to the store to clean out its supply of Cinnamon Bears before driving up to the ranch.

It was a beautiful day with sunshine and blue skies, and the ride was uneventful except for that nagging feeling that comes over me when I'm not sure I'm correctly executing the task at hand. I had no navigator, and this was in the days prior to Siri and Google Maps. I couldn't even call Jon for reassurance because there was no cellular coverage at the ranch except that small square in the field behind the cabin.

Despite doubting myself, I made it to Coalville and, while tempted, passed the opportunity to say hi to Turtle's girlfriend. As I turned onto the road out of Coalville to head toward the ranch, I heard from Jon.

"Where are ya'?" he asked. I told him I was past Coalville and asked him to meet me at the gates so I could get onto the property. It turned out he was still a nice guy and was waiting for me at the gate next to the highway when I arrived at the dirt road.

We went through the painful ritual of opening, closing, and relocking all three gates and continued our hour-long drive up the mountainside to the cabin.

The drive was just as beautiful as I remembered it, with all the hills, fields, forests, and animals.

I relaxed immediately. A feeling of comfort washed over me as I returned to this place that I had grown to dearly love and appreciate. As unlikely as it was, I felt at home and at peace in this place that just two years before had been intimidating beyond description, and even that was light years opposite from how I had defined comfort and luxury back then. I was anxious to get to the cabin and see who was there.

Upon arriving at the wilderness residence, I was greeted by Boy Wonder, Santa, a gentleman who brought his horses (how cool is that?), and a military veteran from St. Louis, whom I had met previously and had come to know as the General.

The horse guy quickly became known as Cowboy and sported a sizable belt buckle and a braided ponytail, which fell right between his shoulder blades. He knew all there was to know about horses and, to be fair, way more about hunting than I did. He was a mild-mannered individual who was clearly eager and willing to help anybody with anything for any reason. He was a team player who was determined to see everyone succeed in hunting before allowing himself to settle in and hunt for his own enjoyment.

Then there was the General. The General was a real teddy bear . . . that is, if your picture of a teddy bear is a six-foot-five-inch guy with vise grips for hands that hung from arms boasting biceps the size of bowling balls. He had a barrel chest, was the picture of fitness (at age forty-four, no less), and had a square jaw, a crew cut, a piercing glare, a really deep voice, and an intimidating look that could melt flesh at fifty feet.

Despite the look, he seemed like as genuine and loyal a guy as I had met. The General was also a freakishly proficient marksman who not only designed and manufactured custom specialty rifles for elite law enforcement and military personnel, but also had an encyclopedic understanding of guns' capabilities and how to maximize their potential. He was a decidedly patient man (to a point) whom you wanted on your side at all cost.

As far as his background, all we knew was that he had served in the U. S. Army and had had additional special training. Beyond that, no one was ever brave enough to inquire about his role. He didn't talk about it and none of us pressed him. A simple "thank you for your service" was all that really seemed appropriate. Other than the mostly obvious, he was just one of us and wanted to be treated as such.

After unpacking and laying all my clothes and gear out in a marginally organized fashion, I retreated to the fireplace, where everyone was gathered and already telling stories.

Before I could even get comfortable, I heard an unmistakably disapproving voice ask, "So, Freddie, I understand you shoot game animals but don't dress them."

I looked up and saw the General addressing me with a very judgmental look on his face.

I am not often lost for words, but I honestly had no idea what to say to that. Clearly, it was true, and, evidently, he was not terribly pleased with or accepting of that practice. I sat there as he stared holes through me, and before I could offer an even partially intelligent response, he said, "Not to worry. You and I will go out tomorrow, and we'll overcome this little issue together."

I would tell you how eager I was for the next day, but, predictably, I was not at all enthusiastic about the idea. I still didn't like blood, and I knew I wouldn't get away with squat if I was with the General. Incidentally, the General knew it too. His facial expression transformed into a sinister grin as he watched me squirm in my chair.

Then we all began to discuss what tags we had; in total, we possessed six antlerless-deer tags, six buck tags, six bull tags, and four cow tags between us. (The state of Utah made a fortune on our trip alone.)

Those tags represented a tall challenge to us and an amazing win for the shelter in SLC, for which we intended to provide food if we managed to fill them. Our work was cut out for us.

We all decided that we would fix an early dinner and then go on a tour of the property to look for the sheep. That would give us an idea of where not to hunt the next few days and help the new guys get their bearings.

While Jon was banished to the kitchen to prepare yet another stellar dinner for his guests, I decided to find out what kind of crowd I had for my unrelenting assortment of inappropriate anecdotes.

I started with a few innocuous jokes with slightly racy punch lines and escalated to some daring ones with great shock value and an obvious lack of reverence in general.

After the test run, it appeared that everyone shared my brand of humor, and that I would not have to observe any boundaries. The jokes, and the laughter, continued right up to dinner time.

"Food's ready!" boomed Jon. "Whether or not you're hungry is irrelevant."

We wandered upstairs to find cowboy rib eyes that weighed in at twenty-four ounces apiece. They were grilled to a perfect medium-rare and served with baked potatoes and all the fattening stuff that made them worth eating, fresh rolls, and, of course, the often-imitated-but-never-duplicated bacon with canned green beans—the beans used merely as a garnish for effect.

Jon kindly brought the newcomers up to speed by regaling them with the most embarrassing tales from years gone by, only to be roasted in return as we shared some of his more infamous moments. Dinner was a riot and everything seemed to have picked up right where it had left off a year ago.

The property tour would have to wait; we were tired from our travel and incapacitated by the feast. It wasn't long before we were all seated in front of the fire downstairs, cards in hand and unwinding before bed. The evening had been a relatively benign experience; no one had done anything displaying particularly poor judgment . . . yet. But, as usual, the expectations were high and we were all ready to call each other out at a moment's notice.

One by one, as we were eliminated from the ritualistic game of Ninety-nine, we retired to the dorm to change for bed. The General took the spoils of victory in the first card game to a playful accusation from Boy Wonder that he had cheated. It must have all been in the delivery because it seemed like Wonder was the only one who thought the comment was funny. In that second, the subsequent look he earned from the General became instantly legendary.

Having heard his integrity called into question, even in friendly jest, the General's look was one of being profoundly offended. It seemingly indicated beyond any reasonable doubt that a similar accusation in the future would not be tolerated and could be punishable by death—likely a slow, painful one.

It was enough to chase Boy Wonder into the other room to change for bed and almost certainly caused him to sleep with one eye open throughout the entire night.

21

PHYSICS INTERACTING WITH NATURE: EDUCATIONAL AND HYSTERICAL

Another dark morning at the cabin and we were all startled awake by Jon's gentle and compassionate, "Get outta bed! Breakfast in twenty!"

Those of us who were used to it merely found it abrupt and unpleasant, but those who hadn't yet been treated to the formal morning experience were less than amused, and we all thought the General was going to pull Jon's limbs off out of reflex before he was fully awake. (Note to self: Don't scare the military guy while he's sleeping. It could end violently.)

At best, we were sluggish getting dressed, but, per usual, the pace picked up dramatically when the scent of fried pig flesh reached the dorm. We all ascended the stairs to find a lovely breakfast, which we were grateful to have once we began to gain full consciousness. The weather was to be mild that day, and the plan was to give the tour to the new guys and end up at the top of the East Road just below the cabin, where we would discuss further plans for the day.

Breakfast was adjourned and we all retreated to finish dressing and collect our gear. We gathered on the driveway in front of vehicles, where we mounted up, three to a car, and headed out with Jon leading the procession.

Cowboy and the General accompanied Jon, and following in the Tahoe with me were Boy Wonder and Santa. With the sun just beginning to lighten the land-scape, we headed to the intersection of the three roads and turned down the West Road toward Box Canyon.

I was in my own world. Everything I saw was as if I were seeing it for the first time. It was awe-inspiring still. The scale of the mountains and the vastness of the meadows and forests were overwhelming . . . again.

Everywhere I looked reminded me of experiences from the two previous seasons, whether it was a hike, a kill, a hunt, or a noise that frightened me.

I was becoming familiar with the ranch and had a bond with it. Granted, it was give and take, but a real relationship had emerged with an environment that had once been so foreign to me, I had been unable to imagine ever being comfortable there or making the connection with it that I had made. Just the tour alone was magical on some level for me — even on this, the third time — though I couldn't quite put my finger on why.

It was a surreal journey around the property, a place that seemed less a mystery to me by the hour.

Of course, I could only imagine what was happening in the vehicle ahead. Jon was undoubtedly telling more embarrassing stories about seasons past. In fact, on more than one occasion, I saw his hand dart out the window and point to a hillside or field and then gesture wildly as he told stories.

Based on our location on the property, I was sure I could guess, with relative accuracy, which story he was telling and whom he was throwing under the so-called bus.

By now, those of us who had been here before had all come to terms with what it meant to be up here in this place where nothing personal was sacred. We embraced, at least to a degree, the idea that it was all part of the experience. But it still didn't allay the anxiety of facing all the ridicule back at the cabin beside the fire. We all knew it was coming; it was only a matter of when and how bad it was going to be. The good news was that we had plenty of ammunition in the form of embarrassing material to fight back with, not to mention a whole week to put dead animals in Jon's Suburban.

We stopped at Box Canyon and had a long look around. It was just as majestic as the last time I saw it, but this time was different in that I reveled in knowing that I didn't have to climb its walls to go after a wounded animal.

I had gotten smart enough to know better than to take a shot that would cost me half the day and half my health to recover the animal . . . or *not* recover the animal.

We were standing there in front of the trucks glassing the canyon's hillsides when Boy Wonder pointed out a sizable bull well past the tree line and some three hundred yards up the mountainside. I immediately declared myself ineligible as a shooter because I was not going to climb that steep hill again.

Despite my caution, a gun appeared and a shot was considered. I tried my best to be realistic and warn of the unpleasant climb should any one of the group kill the animal, but it fell on deaf ears.

After a few calculations and bits of advice from the General, Boy Wonder sat on the ground and directed his rifle at the elk. A hush fell over the group as he carefully planned his shot and zeroed in on the target.

Moments later, we all flinched as he pulled the trigger.

With all eyes on the elk through our binoculars, we saw the impact of the round as it found its mark, knocking the bull off balance and dropping it on the steep hillside after just a step or two. It tipped toward us and began to slide and tumble down the mountain. It gained momentum and glanced off several trees, falling farther and farther down toward the canyon floor. It looked like a cross between poorly executed Olympic skeleton racing and Pachinko.

The animal finally came to rest after sliding more than three-quarters of the way to us. It was a nice five-by-four with a tall rack and a broken G4. We were all thrilled to get on the board so quickly, but we knew it was rare to have it that easy. All that was left to do at that point was tag it, quarter it, carry the parcels about a hundred yards to the vehicles, and fight over which SUV it would get placed in. (For the record, yes, it ended up in mine. I would also like the official documents to reflect that I was not pleased.)

We left Box Canyon and crossed over to the East Road, where we stopped to glass a few clearings. Shortly thereafter and once again mobile, we came up to the daunting switchbacks, but this time from the other side.

Jon reminded me to watch my speed and maintain my concentration at all times.

"It's actually harder going up the switchbacks than coming down," he warned as I adjusted my collar and began squirming in the driver's seat.

Jon put his Suburban in drive, crossed the shallow water, and started up the incline, making the first sharp turn to the left. Up he went at what appeared to be an impossible angle before he reached the second hairpin turn—this one back to the right. I cautiously began my journey up the infamous road (if you can even call it a road) and got more nervous with each approaching bend. I'm pleased to report that I was successful in reaching the top without rolling the Tahoe or injuring my passengers, but I had broken a sweat that must have cost me a gallon of my body's water.

My clothes were damp and I actually felt like I had lost weight. Other than being nervous, a bit light-headed, and most likely as white as a sheet, I was fine and ready to continue the tour.

We continued past the Beaver Hut and the Jack-rabbit's Stage before driving up the hill to the plateau, upon which Turtle had missed his elk-of-a-lifetime the year before. (Of course, that story had to be told.) Then we drove up the road, passing the Bear Claw on our left, crossing the water feature, and winding in and out of the tree stands and forests. Once we reached the top of the East Road, Jon pulled off the road and parked twenty yards from a beautiful four-acre pond.

While we all hopped out to stretch a bit, he pulled out his rifle and claimed that he needed to sight it in. He rushed to set up for a shot as he noticed a muskrat crossing the pond. We looked at one another knowing that the outcome would be catastrophic, at best, if he were to actually hit it.

We all looked on through our binoculars, cringing at the likely conclusion of this exercise. Jon was ready to take the shot and squeezed his finger against the trigger of his beloved hunting rifle. The shot resonated across the property, and we all looked away from the target and at each other in absolute confusion. When the shot rang out, the muskrat vanished without a trace. We looked back out in the water after a moment, and the creature reappeared and could be seen continuing across the pond. We had no idea what had happened and were all suddenly stuck trying to understand it.

"It didn't dive," Jon explained. "When they dive, they put their back end up over their heads and plunge straight down. No way he could have reacted to the shot and completed a dive before the bullet got there."

He shouldered his rifle for another shot. We all stared intently at the muskrat as it paddled along, none the worse for wear. Jon aimed and fired his second shot, and we watched in disbelief as the muskrat disappeared again, only to pop into view seconds later, the picture of health. Everyone was speechless. We couldn't figure out what was going on.

The General directed Jon to take a third shot as he watched through his military-spec binos. Jon squeezed off another round and, sure enough, the muskrat vanished again, only to reappear moments later.

The General started to laugh while we all stared toward the pond with skepticism. He composed himself and explained that Jon was shooting just a touch low. The bullet was entering the water just below the muskrat at such a high velocity that it created suction underneath the animal, yanking it underwater for a moment until it regained its buoyancy and surfaced unharmed. None of us could believe it, so the General offered to shoot Jon's rifle with us all looking on.

Jon told him exactly where he had aimed, and we watched the General take his shot. Sure enough, the gun fired low and the muskrat was pulled beneath the surface of the water so quickly, we could only barely see the motion. All that remained were a few ripples expanding from the epicenter of where the animal used to be. It was simply there one instant and gone the next.

About five seconds later, the muskrat resurfaced as though nothing had happened. We couldn't stop laughing. It was bizarre but absolutely hilarious. To this day it remains the only instantaneous, autosubmersive muskrat I have ever seen. And if we were confused, there's no telling what that poor water rat thought.

Jon adjusted his scope up a click or two, leveled his rifle, and let 'er rip. In that instant, the muskrat became a former muskrat, and we jumped back into the cars and headed for lunch at the cabin knowing that we had just done our part to protect the ponds and lakes on the property from the substantial havoc these creatures cause.

"If left uncontrolled," Jon explained, "rodents can cause a remarkable amount of destruction by weakening the structural integrity of shorelines and destroying the surrounding vegetation's root systems."

Lunch was an easy one. We grilled burgers and piled them high with tomatoes, onions, lettuce, pickles, etc. All of the components of a blue-ribbon burger experience were present with the exception of beer, obviously. (Guns and alcohol make for poor, dangerous, and often illegal bedfellows. Besides, none of us were big drinkers, and, in fact, most of the group didn't drink at all. So the fact that there was no alcohol allowed at the ranch didn't bother any of us.)

The meal started with a passionate yet disruptive discussion about physics and how they apply when bullets strike the water underneath small, swimming, aquatic rodents. We then discussed behavioral expectations from the muskrat's perspective and what it must have felt and observed, as well as the impact it clearly had had on the simpletons shooting at it in the first place. The conversation eventually devolved into questions about previous years, such as how one fails to fill a tag in an entire trip or how many bullets it took to kill a raccoon on the attack.

Even Cowboy jumped into the action and offered, again, to help Santa make sense of a calendar. The horse was out of the barn and the abuse ran amuck through the ranks. This was the beginning of another great week in the woods.

Jon explained that we had the rest of the day and the next before the Village Idiot and his entourage (limited to five people by ranch bylaws, but likely to surpass fifteen) invaded for the weekend. And once that little announcement was aired, he paired us off and sent us out for the first official hunt of the trip, even though we already had one tagged bull hanging from the deck.

I elected to go to Bluebell Flats with Santa while the other two pairs went to hunt off the East Road. Santa and I headed down the Middle Road until we came to our familiar parking spot in the grass next to the creek.

We jumped out of the Tahoe, grabbed our gear, and started our trek across the creek and up the hill toward the trees. After the short twenty-minute walk through the aspens to the field, we set up with the wind in our faces and a perfect view of the Flats in front of us.

We were separated by twenty yards and both had tremendous shooting lanes for the field, as well as the hill rising to the south behind it. We got out our binoculars and began to glass.

I'm guessing it was an hour later when Santa shook my arm and scolded me for snoring. I woke up a bit startled, and he pointed to a pair of bucks making their way into the field at the far corner where the hill surrenders to the woods.

Neither of them were shooters — particularly because mule deer season hadn't yet started. But what followed in the next ten or fifteen minutes was an amazing show.

No less than twenty does walked out of the woods into the field and began looking at the two bucks. It looked like the start of a high-school dance — a bunch of brave, willing participants and two intimidated guys too scared to approach any of them.

By the time the afternoon was in full swing, there were over forty deer in the field. It was incredible to witness and gave us hope for the rest of the trip.

It appeared that the animals were thick again this year, which meant we were in a good position to make a significant donation to the food pantry for the third year in a row.

We watched the group all afternoon (or, in my case, after my nap) as the does cycled in and out of the trees. The two bucks wandered around the base of the hillside for a couple hours, and several button bucks and other yearling deer started to populate the middle of the field. By the time the light was dying down, there were upwards of fifty deer wandering around this meadow.

The glassing was astounding and quite gratifying. But when we stirred to back out, all it took was one doe to react and they all scattered into the tree line and disappeared like the finale of an elaborate magic trick. It was hard to imagine that they could all vanish so quickly. It was as if I had started telling jokes at a party. (I can clear a room in seconds.)

That had to be another in a long line of best hunts ever for me—so much action and so many animals milling around! We were covered in them. Nothing present was in season, no shots were fired, and yet even then it was an incredible afternoon. I thought to myself, *Certainly, I will remember this hunt.*

As if to build upon the "moment" I'd had the year before, I could now fully appreciate the difference between hunters and killers: it wasn't about the harvest at all; it was actually about the experience and how it shapes a person. (Maybe I'm a hunter after all.)

We made the short hike out of the trees and back to the Tahoe to load up. We turned the car around and drove back up to the cabin, taking bets on what we thought dinner was going to be. Truth be told, we really didn't care one way or another what dinner was, as long as we didn't have to endure Chili con Grizzly! Not that it wasn't good, but neither one of us was in the mood to tolerate the two-day deceleration process.

In the end, dinner was freshly harvested and grilled backstrap of elk, kindly provided by Cowboy, who had taken down a large five-by-five within an hour of setting up at the Beaver Hut after lunch.

As if this came as a shock to anyone there, the experience of eating elk was a first for me, and it was delicious. Talk about a farm-to-table experience—this animal had been sauntering through the woods only hours before and was now, in part anyway, on my dinner plate.

The meat had a silky consistency and was very dense. I remember the flavor was extraordinary, the meat very lean and perfectly seasoned. There wasn't much fat to render and give it flavor, but, unlike beef, it didn't need it. It was different from any other protein I had ever tried. And while it may not have been my all-time favorite, I did concede that it was quite good and I finished my plate, which also included scalloped potatoes and a dinner salad.

All the other hunters were ecstatic and assured me that elk was a prized meal. They had all had it before, and they relished every bite. It was a wonderful experience to share with them, particularly knowing that they had shared it with me — the guy who not long ago simply wouldn't have known the difference. Turned out I was more flattered to have been included than anything else. Maybe that's why I liked elk more than I thought I would.

Cleanup was no more of a challenge than usual, and as had become habit, everyone could be found downstairs in front of the fire by the time Boy Wonder and I finished kitchen duty.

After we arrived fireside, we had quite the series of discussions that night about a litany of subjects, from family and travel to hobbies and careers. While it seemed like a bit more reserved a group this year, it was a relaxing change from the conversations that usually occurred at this hour. However, I will admit to being a bit worried that this group was going to be all serious and boring.

To my delight, they weren't. By the time we all hit the rack that night, Jon's bed had been short-sheeted,

Boy Wonder's mattress had been completely wrapped in Saran Wrap, and Santa's rifle had been abducted, as evidenced by the ransom note he found on his pillow.

Additionally, complaints were lodged against the wake-up ritual in which Jon plays a Marine drill instructor and scares the life out of the group, and threats of retaliation were made public.

I was relieved to know the group would be fun, and I took comfort in knowing I'd be pretty safe. After all, I had the General on my side, and one whiney call from me to Jon's wife about anybody in the group and there would be bloodshed—and everyone knew it. So at least I had some insulation from the abuse. I'm not sure about anyone else, but I slept like a bear in December.

22

THE DAY WAS NOTHING SPECIAL . . . UNTIL IT WAS

The day's advent was unusual. We were all gently awakened by the General, lightly shaking us one at a time and signaling with his index finger to his lips to remain silent. Once everyone was awake, we all gathered around Jon's bunk, and on the General's signal, everyone screamed at the top of our lungs.

For once, it was our fearless leader who was on the receiving end of the brutal morning alarm. We not only met our goal to scare the living daylights out of him, but we exceeded it by a mile! He woke up swinging from the proverbial chandelier, and we danced about like school kids at recess, reveling in our triumph.

Of course, it was juvenile . . . but no one felt like going upstairs to get a bowl of warm water in which to put his hand while he slept.

For some reason, Jon was the only one who failed to see the humor in what we had accomplished, at least not until he got his heart to start again. On the other hand, we were all quite proud of ourselves.

As the celebration waned, we started getting dressed for the hunt while Jon, still slightly disgruntled, headed upstairs to make breakfast.

Keep in mind that we're not completely dense. We sent Boy Wonder up with him to make certain we didn't suffer any cayenne-pepper-related retaliation or other food-linked vengeance.

Over our retribution-free breakfast, we were alerted to the impending weather changes. We were also reminded that the notorious Village Idiot and his groupies would be arriving in the afternoon.

Regarding the weather, it was supposed to deteriorate steadily all day and end with snow flurries overnight. Accumulation was downplayed and estimated at less than two inches.

Likewise, it was predicted that our moods would diminish accordingly and in direct proportion to the arrival time of our cabin mates.

When we finally got down to the hunting business at hand, Jon divided us into two groups. He sent Boy Wonder to drive Cowboy and the General down the Middle Road and drop them at the top of Deep Canyon. He then instructed Wonder to meet him at the Beaver Hut. Jon then looked at Santa and me and said, "You pinheads come with me down the East Road."

Jon had undoubtedly associated the morning's shenanigans with the two of us. Naturally, we wanted to set the record straight, but there wasn't a soul in the cabin brave enough to incriminate the General, so we kept our mouths shut and figured we were in for an ugly hike at the very least, or that he could be planning to take us to a remote part of the property, shoot us, and bury our remains in shallow graves.

We suited up after the morning briefing and headed out to the driveway, where we found Jon waiting by his Suburban and Boy Wonder waiting in his pickup. We all piled into the assigned vehicles and headed out.

To his credit and despite the morning's antics, Jon was in a pretty good mood. He was anticipating a successful day and, as he often did, spent part of the morning drive building my confidence and trying to downplay any pressure I might be feeling.

Then the other shoe finally dropped when he explained, with a bit of a smirk, that we were headed to the Bear Claw.

Immediately, I felt every hair on the back of my neck stand straight out and a tepid rush of anxiety overtook my entire body.

"I am going to send you guys in the northern end of the Bear Claw, right where it starts. You will walk straight in from the road, as quietly as mice, heading east. I want you both to walk exactly three hundred yards. Fred, you will stop and find a place to set up on the game trail you find there. You, Santa," he continued, "will walk another one hundred fifty yards and set up in the bottom of the draw near the dry creek bed. There will be a watering hole about thirty yards to the south. Find cover and just sit and watch."

Honestly, I didn't hear a word he said after he announced we were going to the Bear Claw, though I did pick up and manage to understand that I would be sitting alone. I couldn't have been more nervous had I had dysentery and hay fever at the same time.

We got to the drop-off spot, and Jon directed us into the woods after reviewing the instructions. Santa and I turned and stepped into the darkness just before Jon drove away toward the Beaver Hut.

I was completely spooked, despite Santa's company, as we crept through the menacing forest. It felt as though there were a hundred pairs of eyes on us as we tried to sneak into our spots, and the going was slow. After stepping over fallen timber and walking around obstacles, down paths, and through heavy vegetation, we found ourselves at the game trail of which Jon had spoken. Santa noted that the sun would soon be up and that he needed to be in place when that happened. He wished me good luck and pressed on deeper into the trees, disappearing in a matter of strides. His footsteps on the fallen leaves were soon replaced by dead silence that, in turn, gave way to noises I thought only I was hearing.

I tried to dismiss the chilling thoughts that were creeping into my head and focus on doing what I had been told.

I found a gigantic evergreen tree in the midst of the thick, quaking aspens. It stood five yards off the trail and looked to be the perfect spot to lie in wait. I crawled under its branches for cover, just as morning light started to break.

The trail wandered through the dense trees to my left and split to my right. This left me with two trails to watch on my starboard side—one to the ridge line nearly at my three o'clock and one that disappeared down a hill at my one o'clock. The only obstacle in my way was a small two-inch branch that obstructed my view and shooting lanes. I took out the little saw that Jon had insisted I buy (despite my being convinced I would never need it) and quickly cut the branch away. The only task that remained then was to get comfortable and wait.

For the next hour I sat motionless with my rifle across my legs, every little noise caused by the stirring breeze piquing my curiosity and angst. The morning mist hung heavy over the forest floor, and I could feel my heart pounding inside my chest. I recall trying to remember to breathe and calm down, but it was a futile exercise. I didn't know if it was fear, excitement, or a fairly unhealthy combination of the two. But there I sat with my rifle, my binoculars at the ready and my eyes ready to pop out of my head as I watched the trails and scanned the trees in front of me from side to side.

Just then and no less than fifty yards to my left, well beyond the distance I could see through the dense forest, I heard a bugle. It was loud, frightening, and exhilarating all at once. I strained to see through the trees as I heard it again.

Then there were more! I heard another behind me and a third off in the distance to my right. It was like an elk convention had suddenly convened and I was right in the middle of it. I put down the binos and carefully removed the glove from my shooting hand. I then slowly gripped the gun in my lap and better positioned it should I have the need to raise it to my shoulder.

The beasts' chatter continued for ten minutes. I still hadn't seen a thing, but I was in the thick of it and could feel the suspense building. The calls got louder, and I swore I could see the mist swirling to my left, just from where I expected a giant to emerge. However, I soon realized that was just an overly active imagination at work.

I tried to keep my wits about me and continued looking at my surroundings for clues and opportunities. The bugling subsided and I was back to listening to my heart pound away behind my ribcage.

I remained at full alert, hoping that the near encounter wasn't over.

A gunshot pierced the morning's stillness from off in Santa's direction . . . . and then another. I leaned forward from the trunk of the tree I was leaning against and listened even more intently. A couple moments passed and a third shot rang out.

I wondered, *Has a civil war broken out or have the elk been armed and trained to return fire?*

All fell silent again and I assumed that Santa was on the board with his first-ever elk.

Before I even had a chance to take a deep breath and be happy for him, I heard rocks sliding and branches crashing off to my right. The commotion was loud and undeniably deliberate. Something large was in a hurry to get through the woods.

I gripped my gun and repositioned my body under the tree so I was facing the trail that ran toward the far right. I looked up and, as if it had been elevated through a trap door on a theatrical stage, a magnificent bull elk gracefully appeared atop the ridge. He stopped and looked back down the steep grade he had just conquered. He stood there, steam pouring from his nostrils as he took a moment to catch his breath. I raised my gun to my shoulder, pointed it toward the giant six-by-six, and peered through the scope. When I realized I didn't have a clear shot, I began to scan left down the trail to find a shooting lane.

As I found one, I held the gun in place and looked away from the scope to watch the bull. He looked to the trail again and began to trot toward me.

I looked again through the scope to be sure my lane was clear and held the gun as steadily as I could. I then looked just to the side of the scope and watched until he approached the opening. I again gazed through the lens, timed my shot, and squeezed the trigger just as he entered my scope's field of vision.

I had the loudest rifle in the group by far, and it had a unique report, so I had been told. I swear I never heard the shot, but I saw the elk drop instantly, in mid-step, not thirty feet from where I sat under the tree. He went down in a heap and lay there motionless, and I quickly racked another round into the chamber in case it became necessary. I kept the barrel trained on the elk for half a minute, but he never so much as twitched.

I lowered my rifle and realized that my quest, which had started over two years and two hunts ago, had just come to a successful end—and that I had accomplished, alone, what I had set out to do.

In that extraordinary moment, a feeling defying description washed over me, and I had to remind myself to breathe.

It hit me then that I had just conquered a lofty goal I had set for myself—one that I wasn't completely convinced I would ever achieve. Yet, instead of wanting to jump up and down, I was instinctively humbled.

The creature was absolutely magnificent. It was both a powerful animal, as evidenced by its crashing through the woods, and a graceful one as it cantered down the game trail in front of me with all the grandeur and majesty of true royalty.

It left me in awe and wondering if I ever should have pulled the trigger in the first place.

In the instant between releasing the bullet and realizing that I had killed the elk, I felt commanding power and crippling remorse. Perhaps I may have been just as thrilled to have had the experience and missed the shot. I just wasn't sure.

Admittedly, my emotions were mixed and running through my head in indecipherable order. Overall, the feeling was one of great pride, honor, and accomplishment. I even felt a connection to our strong hunting heritage of years gone by. But try as I might, I couldn't corral or stabilize the myriad of thoughts racing in my mind. I was elated. I was exhilarated. I was empowered. I was grateful. I was exhausted. I was emotional. I was wrought with guilt. I was entirely overwhelmed. And I was still alone in the unnerving Bear Claw — and just heard something.

I looked due east and saw Santa walking directly toward me, whistling every few steps so I wouldn't mistake him for game. After he had gotten my attention, I composed myself, stood, and emerged from under the tree as he approached.

"I heard the shot," he said. "Did you get one down?"

I replied, "I did. And I heard what sounded like a combat engagement in your direction. Are you on the board?"

He laughed and said that he was as well.

In a matter of one or two minutes, the only two guys on the trip who had never taken elks before had realized their dreams. We embraced and then I nearly broke my hand high-fiving him before we walked over to my harvest.

"Are you going to tag it?" he said as he smiled.

He knew full well I had forgotten due to my overly excited state. He watched as I pulled out my tag and knife, notched the tag appropriately, and attached it to the animal's antler. Together, we then straightened out the elk (with considerable effort) and held his head up for the first time.

I was speechless. Santa estimated the bull to weigh

over nine hundred pounds. He boasted a mighty six-by-six rack that stood thirty-eight inches tall and was complete with ivory tips. It was perfectly symmetrical and had considerable mass and an inside spread of thirty-six inches. This bull was everything I had hoped for and more.

When Santa asked me where I'd shot him, I said, "I was hoping to shoot him in the neck, but he was trotting from right to left, and my shooting lane was narrow. I honestly don't know where I hit him."

We looked for the hole and found it centered on the left side of his neck, midway between his head and his shoulder.

"No wonder he dropped without a step," Santa said as he put his hand on my shoulder.

"Now, who's cleaning it?" he asked and began to chuckle.

I stood up, tied some hunter's tape to a tree branch next to the bull, and said, "Let's head back to the road. Jon said he'd be there about now, so we should go get him and bring him in. We've got a lot to show him."

Santa and I proceeded back the way we had walked in only hours before in the dark. When we reached the road, there stood Jon and Boy Wonder.

Jon said, "Judas Priest! Did you two take the castle or what?"

Santa told them that we had both filled our elk tags, and the party was on. Jon was excited for both of us, as was Boy Wonder, who also knew that this meant that his day was only getting started.

"Did you mark it?" Wonder asked.

And when I told him that indeed I had, he dropped his gear, picked up his pack, gave us each a hug, and said, "Let's get on it!"

He charged eagerly into the woods and told us to keep up.

As Boy Wonder ran ahead, the rest of us walked in at a slower pace.

Jon asked to hear the stories, so Santa related that he had been comfortably sitting on a rock in the creek bed, shielded by a fallen tree, and was watching the watering hole to the south.

"I had been there for over an hour since daybreak, and I heard a bunch of bugling behind me but never saw anything. Then I heard grunting in front of me by the watering hole and a bugle beyond that. I saw a cow elk by the water's edge and started looking through the scope for the bull. I never did see him, but I figured that I would take the cow while I had the shot. I trained the gun back on her, squeezed the trigger, and she staggered. I racked another cartridge and dropped her with the second shot."

"Okay, that was two shots," said Jon. "I heard three before I heard Fred's."

Santa continued, "When she fell, there was this year's calf standing behind her that I hadn't seen — and I knew something was wrong because it didn't run away. As I approached the dead cow, I saw that the calf's hind leg had been severely broken from an earlier event. There was bone sticking through the hide; the animal was thin and clearly suffering. I didn't know what else to do, so I euthanized her. The third shot was to put her out of her misery, as she never would have survived her injury. I hope I did the right thing."

"I'm sure you did," Jon said reassuringly. "We'll head down there and take a look, but that seems like the responsible thing to do."

Then I interrupted because I was so excited to tell my story to Jon that I could hardly focus on putting one foot in front of the other. I told him the whole story with my lips flapping away at twenty words per second, and when I finished, we were standing at the evergreen. I described in three-part harmony and flailing appendages how it all happened, and Jon said, "Okay, okay . . . I get it. Breathe. Where's the elk?"

I motioned toward the orange ribbon where Boy Wonder was standing, and there it was, still majestic and colossal. While it may not have been the biggest elk anyone had ever seen, I guarantee it was the biggest elk I had ever imagined for myself, and that's all that mattered to me. From my perspective, it may as well have been the world record.

There were high-fives all around before Jon then said, "Congratulations! I'm really proud of you."

That alone truly meant a lot. It was almost hard to hear in that moment. Even to this day, I'm not sure if Jon knows just how much that moved me. In fact, in retrospect, that moment had a larger and more lasting impact on me than killing the bull. I suspect that long after I have forgotten what it sounded like to hear the echo of the gunshot fade, those words of his will continue to ring in my ears.

Then reality was instantly restored with resolute clarity when I heard, "Now, you have to dress it." (In my mind, the party ended abruptly.)

"You know I can't do that, Jon," I said with a bit of shame. "I just can't."

"There's a difference between 'can't' and 'won't.' So which is it, Freddie? And choose your words carefully because this is serious."

I admitted that it was more that I wouldn't, but the reasoning seemed sound to me. It wasn't that I was trying to avoid responsibility as an outdoorsman as much as I was trying to circumvent being covered in blood and physically ill after cutting up an animal with a short blade and combing through its innards with my bare hands. It was hard enough to get to a point where I was comfortable making a decision to end an animal's life like this; now I was in a position where I had to cut open, disembowel, cape, and quarter one? I knew if I did that it would spell the end of hunting for me. That was too much to process. I just wasn't comfortable with the task, and I stood firm after explaining myself.

Jon seemed disappointed, although he said that he understood my position. However, despite his understanding, he held out his knife and said, "You're going to dress this elk, and I will help you."

Again, I declined and said a bit more strongly that I was not going to do it.

"Wanna bet?" he said.

"Sure," I said, "I'll take that bet. Fifty bucks."

Jon immediately agreed and reached out for my hand to shake it. He continued to stare at me and said, "You're going to do this, and now you owe me fifty dollars."

I looked at my buddy Boy Wonder and said, "How'd you like to make fifty bucks?" as I took the knife from Jon's hand and turned to hold it out for Wonder.

"Sure," he responded excitedly. He grabbed the knife and bent down to get to work.

I looked at Jon and said, "You can just give the fifty directly to him."

Yes, I had gotten one over on Jon, but I still felt poorly about the whole situation. I did feel a sense of responsibility, yet I was restricted by my own physical limitations. Ultimately, I did get involved (marginally, but I did help), and Boy Wonder and I walked out together after the four of us (really the three of them) put in over an hour of hard work.

We put all the meat in canvas game bags and tied them off for Jon to pick up with the four-wheeler after lunch.

Boy Wonder threw the caped head and rack on his shoulders and walked out to the vehicles. He carried the head the whole way to his truck without putting it down once, and the terrain did not make for an easy hike. He placed it gently in the bed of his pickup and hopped into the driver's seat. I elected to ride in the back to steady it. That was a long and rough trip back to the cabin.

Meanwhile, Jon and Santa had turned and walked farther into the woods so Jon could satisfy his self-imposed ethical responsibility to tag the calf, even though it was not fit for human consumption. He then turned around to help Santa field dress the cow in the creek bed.

Again, Jon assured Santa that he had done the right thing given the calf's condition. It was clear that the badly broken leg, the visibly spreading infection, and the obvious malnourishment of the animal had caused undue pain and suffering with no hope of recovery. Jon said, "You did exactly what I would've done."

It was over two hours before we saw those two boys again back at the cabin, and even when they showed up, Jon had to head right back down with the four-wheeler to retrieve the meat from the two mature elk. Boy Wonder was appointed to follow with his pickup, as the ATV was good for bringing the harvest out of the woods but wouldn't be able to collect and deliver all the meat back to the cabin.

While they were out being productive, I prepared lunch. I had the easy day as we settled in for sandwiches and chips. It was a blast getting to hear some of the General's hunting stories, although we all listened with a certain amount of caution once we started hearing terms like *velocity*, *windage*, *minutes of angle*, etc. That was intimidating, to a degree, but the guy clearly understood all there was to know about guns and their capabilities. To some he may have sounded like an egomaniac, but he wasn't bragging, nor was he embellishing. He just had a natural gift, some wickedly intense training, and the ability to back up every story he told, as evidenced by a quick demonstration off the porch that left us all with our jaws scraping the tops of our shoes.

We had selected a target well over a mile away, as confirmed by a military-grade rangefinder. He then pulled out his .30 Wolf, made a few adjustments to the scope dials, and casually drilled the target three shots out of three. There was absolutely no more questioning the General about any of his stories, but as you can imagine, we all wanted to hear more of them.

Meanwhile, I was comfortable with my shooting ability, but after hearing him recount some of his experiences, there was no doubt that the General was the real deal. I didn't even come close to being a marksman of his caliber. It wasn't that he wasn't in a different league than I was; he was in a different galaxy.

When Jon and Boy Wonder finally returned, it was with the first wave of cars that signaled the Village Idiot's arrival along with some of his followers.

There were only ten people, so we knew there would be more—again, contrary to the bylaws of the cabin. An hour later, the rest of the parade arrived and, as anticipated, brought the total number of people in their group to fourteen.

Everyone gathered upstairs as a fire crackled in the living room. We were all milling around meeting new people and having a nice time, despite a certain someone's insistence that he knew more about anything and everything than anyone else. The re-emergence of his superiority complex signaled only one thing to me: it was time for him to meet the General. (Yes, I'm evil. But everyone needs a hobby.)

The relationship was off to a blistering start as the General was obliged to listen for ten solid minutes about what an outstanding shot the Village Idiot was. Then it became a conversation (still one-sided) about all the game trophies he had laid claim to on various continents and the miraculous shots he had made to kill them. We could see the doubt building in the General's expression as he patiently listened and tried to suppress his look of suspicion and complete disbelief. An opening in the monologue finally offered the General an opportunity to speak when he was asked, "So are you a good shot?"

He replied with a mischievous grin, "I can hold my own."

The Village Idiot then uttered the words we all knew he couldn't resist: "Well, then, we should have a little competition tomorrow. I'll get a few of the guys and we can shoot for some cash."

The General just smiled and said, "Count me in."

We were all salivating at the opportunity to watch these guys get annihilated on the range. We kept prodding the General to make it fair by shooting blindfolded.

Of course, we couldn't help but stir the pot a bit on the other side, too, by making comments throughout the afternoon about wanting a piece of the action.

The rest of the day went by without incident, and we all just kept to ourselves around the cabin. Our crowd built a fire downstairs and got the daily round of cards started early because the afternoon hunt never materialized. The guys in the two factions of hunters started to relate to one another pretty well as the day progressed, and we all ended up having a huge dinner together and really enjoying one another's company.

We grilled steaks and just sat wherever we could find a seat. The stories were amusing, the food was fantastic, and the funniest part about the night was that we could all tell when the more insecure members of the group had started making stuff up to impress everyone else.

After our meal, the other group kindly took over the clean-up duties in the kitchen, which afforded Wonder and me the rare opportunity to join the boys downstairs for the first post-dinner round of Ninety-nine.

The cards were dealt and the game began, but our minds were all fixated on one thing: the shooting match. Jon confided that he had additional plans that would make the day one to remember, and we were all overcome with anticipation. True to form, however, he played his hand close to his chest and refused to let us all in on it.

The subject turned to Santa's calf, and a deep discussion ensued about responsibility versus wanton killing. We were all on Santa's side and felt that he had done the right thing while conceding that the loss of such a beautiful young animal was tragic. At the culmination of the discussion, an important element of hunting emerged: sometimes hunting with an ethical conscience and actually doing what's right is not black and white, nor is it as easy as it would seem. In the end, the group all learned a very important thing about the characters of both Jon and Santa: they were both ethical hunters with the integrity to do what was honorable. I remember this as one of the more notable experiences of the trip, and it stood out as a significant example of the type of hunter I would endeavor to emulate.

It was bedtime and another day at the ranch was in the books. But this day would always live in my memory as something very special because I had finally harvested my first bull elk.

The lights went off and we all settled into bed, and the last thing we heard that night was Jon threatening any one of us who thought of waking him up again the way we had woken him that morning.

If I weren't such a gentleman, I would tell you exactly what he said. But since I'm a polite and upstanding human being, I will simply say that Jon was quite the wordsmith that night. Though I must also tell you that some of the suggestions and threats he made left us wondering whether or not they were even physically possible. They were either remarkably innovative torture ideas, or he really needed to brush up on his anatomy and the limitations of the human body. In any case, surely, we'd think twice before repeating our brave act of rebellion.

23

CHECK YOUR EGOS AT THE DOOR; YOU WON'T BE NEEDING THEM TODAY

We all slept well, which was obvious given that we were all wide awake before Jon had the chance to scream at us. I wasn't sure if it was because we were all nervous about retaliation from the day before or a product of our excitement to watch the General humble the self-branded expert marksman from the other group. Either way, we were up, dressed, and ready for breakfast ahead of schedule.

As usual, we were treated to a fantastic meal featuring bacon and eggs, along with toast and breakfast potatoes—everything a hunter needs for a solid nap in the woods.

The weather update for the day called for persisting cold temperatures with no break in sight. Notably, and thankfully, there was no snow in the forecast.

Jon split the group by pairing Boy Wonder with Santa and me with Cowboy and the General. Cowboy had been up even earlier than the rest of us, preparing his horses for the day. So it came as quite a surprise to the General and me that the three of us would be riding out on horseback.

Having ridden as a teenager and trained for competitive equestrian jumping, I was somewhat comfortable with horses. However, riding one out on a hunt with a gun was an idea completely foreign to me. I was up for it, though, particularly if it meant I had less hiking and climbing to do.

After breakfast the three of us walked down the road from the cabin to the corral, where Cowboy had parked his horse trailer. He told us which horses we would be on and had us mount up. Once I was back in the saddle, it was like, well, being back in the saddle. I remembered in an instant why I had liked it so much, and also why I had quit and vowed never to do it again.

Well, at this point it was too late to whine, so the three of us on our steeds walked back up to the cabin, crossed the field behind it, and steered straight into the woods toward the steep incline at the base of the crescent mountain face.

The woods were easy if you didn't mind having to be alert for low foliage. (Did I mention it was still dark outside?) I got face-whipped by a branch that was let go by the rider in front of me (thanks for the warning, Cowboy) and ten steps later managed to inadvertently pay it forward to the General. The contact stung but taught us to pay attention as we moved on.

We made our way through the thick trees, and the landscape's incline began to change.

As the morning light started to creep into the trees, we went from a flat trek through the woods to an uncomfortably steep ascent. It didn't seem to bother the horses at all, but it had my undivided attention as I'm only used to riding these giants in a level environment. The gradient increased again, and my nerves became markedly unstable.

At this point, the hill was so steep that my horse's front hooves were entirely above his haunches, and his head was well above my natural line of sight. I felt like I was part of a moon shot, though admittedly at a much more moderate speed.

As I leaned around my horse's neck to look ahead, I could see the path emerging from the tree line into the open, and just beyond that, the ridge line at the top of the hill became visible. I was momentarily relieved until I heard an alarming announcement from in front of me.

Cowboy ever so eloquently articulated that it had become too steep for the horses and we needed to dismount, grab the reins, and lead them the rest of the way on foot. (Oh, wait, there's more . . .)

"Also, I'm afraid my horse is limping a bit," he continued. "I'm going to have to walk her back down. You guys go ahead without me."

My inner voice was suddenly very talkative and extremely unhappy. In total disbelief, but with the utmost compassion for the horse and its issue, my vocal containment skills failed and I finally said out loud what I had been trying to control: "Are you kidding me? I'm not comfortable with you here to help, let alone without you. You can't send us up this mountain on our own."

Before Cowboy could respond, the General said, "We can handle it. Do what you need to do."

I seriously considered shooting the General on the spot but elected not to once I determined, after some serious thought, that it would only serve to make him mad.

I was in shock as I climbed off my horse, pulled the reins down from over his head, and began climbing, sidestep, up the remainder of the mountain.

With each step, my lead foot was as high as my opposing knee, and I felt as though I were dragging this thousand-pound horse, who seemed as pleased and excited to be there as I was — which was as pleased and excited as one might be about having major surgery without sedatives.

I became more contemptuous with each step and had completely lost control of my inner monologue, which, by the way, had the General in hysterics. That only served to provoke me even more.

By the time we reached the top, I was physically drained, and the General had tears streaming down his beet-red face from laughing at me and my inability to adjust to new situations.

After gathering ourselves for a minute, we jumped back on the horses and rode a trail about ten feet from the edge of the now-sheer face to our right. To the left we looked over an unbelievable set of rolling, grass-covered hills that stretched to the southern horizon.

When we looked out to our right — past the cliff's edge, which spelled certain death for anyone who fell from it — we could see almost the entire ranch. It was breathtaking. And so was the fact that the trail was now within a foot of the precipice atop oblivion. (That's what I get for being distracted.)

I stopped the horse and climbed down immediately — on the left side. Even though I knew he was far more sure-footed than I, I felt more comfortable in charge of my own destiny. The General and I walked to the highest point and left the horses to relax in the fields behind us.

The two of us then set up on the edge of the rock face and glassed over the entire property. The vista was truly amazing. I had a bird's-eye view of the place where so many memories had been made these last couple years, and I now had a clearer perspective of all the locations I had explored. I was awestruck.

We glassed for a while and failed to see anything other than the five cows that were standing behind our horses, all of which were clearly wondering what we were doing on their mountaintop.

The General and I started talking and actually ended up bonding a bit. We spent time finding out what interests we had in common besides hunting. We touched on family, childhood, and upbringing, and then he tried to gain insight as to why my sense of humor was so desperately twisted.

Naturally, the conversation eventually circled back to hunting. We shared the highlights of our hunting experiences and ultimately landed on the subject of guns.

I was fascinated to learn how a person goes from being "surgically accurate," as Jon claims I am, to being laser-precise, as I classify the General's abilities, in the face of the challenges including extreme distance, weather, and obstacles — not to mention distractions like life-or-death combat conditions.

He explained, in painfully specific terms, that shooting precision always came down to math and concentration. Half an hour later, after diagrams, examples, and numerous calculations for windage, minute-of-angle, and several other things that were well beyond my pay grade, I was left thoroughly bewildered and drowning in my own ignorance. Each time he tried to simplify all the physics and math, I became only more mystified.

In an effort to tie it all together for me, he decided to show me. He asked me to pick a target at least a mile away. I got out my binos and glassed the adjoining hills for a target. (It would have been the fuel tank of the Village Idiot's car down at the cabin, but the General said that would be too easy.) I selected a rock just above a singular tree to our right. He glassed the hillside and found what I was looking at: a small, flat rock standing upright that had a tint of blue in the upper right quadrant. He said, "I got it. That is 1,710 yards away (according to his rangefinder) and appears to be a sheet of granite about 14 feet tall and 10 feet wide with some sort of colored vein running through it. I will hit the upper left quadrant of the rock so you know where to look. And here's how I'm going to make the calculations to account for the wind, gravity, the curvature of the earth, elevation, etc."

I watched as he calculated the numbers on paper, though he may as well have been writing in hieroglyphics because I understood not one figure he wrote down, nor could I grasp why he was writing it in the first place. He then made a couple of innocent-looking adjustments to the dials on his scope before putting the gun, the .30 Wolf that he had designed and built himself, to his shoulder and began to breathe slowly and deeply.

"Look at the rock through your glasses," he said, "and tell me when I hit the target."

He then asked me to count to three, which I did. "One . . . two . . . three."

BANG!

I stared at the rock and observed nothing. Just as I went to open my mouth and report that he had missed the target, I saw a puff of white dust rise over the rock from the upper left corner. It was equally humbling and fascinating to have witnessed the results of science behind the General's incredible shot, even if I hadn't followed it on paper.

"Stick around this week," he told me. "This knowledge allows me to make unbelievable shots. I'm happy to teach you this stuff if you'd like to learn."

Before we knew it, we had chatted away the entire morning up there on that ledge, solving the problems of the universe. Seemingly the only thing we couldn't solve was our hunger, which indicated that it was time to head down to the cabin if we wanted to be there in time for lunch.

We strapped all our gear on, collected the horses, and rode over to the trail we had ascended at daybreak.

That first step looked impossible. It was like stepping off Angel Falls. And as if it weren't uncomfortable enough, we were walking the horses down behind us. (Think about it. They're smart enough not to voluntarily walk off that ledge first, and if they're following us, the natural assumption is that they may lose their footing and crush us. Sounds like a lovely alternative, doesn't it?)

The General led his horse off the ridgeline first, and I followed a minute later after they were clear of the landing and/or potential mash-to-a-pulp zone. I simply closed my eyes, said a short prayer, and took the leap of faith, pulling the horse behind me. I landed and my momentum carried me a step or two. I cringed and waited for the horse to flatten me. When I felt nothing, I turned to see him standing there, just staring at me as if I were somehow mentally incapacitated.

Taking my cue from the animal that wasn't smart enough to be scared, I began to follow my hunting partner down the path.

We led the horses all the way down to relatively flat ground before mounting up and continuing toward the corral.

We arrived at the trailer and dismounted, each passing our reins to Cowboy, who had been re-shoeing the front axle of his favorite horse.

We climbed off the beasts, helped remove the saddles and bridles, and gave the horses a well-deserved brushing. After enjoying a few carrots, they seemed good as new and Cowboy put them in the small paddock. Then the three of us walked back up the hill to the cabin.

It had been a morning to remember on all fronts (despite having accomplished slightly less than nothing with regard to harvesting animals for the benefit of the food pantry), and we were starving.

As we approached the cabin, we were just in time to see two elk getting hoisted onto the beam by the other group's crew. They had had a wildly successful morning and bagged a big beautiful six-by-five bull and a sizable cow elk. Apparently, it was a fruitful morning . . . for some of us.

But as attention turned to food, the looming shooting showdown was the talk around the room.

While Jon was making lunch for us, members of the other group were running around trying to find targets to place at long distances. They agreed to use brightly colored plastic plates as their targets and intended to shoot in a field off the West Road, where there was a safe field of fire for well past twelve hundred yards.

Boy Wonder, the Village Idiot, and the General took the rangefinder and left in the pickup to place the targets at hundred-yard increments starting at one hundred and extending to one thousand. Four plates were set up at each distance, and the agreement was that each challenger would have one shot to pass the level before moving to the next distance. Each shooter would also have one mulligan, to borrow a golfer's term, to use at his discretion. By the time the target crew returned, the cabin was abuzz with bragging rhetoric, and the trash talk intensified exponentially.

Interestingly enough, as often happens, the guy who had the most to brag about sat quietly at the table and ate his lunch while the others baited him.

Finally, when one of the contenders reiterated that there ought to be a monetary wager involved, the General casually put his sandwich down, took a sip of his water, and stood up from the table.

"I thought this was just going to be a friendly little shooting match," he said.

"Ahhh," came the reply from the peanut gallery. "He gets uncomfortable when money is at stake."

Jon was just shaking his head at this point because he and I were really the only ones on the mountain who knew what the General was capable of.

"You can bet whatever you can afford to lose," said the General to the overly confident group. "I have a thousand dollars cash on me. What's the bet?"

That quieted the group a bit, but they seemed excited and acted like they had the General right where they wanted him. It appeared that there was no holding the event at bay any longer, and people started to congregate by their cars in anticipation of the short drive to witness the contest.

Ultimately, three guys from the other group wanted to challenge the General, and they stood at the door with their rifle cases. The General retrieved his from the cabin and met them by the cars, and we all started to head down to the field.

Once we were there, the wager took shape. One member of the other group suggested that each man put up hundred dollars, and the winner would take the spoils. Everyone agreed, handshakes were exchanged, and the game was on.

The first contestant who stepped to the firing line leveled his rifle and, without much effort, hit his first target at a hundred yards. The second enjoyed the same success. The third, the Village Idiot, missed the target low and made the excuse that he forgot to adjust for the distance. The General allowed him to shoot again without losing his extra attempt. That was followed by more excuse-making and delay tactics as he tried to garner the respect of those around him. He then promptly missed again. More justification flowed from that opening in his face, but less and less of it made sense as the rant went on. He declared that he was using his mulligan shot and played with the dials on his scope again. For a third time, the group fell silent and everyone looked through their binos at the target.

Idiot's third shot rang out with the same result as the first two. He had choked. His day had ended before it started. He jumped up and said, "Well, I don't know what happened. I guess someone messed with my scope. I'm not involved in the bet anymore." (So much for integrity.)

Then the General stepped up and, without much delay other than a deep breath and a moment of concentration, poked a hole through the center of his target and stepped back.

Another challenger fell out of contention in round five, and the last failed at the nine-hundred-yard mark. The General then effortlessly drilled his nine-hundred-yard target, as well as the remaining four at a thousand yards without a single errant shot.

Just as we'd expected, he'd dominated the event. And, just as we'd reckoned before the first projectile ever made it down range, nobody coughed up the dough.

The General wasn't worried about it because, aside from knowing that he wasn't going to collect even before taking his first shot, he had enjoyed the exercise and taken pride in giving people pointers on how to shoot at distance. At the end of the day, he just liked spending time doing what he loved.

But it sent a real message to the cocky renegades who could no longer brag about what great shots they were. They were embarrassed, and rightly so, not only about their ability to hit a target, but really about what their handshake and their word meant. Unfortunately, the writing was on the wall, and we quickly realized that the next several hours of dialogue were going to be abundant with excuses and other talk suggesting a slanted playing field. Certainly, no one would've mistaken this group for honorable adults.

And speaking of childish behavior, Jon called us all down to the dorm for some assistance. He asked us to carry six plastic containers out to the driveway and place them opposite the deck on the southeast side of the cabin and at the foot of a specific pine. It was a towering pine that, sadly, was well on its way to arboreal heaven. I'm sure that in its prime it had been quite a grand tree. Now, however, it was a browning, sparsely needled tree with obvious signs of decay and distress. There were spots on the trunk where fallen branches had left holes, and there were numerous scars weeping sap. It was Jon's idea to use the tree as a prop to capitalize on imaginations and call out some of the more outspoken members of the other group by playing to their adventurous spirit and self-proclaimed worldly experiences.

The targets we carried up were filled with dual-agent explosives. (A product that is completely legal and readily available at gun stores everywhere.) The two powders alone were not volatile, but mixed together and struck by a bullet traveling over fifteen hundred feet per second would release roughly the same amount of power in an explosion as a stick of dynamite. So while we placed these soda-can-sized containers with the mixed materials in various nooks and crannies of the tree and covered them with paper targets, the General and Jon, as they set the trap, dis-cussed a new, classified, devastatingly powerful round that the government had given him to test.

Mind you, they were discussing this highly sensi-tive and top-secret round within earshot of a certain person who simply couldn't help inviting himself into the conversation with, "Explosive bullets? With that kind of release? Wow! I really need to see those in action. Do you have any?"

Naturally, we had boxes of ammo around the cabin that met the required velocity to set the charges off, and the General just happened to have 10 or so of the "special" rounds in his pocket that he had loaded himself with special tips so as to make them appear different from the average shell.

"We can shoot these but I have to swear you to silence," the General said. "This is a highly classified project."

Of course, there was indeed no secret government project, nothing special about the rounds other than their appearance, and there was no need for all the cloak-and-dagger behavior other than to wind up the know-it-all.

After the Village Idiot swore up and down to take the information and what he was about to see to his grave without telling a soul, the General told him to meet us on the back porch in a minute.

By the time our group arrived, his entire group was gathered around the back steps to the deck. As had been predicted, the first thing that the Village Idiot did after swearing to tell no one was to tell everyone. They were eager to watch what they all thought was the evolution of advanced combat ammunition.

I handed my rifle to the Village Idiot, and the General handed him one of the "special" .270 Weatherby magnum rounds, which he referred to as a "Wolverine" bullet, and told him to rack a shell and shoot one of the targets on the tree.

"Handle it with care; it has an explosive head," he warned for effect.

We were all certain that even Dingle Snort could hit a soda-can-sized target at fifty yards, so we all braced ourselves as he peered through his scope with all the concentration he could possibly muster — and missed the target.

"What happened?" he complained.

The General quickly explained that since this was all in development, the manufacturing of the bullets had not been perfected, and sometimes the impact of the bullet damages its detonating device and the charge fails.

"Try again," he offered as he slid another round into the weapon. Again, the concentration was at fevered pitch. The shot was taken with no result on the other end.

"These rounds don't work," V.I. declared in disgust.

Jon then casually suggested that I take a shot.

I took my rifle from Amateur Hour and carefully placed another cartridge inside the action, closed the bolt, and raised it to capture the target in my scope. I placed the crosshairs directly over the target and squeezed the trigger.

The rifle's report was loud, but the tremendous explosion from the container hidden behind the paper target reshaped my eardrum, and the concussion hit us all in the chest like a twenty-pound weight. A smoke cloud rose from the tree, and splinters and bark rained down from the skies. It was shocking how much energy was released when that target was breached.

There were cheers and a throng of volunteers to shoot the next one. A couple of the guys were allowed to take shots, and, of course, their bullets "worked" like a charm. But, sadly, when the Village Idiot was given another opportunity, he had another stroke of bad luck when his bullet was, again, "defective."

By the time we had detonated all six containers, we had multiple requests to fill purchase orders for the "top secret" Wolverine projectiles, not to mention a lifetime supply of toothpicks. We also had what was left of this beloved tree, which had just given its all for our entertainment, for we surely had hastened its demise. I would say that our mission of mercy was a glaring success judging by the amount of sawdust in the air alone. Besides, we'd also proved that a certain someone who loves to shower himself with accolades about his shooting prowess couldn't hit the broadside of a barn with a howitzer at point-blank range, and that the safest place to stand while he was shooting was most likely the very spot at which he was aiming.

It was safe to assume that, after what must have sounded like World War III, there was not likely to be any wildlife within a fair distance of the cabin. Between that and the fact that it was nearly half past three in the afternoon, the General was not keen on heading out for the afternoon hunt in fading hopes of filling his elk tag — the last one remaining from our group.

The rest of the day was spent relaxing, playing cards, and taking cheap shots at everybody — all in good fun, of course.

The cabin was really rocking and everyone seemed to be mixing well. There was even another collective dinner during which we all ate together and spread the abuse evenly.

The day ended hours later around the fire, when none of us could keep our eyes open any longer. We all cashed in and headed toward our respective rooms.

There wasn't much chatter from this bunch of tired guys who had eaten too much.

Before the lights went out, however, there was one matter that had to be addressed, and we all elected the General to address it.

"Jon," the General advised, "tomorrow is the off day between seasons, so I assume there will be no hunting. I represent the group here when I tell you that we are going to sleep in tomorrow, and, out of respect for us all, we want you to honor our wishes. I am personally declaring that I am not responsible for my actions if I am awakened before eight o'clock."

Snickers arose from around the room as visions of the General getting defensive ran through our heads. There was no telling what could happen to a person who awakened the General from a deep sleep.

To his credit, Jon agreed, and there was relief in the dorm. We could all sleep better knowing that we had a late morning ahead. The lights went out and so did we.

24

THE OFF-THE-BEATEN-PATH PATH

The group awoke to the smell of sausage and eggs, coupled with the distinct aroma of hot chocolate wafting down the staircase and into the dorm room. What an amazing shift from how we had woken the previous days. It was pleasant, comforting, and, most notably, at eight-fifteen a.m.

As with most circumstances, however, there was an exception. Boy Wonder was still sound asleep.

Now, to be fair, he was the one among us who had worked twice as hard, so his exhaustion was understandable. But as you may have guessed, that only garners so much sympathy with this group. If we were up, then he should be up as well.

This occasion called for strategy and creativity. Not unlike most devious pranksters, we allowed him to sleep just a bit longer while we devised a suitable scenario to release him from those pesky REM cycles.

We all left the room to plot over breakfast, and with the help of our trusted comrade and host, whose creativity regarding stunts like this was highly respected, conjured a plan that would most likely keep the Wonder from sleeping at all until he returned to the security of his own bed at home.

After eating breakfast, including his, we returned to the peaceful scene in the dorm. Wonder hadn't moved a muscle since we'd left. He looked so relaxed and comfortable as he lay on his side, drooling all over his pillow.

It was all we could do to keep from laughing as we all stood at the side of his bed watching the General hold a shoulder-mounted bull elk's head (which he'd borrowed from the living room upstairs) about twelve inches directly in front of Wonder's nose. Jon then made a couple of audible mews through his call and Wonder began to stir. Jon mewed again and Wonder opened his eyes.

As he emerged from his slumber and his eyes came into focus, he saw this enormous elk staring at him. His eyes almost popped from his head and he let out a piercing shriek, then ripped the blanket up over his head — as if that was supposed to protect him from what he recognized as a thousand-pound animal about to crawl into bed with him.

We were all quite proud of ourselves and enjoyed a good laugh at our friend's expense. Yet Jon conceded, through his own fit of laughter, that the plan was ill-conceived and we probably shouldn't have done it. And just when we thought there was an apology forthcoming, Jon suggested that we should have used two elk heads, as that really would have helped seal the deal.

We were glad that Boy Wonder, who couldn't help but see the humor, was being a good sport about it all. To give credit where credit was due, this was a big step for him, which did not go unnoticed by the rest of us.

While Wonder tried to remember where he was, I went upstairs to make some breakfast for him and the rest of the guys joined the other group butchering the elk and packing the meat in coolers. He and I sat at the breakfast table for hours entertaining members of the other crew with jokes and the stories of our hunts from before they arrived. In other words, while the rest of the guys got dirty, we were thrilled to find somewhere else to be.

By the time the boys managed to break down two of our five elk, it was about time for lunch. Jon prepared and grilled his infamous burgers and made enough for the entire cabin. He then announced to our group that after lunch we would be going on a little adventure.

"Bus leaves in an hour," he said.

After consuming his legendary burgers, we all put on suitable clothing and piled into the Suburban. Jon announced that our quest would be taking us to Shingle Mill—an old, abandoned cabin, or mill, across the property off the West Road. He said it had been standing for at least a hundred years. We rumbled down the West Road in anticipation of seeing this dilapidated shack, and Jon said that of all the places on the property, this was the place to go to find moose.

It took us thirty minutes to get there. And when we did, we exited the vehicle and walked around a weathered relic of a structure, or at least what was left of it.

The shack stood in a rolling field with unimaginably thick woods immediately to the east and a brook to the north that had been dammed multiple times by beavers. The water calmly trickled by before disappearing into the trees.

The surrounding environment wasn't exactly welcoming either. The trees were gargantuan and the forest was dark. The dirt road disappeared into the timber about sixty yards northeast of where we'd parked, then, as Jon noted, headed off toward the base of a towering rock formation that was shrouded in dense woods and severe creepiness. It was eerie standing there in the shadow of that derelict edifice, looking into the trees and trying not to imagine what might be looking back.

Jon explained that he had spent a lot of time hunting back here because the area was loaded with elk, but the forest was so dense that, while he could smell them close by and hear them all around, he rarely was able to lay eyes on one.

The moose, also plentiful in the area, were a different matter. While Jon was telling us about their general curiosity and propensity for walking along the forest edge to keep an eye out for what was going on, he spotted one, interrupted himself, and told us all to turn around slowly and not make any sudden movements.

We all eased around to see a huge bull approaching from the edge of the timber. While the animal wasn't showing any signs of aggression, Jon advised us to slowly return to the Suburban just in case.

We did as we were told and gently shut the doors.

By the time Jon started the car, the moose had walked toward the truck in obvious defiance. Now he was showing signs of relative displeasure over our decision to intrude upon his afternoon.

We pulled away as he stared us down, and we pushed farther up the overgrown trail into the dark timber. There we accessed a narrow logging road that I had never known existed. It turned out that it was the back way into the Box Canyon.

The road was dark under the canopy of trees — pines that reached a hundred feet or more towered over it. As we forged ahead down the path that was only a quarter of a mile long, Jon pointed out the intimidating entrance to the other side of Box Canyon. We stopped merely feet inside when the road simply ended in the middle of a creek.

We all got out and looked around. The perspective was all turned around, and I couldn't imagine that this was the same canyon I had visited several times over the last couple years. From this side it looked like a completely different place.

Once we had explored the site a little bit, we returned to the SUV, turned around, and headed back down the dark lane again toward the Shingle Mill.

Jon had us get out of the car and wander just off the road for a moment. Within steps from the road, the hairs on my neck stood at attention and that sixth sense that some of us have distracted me so badly that I could hardly give anything else my attention.

As I looked down, I noticed elk sign everywhere and noted tracks in the dirt that were too numerous to count. I'm not sure why I was so jumpy, but I returned to the security of the vehicle feeling very uncomfortable.

Once back in the Suburban, we spotted several moose now stalking through the woods, seemingly watching us as we drove. It was as though they were sentries guarding some secret deep within the forest. It was an odd feeling to have these monstrous four-legged beasts clearly and purposefully escorting us out of their woods.

In all we saw three moose. And Jon said that for the three we saw, there were probably three more that we didn't—but they definitely saw us, and the overall message we got was that we were not welcome.

We started driving back up the mountain and detoured down the Middle Road. We drove for a short distance before Jon parked the truck and led us into the wood line near the top of a deep canyon. He said he was in search of a cave that he had wanted to show us.

We wandered down a barely discernable path and began descending as it meandered around rocks and other obstacles, oftentimes requiring us to rely on others to steady or spot us so that no one slipped and fell.

The trail was not an easy one, supporting the lore Jon had spoken of, that the cave was a safe haven for people to hide contraband, loot, or even each other while they were on the lam or otherwise wanting to avoid discovery or capture.

As we got closer, the creep factor swelled within each of us and became distracting enough that we started to wonder whether we might find something, or someone, in there when we stumbled across the mouth of the hollow.

The trees were strangling the sunlight, which made this adventure far from relaxing, and the path was getting harder to navigate as we got closer to the now-audible rippling of a stream somewhere in the trees below.

Just then Jon was kind enough to point out fresh lion tracks in the mud, and that's when I seriously began to contemplate turning around. I'm all for an adventure, but I don't do fear particularly well.

We then came upon a fallen tree blocking the path. There was no way to get around it, so the decision was made to turn back some twenty or thirty yards (according to Jon's recollection) before reaching the mouth of the underground chamber.

While there was enough disappointment to go around, I, for one, was quite content to retreat while I was still intact. Nobody will ever know what we could have disturbed as it was enjoying the comfort of the cave. And I don't know about the others, but I wasn't going to lose any sleep over that mystery.

We made our way back up the trail to the SUV and noted that dusk would soon be upon us. That, in turn, signaled that food should be on our radar.

We climbed into the Suburban and returned to camp to start prep work for dinner, and for the opening of mule deer season the next day.

We arrived back at the cabin to what appeared to be the equivalent of happy hour. Everyone from the other group was upstairs socializing in front of the fire. We walked into the room and were promptly and generously invited to join the party.

Surprisingly, it turned out to be quite the relaxing evening as Jon worked diligently in the kitchen to produce another inclusive feast.

Once more, everyone seemed to be interacting well; the mood was hospitable, the conversations were casual, and there was none of the usual one-upmanship. The competitive spirit had diminished to a point where we could all just be ourselves. It was a tranquil atmosphere (not to mention a welcome change of pace), and the stories and laughter flowed naturally.

Dinner was a casual affair, with grilled bratwursts and franks, freshly cut fries, a huge bowl of salad, BBQ beans, and a colossal chocolate sheet cake — courtesy of the big group. We all had a great time that night, as a single group, including a Ninety-nine tournament for the ages.

Before we knew it, it was pitch black outside, the temperature had plummeted, the wind was howling, and we were all up an hour past our customary bed-time. After a brief but necessary walk outside, I was elated to be back inside and on my way to the warmth and sanctuary of my bunk.

It looked as though mule deer season was being ushered in by a welcome cold front. All the experienced hunters were excited, meaning I had that much more to look forward to. I remember sleep being harder to embrace that night; I felt like a kid on Christmas Eve anticipating presents at dawn.

But I knew that before I would be outside looking to fill a tag, I would have to endure another jolting morning sponsored by Jon—the most abrasive alarm clock in captivity. I had not even five hours to sleep, so I had to make it count. Sleep finally came to me, but it was a short night.

25

YOU CAN'T FIX INCOMPETENCE, BUT AT LEAST IT'S PREDICTABLE

I was always under the impression that even idiocy had its boundaries. This would be the day I realized just how much I had woefully underestimated the determination of some people to stretch that threshold past any conceivable measure.

The day started like most others. We all woke up to the sound of Jon yammering about breakfast; it was still dark outside, and we all wanted to stay in bed and sleep. Everyone knew the unpleasant consequences that the sleeping-in road led to, so we all got dressed in spite of the fact that we were so tired we had trouble remembering who we were or why we were there.

But once we were dressed and congregated upstairs for breakfast, something extraordinary happened. One of the gentlemen from the other group had brought his father-in-law along on the weekend hunt, and Jon now remarked that he didn't look well.

Our resident host (and former EMT) sat down with the older gentleman and started asking him some questions. The man seemed very drowsy and a bit out of it. Jon took his pulse and some other vitals (all he could do without a blood-pressure cuff) and spoke with the man's son-in-law, who mentioned that other than having diabetes, the older man was perfectly healthy.

"He's diabetic?" Jon asked with some degree of concern. "Where is his blood-test kit?"

He told Jon that the kit had been inadvertently left at home, along with his insulin.

Jon became understandably alarmed and told the guy that he had to leave immediately and get down to SLC before his father-in-law had a hyperglycemic crisis.

"He'll be fine," the young man assured Jon. "We're heading back tomorrow, and he can get stabilized then."

Now, I'm no more a doctor than an astrophysicist (which, ironically enough, might be considered a doctor as well, but you get my point). However I understood that this man was well on his way to having a medical emergency that had the potential to land him in a coma, or even the morgue.

Jon told him, "Look, he doesn't have time to wait until tomorrow. He needs attention right now, and the only facility that can help him is hours away. You need to leave now or you're going to have a tough time explaining his death to your wife."

At this point, even the most challenged person should have gotten the clue that this was a serious medical matter that needed immediate attention.

"This happens to him sometimes," the son-in-law persisted. "It'll be fine."

Finally, Jon pulled the man into another room and explained his position as clearly as he was able: "You and your father-in-law will leave this mountain in the next five minutes in pursuit of immediate medical attention, or I will summon an ambulance up here for him, and the police for you for endangering the welfare of an elderly person. This is not a negotiation. He needs help."

With a frustrated look on his face, the stubborn son-in-law headed downstairs to pack while Jon continued to watch the soon-to-be patient. Within minutes, the elderly man vomited twice (disgusting graphic content warning), producing a white, milky substance that, according to Jon, is an indication of the blood sugar spiking as well as a warning that the person is terribly sick and on the verge of a very serious issue.

Thankfully, within ten minutes, they were headed down the mountain, and we were all left sitting at the table wondering how, and in which universe, hunting takes priority over someone's health.

And just when we thought it couldn't get any worse, along came the Village Idiot, who addressed Jon in a rather short tone and demanded to know why he had sent his friends off the mountain.

Jon carefully explained that the situation was dire and that the man needed medical attention. We all figured that this would clear up any misunderstanding and all at the cabin would return to normal — whatever that was.

However, after Jon explained the issue, which seemed pretty straightforward, he was rewarded with, "Well, you had no right. They were really looking forward to today."

I wasn't sure I had ever witnessed a disconnect quite this significant.

Jon just put his arms up and said, "I thought saving the man's life was a priority."

We were all capable of predicting this man's inept behavior; we just had no idea the depths to which it sank. In any case, their group was collectively two men down when the morning hunt began, which essentially meant that our group felt correspondingly more comfortable knowing there were two fewer guns from their group on the mountain.

We walked out to the cars as the sun was creeping over the horizon, and our group split up for the hunt. The General and Santa headed to the East Road to hike down into Deep Canyon, and Jon and I drove down the Middle Road toward the Weather Station. In fact, we hunted near where Boy Wonder's standoff and ensuing firefight with the territorial quadruped had occurred two years prior.

Meanwhile, Cowboy was going to leave with Wonder for the woods west of the water feature off the East Road.

Jon and I spoke of the morning's events all the way to our destination and continued even as we tried to quietly hike in to our spot. We were in utter disbelief, which, thankfully, turned quickly to excitement when we stumbled upon a small herd of deer. There had to be twelve of them standing right on the edge of the tree line. Luckily for us, the wind was in our favor, and we remained undiscovered at two hundred yards.

We hadn't even had an opportunity to set up, yet we found ourselves in the right place at the right time.

We slowly set our gear down and prepared for a shot.

Jon was glassing for the prize while I fumbled around trying to load my rifle and get it up to my shoulder.

It took Jon a few attempts to direct me to the buck he had identified, which was standing in the shadows behind all the does. He was quartered perfectly for a shot; however, there were two trees obstructing my view, and I could only see his rear quarter and his head. This made any ethical shot impossible.

I slowly stepped to my right, the rifle still up and in shooting position. The moment I was clear of the trees and had a shot at his neck, I stopped, took a deep breath, and released my safety. My heart was beating so hard it was distracting me, and I couldn't seem to control my breathing—two critical issues that almost always result in an unsuccessful shot.

Meanwhile, Jon was in my ear telling me to shoot, "Sometime today, Freddie."

I finally settled down as I concentrated on my breathing. I cleared my head, closed my eyes briefly, and refocused on the target through the scope. I placed the crosshairs midway down his neck and calmly squeezed the trigger. The eight-point buck dropped to the ground as the other deer scattered into the trees.

Naturally, Jon could barely hold his composure. As for me, having the opportunity to finally be with him when I harvested an animal was quite special. It was nice to show him that I had actually listened to all that he had tried to teach me. It was a harvest that I was very proud of, mostly because I got the chance to do it in front of my mentor. It was a good day. (At least for me . . . the jury was still out on the older gent now headed to the hospital.)

Now, all I had to do was figure out how I could avoid dressing this deer. (Had I thought the whole situation through, I probably would have missed the buck on purpose.)

We walked across the field from one cut of trees to the other and found the monster lying on the ground. I picked up its head by the antlers and was really impressed with the deer I had shot.

He was heavy with a tall rack and narrow spread, solid mass, and numerous nicks from fighting. His neck was scarred from run-ins with other challenging bucks, and his face was adorned with a white chevron just below his eyes, making him look like a warrior wearing face paint.

I figured I had to pay the piper at some point, so I addressed the issue straight out with Jon.

"How about this," I negotiated. "I will make every effort to do my best to help you dress the deer. Just don't make me cut or get bloody. I will hold the legs out of your way, I will pull the deer forward to allow the gut pile to fall out, and I will help carry it to the road. Deal?"

He hesitated for a moment and said, "Deal. But with one caveat: you stop talking and get your tag on that deer."

Despite being in such close proximity to the butchering, the only hurdle was not throwing up. It wasn't pleasant, but I survived, and the deer went on to not only ride in Jon's Suburban (clearly a bonus for me from the humor perspective), but also to hang proudly from the beam under the deck.

As luck or raw talent would have it, another addition to the beam had just been hung by Cowboy (a giant ten-point) to the cheers of the others gathered around.

After cleaning up and descending upon the lunch table for homemade vegetable soup and sandwiches, we all shared our stories from the day and took pot shots at each other when opportunities presented themselves. When the progression of stories got around to Cowboy, he told us how he'd bagged his buck while it casually strolled down a game trail near the Beaver Hut.

What struck me as funny was his inability to tell a coherent story as he tried to eat his sandwich at the same time. Apparently, he was more enamored with his lunch than his successful hunt because the next bite frequently took precedence over his finishing his sentences. It was very hard to follow his narrative and distinguish between the buck on the trail and the bologna in his mouth. And that is saying nothing of the food that was repeatedly getting caught in his moustache.

By the time lunch ended, and once we were all satisfied that we had given Cowboy enough grief over the accounting of his morning adventure, it was time to get down to business and organize the upcoming hunt.

The afternoon pairing was as follows: the General was to hunt with Boy Wonder, Santa was with me, and Jon and Cowboy were left to their own devices. The two of them went off to an area near Box Canyon, Santa and I went to the very top of the Bear Claw (which for me was still as unnerving as touring the cradle of fear itself), and the General and Boy Wonder went off behind the cabin to a unique field at the base of the crescent mountain.

The field opened up as a clearing surrounded by dense woods and was in the near-perfect shape of a baseball diamond. The trees all around the meadow were the bleachers and the mountain in the background was the grandstand. It was almost like being in a stadium, hence the name: The Ballpark.

The Ballpark had been home to sightings of some of the largest trophies ever seen on the property, and it felt as though we were standing on the Field of Dreams-West, perhaps waiting for Mickey Mantle and Babe Ruth to walk out of the timber. (To be honest, it's a bit eerie. Even still, I wished I had remembered to bring my baseball glove that day, just in case.)

Up in the southern portion of the Bear Claw, my imagination persisted, causing me to be so concerned about what might be lurking just beyond what I could actually see that I failed to see animals that were present, visible, and within range.

A doe bolted from a cluster of trees behind me as I leaned with my back against an aspen. She had been spooked by Santa shuffling around in the timber. I heard her running toward me, and she passed by in a flash and at such a close distance that I literally could have tripped her by sticking my foot out from behind the tree (which I would have done had I not been so busy thinking it was a bear).

But in that moment of terror, I remembered something. I raised my gun quickly and shouted, "Hey!" And I'll be darned if that deer didn't stop on a dime and turn around to look at me. I was so shocked that it had worked, I almost forgot to pull the trigger. Almost.

I was officially tagged out (that is to say, after she ran for twenty yards and dropped behind a stand of evergreens). I approached the doe and, making sure she was deceased before I knelt down, cut my tag and asked Santa to tie it through her rear leg before he gutted it. (Have I mentioned what a great guy Santa is?) We dragged her to the roadside and then did the unthinkable . . . we actually went back into the Bear Claw.

Now, at this point, Santa still had his buck and doe tags. However, I was no longer a hunter because I had no tags left, so I suppose I shouldn't have continued to carry a gun. But my logic was that because I was entering (in fact, re-entering) a dangerous area with large predators and ironclad indications that they were present and active, there was no way anyone was going to get me to put my rifle down without shooting me first. Santa agreed and off he walked back into the trees, me following behind like a lemming being led to the cliffs.

The rest of the afternoon was intense as we stalked around in the Bear Claw. The noises were unnerving, the lighting was spotty and throwing shadows everywhere, and my eyes were playing tricks on me—to say nothing of what my mind was doing.

Suddenly, Santa grabbed my arm and froze in midstep. I was convinced my life was nearing a very uncomfortable end. I glanced at his face through the corner of my eye to see which direction he had noticed death approaching from, and slowly turned my head to look that way myself.

I couldn't see anything, but he lifted his gun slowly, acquired a target in his scope, flipped the safety off, and squeezed the trigger.

The shot broke the silence in the Bear Claw as if to announce to all predators in the area that the buffet was open and human delicacies would be awarded for free to the first arrivals.

Santa was pumped, yet I still had no idea what he had shot. We approached slowly, and, finally, through the thick trees, I saw a thumper of a buck with a colossal rack. It was a grand ten-pointer with a drop tine and mass I couldn't wrap my hand around. (I have small hands, but still.) His body was huge, suggesting he could've been a walk-on for the D-line of the Pittsburgh Steelers.

Santa eagerly cut his tag and affixed it to the antler before looking at me and offering me the knife.

"Not only will I politely decline that lovely gesture," I answered, "but how's about we drag this deer out of this, the Garden of Lost Souls, before you dress it?"

"That's okay," he replied, "I'm fine in here. You just stand over there — *by yourself*. Let me know if you see anything scary."

By the time twenty minutes had passed, my nerves were completely shot.

"Let's get out of here!" I begged. "Seriously, every creature in these woods knows that we're here by now — cutting up a second dead deer, which they can smell! Can you please wrap it up so we can go?"

Santa replied, "Oh, I've been finished for almost ten minutes. I just thought you were relaxing."

I approached the deer, grabbed one of the legs, and started toward the road, which was just over the ridge . . . and two hundred yards away! I bet I could've dragged that deer out by myself in four minutes flat with the level of fear I had building up inside. I could've done it in even less time had Santa simply uttered the word, "Bear!"

He grabbed another leg, and we dragged his deer out together, though still not nearly quickly enough to suit my taste.

Despite my heart nearly stopping on multiple occasions in there, we emerged physically unscathed. (Though my therapist feels I paid a far greater toll emotionally, which would explain why I now feel the need to pack heat at petting zoos!)

Santa and I loaded the Tahoe with the two latest donations for the food pantry and set off for the cabin while congratulating ourselves on a job particularly well done.

There was no mention, however, of such accomplishments being achieved bravely and in the face of potential danger, mostly because, at least in my case, bravery was clearly not part of the picture.

We hung the two deer back at the cabin alongside a doe that Boy Wonder had shot at (three times, if I recall correctly) and had likely died of a heart attack rather than as the result of a bullet wound. We concluded that maybe the creature had disguised itself as a raccoon.

Dinner that night was the last meal for the other group since they were headed off the ranch the next morning. The dinner was fun as we all gathered over a smoked pork roast roughly the size of Rhode Island. Accompaniments included mashed potatoes and gravy, a salad, and canned green beans with, get this, no bacon. (Tears. Anguish. How sad was I?) We were out of bacon! As in no more, unavailable, depleted supply, end of resource, exhausted reserve, conclusion of stock, total and potentially criminal absence of bacon.

"Who's in charge of this circus? I demand answers! This is unacceptable!"

(Where was I? Ahh, yes . . . dinner. Sorry.)

There were stories shared about the day's hunts and talk of how many tags we had left to fill, but the majority of the conversation was over concern for the older man who had left the mountain that morning with his dimwitted son-in-law.

Dinner ended on a high note, literally, as I accidentally knocked my glass of ice water into Boy Wonder's lap.

Amid the usual jokes, he and I cleared the dishes, reconstructed the kitchen, and managed to arrive on the couch in front of the fire to cheer on our favorite player — anyone playing against Jon.

Naturally, the card game was well underway, but another sad announcement floated over the group. After first hearing and coming to terms with the bacon tragedy, we now had to overcome the fact that the supply of Cinnamon Bears had been fully spent. (Oh, the humanity!)

The living conditions were reaching thresholds that the Geneva Conventions should be obligated to address.

Eventually, after several additional logs were sacrificed and burned for our amusement and comfort, we all succumbed to the promise of rest, our bunks calling to us like the alluring sirens from Greek mythology. (See what happens to a man when he has no bacon? Delusions are just the start.)

We all piled into our beds wondering, with only a couple more days to hunt, whether we would limit out for the pantry. As everyone started to fall asleep, my thoughts took a more selfish bent: how would our twisted host awaken us in the morning? Should I sleep with a gun? Ear plugs? I couldn't believe the hunt was almost over and that I would have to go home in just a couple short days. Where had the week gone?

Deep breath. Thoughts quieting . . . Zzzzzzz.

26

THE DAY BLOOD RAN COLD

Morning was a hard reality to come to grips with, both in terms of cumulative fatigue and the reality that there would be no bacon for breakfast. Even Jon lacked that special energy in his voice that conveyed the delight he normally took in interrupting our slumber at four a.m. every morning while normal people were still enjoying the serenity of their night's tranquility.

"Get up, guys. It's cold again. Breakfast in twenty," he muttered indifferently.

I stirred, rose, got dressed, and started to make tracks outside when, not even halfway there, I was already thinking, *My long underwear needs long underwear!*

It was the kind of cold that made your lungs seize when you drew a breath and burn when you exhaled.

I reached my destination, locked the door, disrobed, and immediately regretted my situation. I had just left the warmth of my sleeping bag and now, not five minutes later, wasn't just cold, I was going numb.

Needless to say, the cold was certainly a motivating factor. The entire mission took only minutes, yet my teeth were chattering uncontrollably and I was decidedly uncomfortable as the skin on my face felt like it was about to shatter.

While I thawed and waited for my lips to turn from blue to a color that gave some indication the flesh was still alive, I put on another layer of clothing. I showed up at the breakfast table, where we all sat with eyelids at half-staff and enough clothes on to make us look like Michelin Men.

By the conclusion of the meal, I was sweating profusely and thinking that certainly I would be a candidate for pneumonia before this was all said and done.

The hunts were set and the breakfast meeting concluded. Jon and the General had agreed to head out together in an attempt to fill their tags. Santa was sent out with Cowboy to harvest his doe, and I was volunteered to spot for Boy Wonder as he attempted to punch his buck tag. The other group had already headed off the mountain after waking, so we had the place to ourselves for the remainder of our stay.

Jon and the General drove up the East Road and walked farther east into the woods near the water feature. About two hundred yards straight through the trees were several secluded fields, which usually held game due to easy access to watering holes and wallows in the vicinity.

Santa and Cowboy headed halfway down the Middle Road to the timber just below Bluebell Flats, and the Wonder and I drove all the way to the end of the East Road and down the switchbacks (because I needed that anxiety in my life at least one more time) to hunt the lower portion of the property.

He and I decided that we would start by walking right into the lower end of Deep Canyon, at the base of the switchbacks.

While walking atop the newly frozen stream to gain access, we were careful not to fall through the ice as we gingerly stepped toward the canyon's lower end. Once we ducked under the vegetation at the canyon's lower access point, we had to squeeze through a narrow rock passage formed by the tapering walls of the gorge. Once past that obstacle, we slowly advanced. It grew darker as the light was barely able to sift through the tree cover and illuminate the slender channel.

We trekked thirty yards in and were back on dirt, rather than the slick rocks layered with thin ice or the equally treacherous moss that carpeted the streambed where the water hadn't yet crusted over.

The canyon walls widened the farther we walked, but by normal standards was still quite narrow. It would be another fifteen minutes on foot before we would reach a place where the canyon was wide enough that we wouldn't be able to see the walls from the center.

I remember thinking about the advantage we had over the wildlife here in the bottom of Deep Canyon. The animals were somewhat trapped in here, their only exit being behind us in a funnel, or ahead of us after a brutal climb up and out of the canyon. So I figured the hunt would be relatively simple since the animals couldn't escape by moving laterally. Just as I was enjoying that encouraging yet completely misguided thought, we heard a most unusual and unsettling sound — the most wicked and disenchanting vocalization either of us had ever heard in the wild.

It was chilling, it was close, and it suggested that we were not at all welcome. We instantly felt as though we were in imminent danger.

We stood motionless, with eyes the size of wagon wheels, looking at each other and wondering what had made that unearthly and disheartening noise.

"What . . . was . . . that?" I inquired with alarm.

"We don't have time to discuss any theories," Wonder replied, "and I'm not waiting around to see what it is."

He reached into his pocket and handed me his Glock.

I racked the slide and we both turned and urgently made our way back down the path.

I was now terrified by the very thought that had given me comfort only minutes before. There was no path for our escape except the funnel we were running toward, and something very large and unhappy was possibly closing in on us.

When we heard the horrific shriek again, I remember thinking that, shockingly, I wished I was in the Bear Claw.

Fear gripped my very soul as we continued our decidedly more rapid pace down the trail, looking over our shoulders every few steps. As we approached the narrow gauntlet where the walls of the canyon formed the slimmest of passages, our pace slowed again, our retreat suddenly requiring more precision and concentration because now we had the slick rocks and ice beneath our feet.

I went first through the constricted egress, and once I squeezed out the other side, I simply ran down the center of the iced stream, punching holes in the surface with each stride. Boy Wonder soon followed, mirroring my footprints as he ran out of the chute and emerged from underneath the scrub.

We soon found ourselves standing near the car, still on full alert and each with weapons trained on the mouth of the canyon. To this day, I'm still not sure why we didn't jump into the vehicle for safety. Apparently, fear modifies one's thought process and magnifies the propensity for poor decision-making. When we caught our breath, we thanked our lucky stars that we were in one piece.

Just as we began to talk about it, we heard the grotesque wail again, although this time with some distance between us.

It sounded like a woman screaming in terror as she was being torn limb from limb. We decided then and there that we would not be walking into the canyon like that ever again.

We got in the car (good thinking, huh?) and headed to a different patch of woodland near the northern stretches of the Middle Road. Though, as I looked back on the event and replayed it in my head, running across slick surfaces with a loaded firearm certainly was something I never wanted to repeat. Fear and urgency certainly had overshadowed my judgment on safety.

The rest of our day was quiet regarding animal encounters, mostly because neither of us could shut up for one minute about what we had heard earlier.

I was noticeably uncomfortable and still had the imprint of the checkering from Wonder's pistol grip in the palm of my hand.

Though we joked about what could've been the source of that cry we'd heard in the canyon — perhaps a feral cat trying to clean a porcupine by repeatedly licking it in the wrong direction—we were happy enough never knowing for sure.

We called an end to our morning hunt and returned to the cabin to find Jon and the General hoisting a nice doe onto the beam.

Lunch was about to get started and so was the narrative of our horror in Deep Canyon.

The more experienced hunters listened to our harrowing tale and weighed in on the near-confrontation. The consensus (over double cheeseburgers and crinkle fries) was that it most likely had been a mountain lion and that we were most definitely a sad pair of cowards.

"You're the ones that were armed with a high-powered rifle and a handgun. What did you have to be afraid of?" Jon questioned.

I said, "Oh, you mean besides getting eaten? Let's review: we have guns, but history has shown that when a certain one of us is in panic mode, he couldn't hit water if he fell out of a canoe. And the other was worried, and rightly so, that wounds from a 9mm would only serve to anger whatever unholy creature was lurking in the woods near us and voicing its extreme displeasure. Either way, I wasn't about to waste time weighing the odds, debating our options, or rolling the dice. I thought the better course of action was to save my tail by running away from the threat."

Everyone around the table laughed at us, not that it made any difference.

"It was fight or flee," I continued, "and I voted to flee. I'm quite comfortable with my decision. The fact that I'm here to talk about it substantiates my thought process."

In the face of judgment by members of a court who weren't there, I stood firm with my decision to retreat.

I was then excused from the table so I could organize my gear for the afternoon outing and bite all my fingernails down to the quick.

The late hunt was fast approaching, so we paired off again as we had for the morning, and Wonder and I headed for the hillside overlooking Deep Canyon.

We were set up amid the sagebrush with a three-hundred-sixty-degree view but camouflaged by the low bushes.

As we sat on the hill and glassed all around us, I noticed a large bird circling overhead. It was pretty high up in the sky, but I could tell it was a large bird of prey.

As it casually descended in lazy circles over us, it was apparent that this was not a big bird of prey — it was an enormous bird of prey; it was the first golden eagle I had ever seen, and as it got lower, its true size became evident.

The bird's wingspan was well over seven feet; it was dark in color, with a light brown head, yellow feet, and grace that was indescribable.

It was captivating to watch this bird in flight, and I thought maybe we would have a front-row seat to watch this raptor hunt and kill an animal on the ground.

Wonder and I were mesmerized. But even better than watching it hunt, we got a chance to see a really fascinating behavioral custom. Another golden eagle joined it overhead and we witnessed a mating ritual, a courtship flight, in the sky directly in front of us.

The two birds would ascend a couple thousand feet into the sky and then fly into each other, grappling and freefalling (helicoptering) together until nearly hitting the ground. They would then separate and gain altitude again to repeat the spectacle. It was an impressive demonstration in agility and courage and far more impressive than dinner and a movie.

Activity on the ground was static, but it wasn't quite time for animals to have started moving around . . . except for Jon, who appeared out of nowhere.

"Are you guys deaf?" he asked. "I walked down here certain that one of you pinheads would have heard me. I tripped over a sagebrush root and nearly fell, and I kicked a rock that rolled down the hill right over there."

Turns out he had been driving around the property and had seen the birds tumbling in the air. When the show was over, he had decided to come down to harass us. While we chatted, the sun started to set, suggesting that opportunities would soon have to present themselves if today was going to hold success for Boy Wonder.

Jon advised that while watching the ridgeline the last few times he was out there at dusk, he had seen a buck emerge from the canyon just before shooting time ended.

We all watched the ridge intently, and with about fifteen minutes to go before shooting time was called, there was a grunt from just below us.

Jon told Wonder what to do, and Wonder shed his gear as fast as he could, rolled to his stomach, and, with his rifle on his back, belly-crawled toward the ridge thirty yards in front of him.

Jon and I remained where we were and glassed the top of the ridge. Another grunt came out of the valley, this time a little louder and a little closer.

Wonder was nearing his destination, and the environment was cooperating perfectly. The breeze was in his face, there was still plenty of daylight, and this deer was about to pop up over the ridge.

He reached the side of a large sagebrush and spun into a seated position. He pulled his rifle from his back, worked the action to ease a cartridge into the chamber, and started trying to control his breathing.

Another call pierced the tense situation, and Jon motioned with his hand to suggest that the buck was directly below Wonder, who was about six feet from the drop-off.

Boy Wonder slowly rose to his feet, using the brush as cover, and then peered around it.

He raised his gun to his shoulder, took one very careful step to the side, and froze. Meanwhile, Jon and I were holding our breath. And then we heard it . . . . *Boom!*

He quickly jacked another round into the chamber and stood motionless and at the ready, looking over the edge. Jon and I waited a minute before getting the all-clear from Wonder. Once we got the thumbs-up, we walked over to meet him.

He was a happy hunter with a buck down at thirty paces. One shot to the neck had put him down on the spot.

He was a big, solid mule deer, sporting a perfect ten-point rack with a nice spread and broad shoulders. After all the congratulations were extended, I generously offered to get the truck for transport, mostly because I would've hated myself for stealing all the fun by insisting on dressing the creature.

I bolted up the hill to retrieve Wonder's pickup and brought it as far down the hill as I dared. I left us a manageable drag of just about a hundred yards.

When we finished loading the deer, we headed back to the cabin, fulfilled, having had another great day, and now able to claim that we had filled another tag.

Upon reaching the cabin, I supervised while the other guys made hoisting the two-hundred-twenty-pound animal onto the beam look easy.

As it turned out, we'd had the only success story of the afternoon.

After changing clothes and getting the fire going in anticipation of playing cards, Jon walked in and made an announcement: "With only one full day of hunting left, some of the guys who have limited out should stay here tomorrow morning and help butcher the elk so we can pack the meat in the coolers. This will save room in the trucks on the way back into SLC. Thanks Boy Wonder and Freddie for taking care of that."

Naturally, I immediately offered to spot for someone on the morning hunt, leaving my colleague to do all the hard work. I managed to beg my way onto a morning hunt with Cowboy while everyone else decided they would pair off in the morning.

We all opted for an early dinner. We were a hungry bunch that night, and it was a simple menu consisting of sub sandwiches again, which was fine with all of us, especially those of us who had to clean up afterward.

It wasn't long before we were all in front of the fire, telling jokes and ribbing one another — standard practice at this point for six fatigued, smelly, disreputable characters.

The exchanges were brief and unmemorable as we seemed to be tiring and losing our offending touch. At the end of the night, it was just six exhausted friends sitting around talking to each other. It was sad, actually. It seemed to mark the occasion as one of maturity — as if a bunch of adults had grown from the group of repugnant, insolent, generally derisive rebels.

It was almost as if the antagonistic element had been completely sucked out of each one of us.

We went to bed that night having come to the conclusion that we had all finally been bested by the outdoors. We committed ourselves to getting a good night's sleep and vowed to wake up ornery and difficult the next day — something more in keeping with what we had all come to expect from each other.

I could only hope we hadn't lost our edge. (If I had returned a nice, calm, caring, mature individual, my wife would certainly not have recognized me.)

At least I knew I was still up for the challenge. I spent what time I had to myself as I fell asleep, creating the story I was going to tell Jon's wife about how mean he had been to me. I figured it would be worth at least two bruises on his upper arm if I put my best effort into it.

27

JUST CALL HOUSEKEEPING; I'LL BE AT THE BEACH

In breaking news: we were awake, and it was still dark outside . . . . again. (This was cruel and unusual punishment.) Certainly, I am not alone in disliking the notion that nearly all hunting stories start with, "I got out of bed hours before the sun came up," nor should I be.

I thought that among the perks of being the enlightened species of the earth's inhabitants was the privilege of sleeping in—at least, it certainly ought to be. Yet somehow, with this hunting business, that idea has been categorically ignored—something I plan on taking up with my congressman right after my nap this afternoon.

But as every hunter will eventually learn, while we can hunt whenever we choose to, the time that gives us the best advantage happens to be very early. So as unpleasant as waking up in what most of us consider the middle of the night, the ritual is merely one of many odd things we hunters do for the experiences we love.

We crawled out of our bunks onto all fours, whining and moaning about wanting more sleep. (It was pathetic, really — a bunch of "adults" crying about more sack time when we had all known going in what we were signing up for. Please don't be misled, however. I'll be the first to admit that I was personally leading the charge for more z's.)

Once we cleared our burning eyes, we attempted to get dressed and head upstairs for breakfast. The first meal of the day was rather abbreviated on this morning, but biscuits and gravy were a crowd pleaser nonetheless. Jon clearly had this dish down to a science.

As we were wrapping up the morning events, I nominated myself to be Cowboy's spotter for the morning hunt, just to go on record in case anyone had forgotten the plan agreed to the night before. Jon and the General paired off, and Santa offered to stay behind to break down the elk and pack the meat in coolers with the Wonder.

We were excused after hearing the mild weather report and returned downstairs to finish getting dressed for the hunt. Cowboy grabbed his gun, I took the keys to Wonder's pickup (with permission, of course), and we left the cabin for our walk through the aspens. We were headed to just below the points overhanging the forest, west of the East Road and east of Deep Canyon. We turned on the East Road and parked at the end of the first open meadow before the landscape started to undulate.

At first light, we were at the tree line, ready to start into the woods.

With the wind directly in our faces, Cowboy led us slowly, deliberately, and as quietly as he could, exercising utmost care with every step. (Imagine a turtle trying to walk through a puddle of molasses.)

We must have covered the entire length of a car in only ten minutes.

Now I can appreciate wanting to be stealthy, but at this pace, we wouldn't have reached our spot until spring.

I eased into the lead and accelerated the progress to a reasonable yet appropriate tempo.

We made our way into the trees as gracefully as we knew how. We would stop and listen every fifteen steps, glassing periodically, and then proceed farther down the slope. Once we had walked a couple hundred yards into the aspens, I placed him near the intersection of two game trails as they merged into one, and I then backtracked to the left for a broader view of the hillside.

Once I found my spot about forty yards from Cowboy, I made sure we had a line of sight between us so I could signal to him should I see something coming his way. We weren't hard to distinguish from the yellow leaves of the aspens, given our mandatory contrasting fluorescent orange accessories.

There we sat for hours, glassing the trees and the nearby watering hole, of which I could see half through a void in the cover.

While we looked over the scenery, the smaller residents were making all sorts of noise. The squirrels were barking, running about in the trees, and scurrying through the leaves on the ground while a nearby hawk was screeching as he floated somewhere overhead. But there were no indications that suggested any action approaching for Cowboy and no apparent activity by the watering hole.

Then I spotted a trio of cow elk that had seemingly appeared out of nowhere. I subtly gestured to Cowboy and directed him to look downhill to his right. I froze so as not to spook them, and the two of us just watched intently for a minute before they took a few steps and inexplicably vanished into thin air like ghosts. We never heard them, nor did we see them approach or leave. It was surreal and better than any David Copperfield illusion I had ever seen. We were left looking at each other, wondering if we had just seen what we thought we had just seen.

The morning continued to yield very little to be excited about until Cowboy slowly turned to look at me and signaled that there was one deer out in front of him at a hundred twenty yards. I glassed as best I could but failed to see what he was looking at due to my angle among the trees. I slowly started to reposition myself and eventually saw a solitary doe standing halfway between Cowboy and the watering hole. I gave him the thumbs-up and looked through the binoculars again. She was completely unaware that anything was out of place as she grazed delicately along the path on which she was walking.

Cowboy raised his rifle and steadied it against his shoulder. There was a brief pause and then the distinctive crack of a gun discharge echoing across the hillside.

The doe scurried down the path and glanced off a tree before succumbing in the leaves littering the forest trail. She was down.

We approached confidently and affirmed our suspicions. Cowboy had tagged out.

He set his rifle down, pulled his tag from his pocket with one hand and his knife off his belt with the other, and notched his paperwork. He attached it to the deer's hind leg and then began to dress it.

Afterward, all that remained was the hike back to the truck. Naturally, it was uphill and hundreds of yards through the trees, but knowing that we had another deer to donate made it easier.

We talked about the three elk all the way to the SUV, unable to explain it with any level of satisfaction. Even to this day, the brief encounter and disappearance remain a mystery.

When we finally reached the vehicle, we placed the deer in the bed and drove to the cabin to hang it.

Upon our arrival, Jon and the General were hanging a very respectable buck, and the guys were almost finished breaking down the elk and packing the meat into the coolers. We lifted Cowboy's deer onto the beam next to the General's latest addition and headed inside for lunch.

Big pork steaks highlighted the menu for our last midday meal on the mountain, and Jon had been kind enough to take the time to do mashed potatoes (possibly one of the greatest inventions of all time), either to enhance our lunching experience or perhaps because he was worried that we hadn't yet gained enough weight despite hiking in the cold with twenty pounds of gear every day. (Honestly, it made no difference to me; I was fat and happy either way.) We devoured lunch as though we hadn't seen food since, well, breakfast. What can I say?

After the feast, we laid plans for our departure the next day. We planned to leave the mountain around midmorning to allow ourselves plenty of time to get our harvest donated to the food pantry (via the slaughter house) and then get to the airport with considerably more of a time cushion than what we had left ourselves the year before.

The cabin still had to be cleaned, the gear had to be packed, and the scattered pieces of the beloved evergreen tree had to be cleared from the driveway (and the field, and the cabin's roof . . . you get my point). Additionally, the animals had to be loaded into a truck other than mine, and we still had tags to fill, which I imagined would be attempted during the afternoon hunt.

While I was right that a group would head out for the afternoon, I was incorrect in my assumption that they would return with any game. From what I understood later, Jon, Santa, and the General had headed out to some corner of the wilderness and told stories the whole time, making so much noise laughing at each other that they'd have been more likely to be mistaken for partygoers than hunters.

I certainly don't begrudge anyone a chance to blow off some steam, so I was happy to hear that they got to relax for a few hours.

I took advantage of my last afternoon by hiking through the woods east of the East Road. I climbed a somewhat formidable hill to what for three years I had heard referred to as The Reservoir.

I wasn't sure what to expect after all the other names of locations around the property. Those areas had unique names, and most were accompanied by great stories. This made me particularly interested about what I would find. I tried to picture what was atop the hills, wondering all the while why anyone would name an area "The Reservoir."

My curiosity was growing as I tried to climb these knolls before my legs fell off.

The following trek through the woods wasn't bad until I began having to climb over deadfall. And beyond that, a final incline came into view, which seemed like just what my thighs needed.

As I neared the top of the hill (and the bottom of my energy reserves), I remember thinking that I wished I had explored this area earlier because perhaps it would have been a good place to hunt; no one had ever hiked up here in the three years I had been to the ranch.

Just then, as I reached the apex of the hill and took it all in, I felt cheated. It was, ironically, a reservoir. (At least I now knew the story behind the name.)

It was immense. It covered hundreds of acres, was roughly a mile long and half a mile wide, and had enough pristine blue water in it to supply a city. The wind blowing over the top of the water created small whitecaps, and the only cliché missing on the post-card-like setting was a marina filled with Hobie Cat sailboats. It was a beautiful sight, and I was thrilled that I had taken the time to walk up there, but I still felt foolish. I had expected more woods and rolling hills, with surplus game animals somehow trapped within by unique land features, thus earning its name. But no, it was actually a water-retention feature. How odd to now think of Jon as being obvious and, by all accounts, practical.

I must have sat on that hillside looking down at the water for twenty minutes while I reflected on my time at the ranch. It was a peaceful place and the water was both beautiful and comforting. Granted, it wasn't Palm Beach, Florida, in March, with the warming Atlantic Ocean lapping up on the hot, sun-kissed sand every ten seconds (which, incidentally, is hard to beat), but it was a beautiful and soothing expanse of water and certainly one I had not expected to see in the mountains of Utah. The contrast of the bright blue water against the rugged backdrop of the landscape was simply hypnotic.

I stowed my thoughts and hiked back down to the Tahoe, though I became slightly delayed by a moose that was making her way toward the Bear Claw. I figured that since I was unarmed, I would take cover until she was well past my route. (I mention that so casually, as though I wasn't shaking in my boots and recalling the last time I found myself in close proximity to a moose.)

I then drove back to meet the boys, knowing full well that a thorough cleaning of the cabin would soon be underway. I also correctly surmised, based on previous experience, that the effort would be staffed by a bunch of guys who would do nothing but get in each other's way and delay an already-tedious process. I figured if I could get back and commandeer Cowboy and Boy Wonder before the other knuckleheads returned, we'd have a fighting chance of getting things under control without tripping over the rest of the group.

As I had hoped, half of our circus was still out scaring wildlife somewhere on the property, so the three of us got down to business, tackling the common areas first and then all the windows.

The tree detail was next, and while it really wasn't a big commitment, it did require the three of us to move one of the branches that had succumbed to the heavy ordnance it had sustained. We moved the larger pieces of debris and elected to leave the countless splinters where they were. All that was left at that point was to vacuum the lower level (which fell to Boy Wonder), clean the kitchen (a duty I claimed), and straighten the dorm. This last item was one we really couldn't touch until all the gear was packed the following morning.

We built a big fire and relaxed until Larry, Moe, and Curly returned from whatever they were doing on the sprawling property.

Cowboy loaded all his gear, got his horses in the trailer, and bid us all farewell, as he was anxious to get on the road.

We were now down to just five guys looking ahead to our last night on the mountain for the season.

Thankfully, we had escaped Chili con Grizzly this trip (something for which the guys returning from years past were grateful), and the harvest was a glowing success. We filled three of six bull elk tags and two cow tags, including the wounded calf, which, sadly, was not fit for consumption. As far as the mule deer were concerned, we had filled five of the six buck tags and three of the antlerless tags. As Jon pointed out, we still had tags for three does and a buck.

"There's still tomorrow," he said.

We all looked at each other, knowing full well that that meant we needed to leave even earlier than planned so an effort could be made to fill a tag or two on our way off the property.

It had grown dark outside and dinner time was upon us. The last night featured another classic roast served with scalloped potatoes, a salad, and the last four cans of green beans. (Naturally, I boycotted the green beans due to their anxiety-inducing lack of bacon.)

As had become common practice, the conversation was focused around hunting stories including derogatory, demeaning, and demoralizing comments about one another—stuff that was rarely appreciated and often repeated. And, as usual, by the time dinner was over, our sides were hurting from having had such a good time.

Boy Wonder and I took one last run at the kitchen, and the rest of the group headed down to the fire.

When we made our way down to join them, Wonder excused himself to the dorm momentarily and suddenly displayed cause for alarm. He had discovered that all of his gear had gone missing and that nothing but the sheets remained on the bunk where his clothes had been. Even those had been neatly straightened to look as though no one had disturbed them for years. His lower bunk was the same. It was neat as a pin and offered no evidence of any belongings whatsoever.

As had been predicted by the others with a wink and the comment directed at me, "Wait for it," we started to hear a fit brewing in the next room. When I heard Wonder's frantic rhetorical questioning regarding the whereabouts of his things in a decidedly panicked and distressed tone, I looked at the guys and asked what they had done. Having been partially let in on the joke, I remained calm as the rest of us relaxed in front of the roaring fire.

Wonder came storming out of the dorm and demanded to know where his clothes were. His appeal was met by a chorus of silence from the four of us who just stared at him with quizzical expressions.

After a moment, the General reached nonchalantly to the floor beside the couch and picked up a camouflaged shirt that looked very similar to one that belonged to our flustered camper. He casually wadded it up, tossed it deliberately over the card table into the blazing fire, and said, straight-faced, "I have no idea what you're talking about."

Talk about a short fuse. I thought Wonder was going to have kittens!

"My shirt! Are you serious with that? Did you burn all my stuff?" he screamed.

He started running around the room trying to save what may have remained yet found only a small pile of socks and other relatively inconsequential articles, which had been carefully placed on the floor next to the couch by the General. The poor kid almost lost his mind right there in front of the group when he found what appeared to be all that was left of his clothes.

He was beside himself, with a face as red as an apple and absolutely no ability to clearly articulate his thoughts—which, in front of the General, was probably a glitch that saved his life.

Once the moment had passed—or, that is, once the first person caved and started laughing—we let him off the hook. Jon explained that they had placed all his gear in the other dorm for safekeeping, with the exception of the pile of socks and T-shirts next to the couch. The camo shirt that had been sacrificed in the fire belonged to the General, who had declared it too small and a candidate for the trash. It was simply repurposed to sell the prank.

An assortment of obscenity-laden rhetoric and venomous invective were hurled at the group (which was admittedly well-deserved), but the humor prevailed and was appreciated by all, Wonder included, once he recovered his belongings.

There was one last thing to address before breaking the party up for the night, and that was who would reign as the Ninety-nine champion until the next hunt.

The cards were dealt one last time, and the game came down to Wonder and the General.

Despite numerous threats from the General, Wonder was victorious, so at least he had his Ninety-nine title to hold over everyone's head until we were all together again.

Sadly, the fire was reduced to nothing more than dimly glowing cinders, and it was time to go to bed. We headed into the bunk room, where it wouldn't be long before we were all unconscious.

I remember thinking, as I lay in the silent room before nodding off, that it would feel good to sleep in the next day and wake up when normal people wake up.

Just to make sure we were all on the same page, I said to Jon, "Since there is no hunting early tomorrow morning, please feel free to resist the urge to wake us up before it's light outside.

There was agreement among the rest of the group, and even an acknowledgement from Jon before the room fell silent again. I can't speak for the others, but I was comforted by what I had interpreted as an accord.

I remember looking forward to the extra couple hours of sack time as I sank further into my pillow. Then thoughts of the day's amazing scenery filled my head and made me smile.

It wasn't long until sleep held me firmly in its grasp.

28

BEST-LAID PLANS

No matter how hard or to what degree of detail you plan, it seems that the world order always has the last word — and it's usually something along the lines of, "Nice try, know-it-all. Don't quit your day job."

The "alarm" sounded, and as we all stretched and tried to wake up, Santa returned from a short morning walk. He reported that it was still dark outside and thus declared Jon a cruel and twisted individual for waking us early.

"I thought we were all going to sleep in today," offered the General.

The "cruel and twisted" title came as no surprise to any of us, including Jon, since that's part of what makes him so fun to be around — just not at four o'clock in the morning. (Please don't think that I'm singling out anyone in particular. Let the record show that at four o'clock in the morning, I don't want to be around anybody.)

Somehow, we managed to grasp and embrace consciousness long enough to dress (at least to some degree) and stagger upstairs to the kitchen. Still unsure why it was necessary to be awake at that hour, we sat and enjoyed enough scrambled eggs to feed a small village, along with ham steaks, toast, butter, jam, and orange juice—all of which I was counting on to provide enough energy to keep me awake long enough to beat Jon senseless for dismissing my clear attempt to buy us all some much-needed rest.

Not surprisingly, breakfast was a bit quiet. I'm not sure we were all there despite all being there, if you know what I mean. But as the neurons started to fire and we began to get feeling in our eyelids again, we perked up a little bit and began the inquisition.

"So why are we awake right now?" the General pressed.

Jon said, "Well, I was awake and bored, so I thought I'd get you all up for company."

The General quickly pointed out that if that were truly the case, Jon's life expectancy had decreased to a fraction of what it had been prior to the question's answer.

"I got you clowns up," Jon admitted, "so we could take one last drive around if you wanted to. I'm going to try to fill my tag, so if anyone wants to go, they can. Otherwise, stay here and finish packing and cleaning the dorm, and we will leave around ten."

Most everyone volunteered to go . . . back to bed, that is. But seeing as how this was my last opportunity to cruise the ranch, I figured, why not have one last hunt with the guy who had taught me how to appreciate all of this? I jumped at the chance, which is to say that I reluctantly raised my hand as far as it would go that early in the morning—just about shoulder height—and expressed my desire to go along by grunting once. (At least I got out of kitchen duty.)

By the time we were ready to go, most everyone else was happily fed and back in the rack. Jon and I loaded up in his Suburban and drove off down the Middle Road.

Due to the northerly wind, his plan was to drive almost all the way down to the gate, cross over to the bottom of the East Road, and come up the switchbacks so he could approach the Bear Claw from the north. The last hunt of the season was officially underway.

Around the first bend in the road, there stood two good-sized does at the tree line. We couldn't have planned it any better if we had tried, except for the facts that it was still dark outside and we'd be shooting them from the road. Other than that, it was a great opportunity.

We watched them for a while and mused at the notion that they were acutely aware of when it was safe to be seen and not seen. Eventually, they wandered into the trees, and we continued our slow drive down past the Darning Needle, Bluebell Flats, and all the other woods and fields that I had grown to love over the past few years.

Our drive was rudely interrupted as we rounded a bend and encountered a large Shiras bull moose that glared at the vehicle from the center of the road, as if to suggest that we were somehow intruding on his morning stroll.

Again, we paused and watched from the safety of the truck. Eventually, he too ambled off into the trees.

We continued farther down the mountain, and the light of day started to peek through the morning mist. Shooting time was getting closer.

With hope that we would surprise any game that was taking refuge within, we pulled over to investigate a couple secluded fields that were still shrouded in thin layers of morning haze. However, both sorties into the woods failed to yield any opportunities.

Once back in the vehicle, we turned onto the lower end of the East Road and drove toward the always-entertaining switchbacks. The climb was predictably nerve-racking but ended at the top without incident.

After reaching the safety of less-treacherous roads, Jon and I switched seats and I became the chauffeur.

We slowly drove up the road and bumped (figuratively, not literally) into three bucks, a small herd of elk with one shooter bull, and an extraordinarily unhappy porcupine — presumably headed home after a late night out.

It was a remarkable sight, but our only interest was in a legal doe, which, as you may have noticed, wasn't among the cavalcade of game that we had seen so far on this, the last roundup.

We elected to park and wander through the tip of the Bear Claw. (Well, that's not entirely true. Jon suggested it, and when I started backpedaling like a nine-year-old being taken to the doctor for his shots, he ordered me out of the SUV.)

So here I found myself venturing into the Bear Claw one last time — unarmed. I was promptly overwhelmed with panic.

As we approached the tree line, I began experiencing a level of hyperawareness that was, quite literally, nauseating. I was still very uncomfortable in this dark timber.

We cut in fifty yards from the road and then walked upwind, hoping to run across an unsuspecting doe before becoming breakfast for some creature that was likely stalking us. We crept through the shadows of the trees but never saw anything apart from my life flashing before my eyes. And when Jon finally decided to give it up, he could tell how terribly disappointed I was by the rush of calm washing over me as I happily sprinted back to the truck.

When we arrived at the cabin empty-handed, no one really seemed too concerned. I'm convinced that they all knew the trip down the mountain would be the final hunt anyway.

I packed all my hunting gear and changed into some clothes more suitable for travel while the rest of the group finished loading the vehicles with their gear and the animals from our harvest.

It came as no shock that half the deer ended up in the Tahoe again, although at least there was no fresh blood this time . . . yet, anyway.

Within an hour, the loading process was complete and seemed to have been carried out with some degree of care and consideration. The cabin was spotless, and even the generator had been cycled down.

Another wildly fun hunting season had come and gone, leaving us all staring down the barrel of a drive into SLC.

We got in our respective vehicles—Jon with the General, Santa with me, and Wonder in his own pickup.

We headed down the mountain, and Santa and I placed a gentlemen's wager on whether or not tags would be filled on the way down the hill. We both felt that someone would kill but that it was unlikely we would reach our collective limit.

The caravan was halfway down the mountain when, right on schedule, I saw Jon's brake lights go on and his reverse lights flash as he put his gear selector into park.

"Here we go," I said to Santa.

Jon jumped out of his car, pulled the rifle from the back seat, and walked off the road. He glassed up a big hill to our left and then loaded his gun.

Boy Wonder hopped out of his truck and spoke to him before they both disappeared into the trees, leaving us waiting patiently on the road.

Meanwhile, we were glassing the hill as well, but none of us saw anything other than one doe way up the mountain and in another zip code. We were certain Jon wasn't after her. We were good for our flights, but had not allowed enough time for an excursion like that.

After fifteen minutes of silence, Santa and I started to glance at our watches and recalculate our times, knowing that our flights would leave without us if we failed to get to the airport on time.

Just then, a resounding *boom* made us all turn around and glass the hillside again. Sure enough, it was the doe that was standing three counties over, so we would now have to wait for the two mountain goats to climb the hill and then tag, dress, and recover the animal. As if that wasn't bad enough, that list of to-do items didn't include consideration for the time it was going to take to bring the animal from point A, where it had been shot, to point B, where the vehicles were. (So much for sticking to the plan.)

It would be at least an hour before we saw the whites of their eyes, and we were already feeling the pressure. All that was left to do was get into Jon's car and blast the distinctive tunes of ABBA with the doors open. (Why not? If I could scare the rest of the remaining wildlife, we wouldn't stop again on the way to the gates.)

After an insufferable wait, Boy Wonder emerged from the trees with a tagged doe on his shoulders, followed by our very-out-of-breath host.

Though we were all a bit lacking in the patience department, we were excited that Jon had gotten his doe and that now we'd be able to feed more people who might otherwise go hungry.

The fresh one was loaded into Jon's Suburban (because I'd locked my doors), and he remarked that he could hear "Dancing Queen" halfway up the mountain. (Everybody should be so lucky as to be able to track deer with ABBA playing in the background.)

We piled into the vehicles one last time and drove down the hill, leaving in the rearview mirror one of the most beautiful and placid places I had come to know and love . . . and the Bear Claw.

We exited the gates, one by one, locking them as we cleared their thresholds. Each car then turned onto the paved highway toward Coalville.

Sadly, there was now no time to stop and see Turtle's conquest from last year, nor was there time to waste getting a little thing I like to call lunch. We did, however, manage to spare ten minutes to fuel up at the closest gas station, where I was fortunate enough to procure a soda and some powdered-sugar doughnuts stamped, "Best if eaten before the Napoleonic Wars."

I returned to the Tahoe and immediately started in on the doughnuts. Sadly, after nearly losing a tooth biting into one of those doorstops cleverly disguised as tasty little miracles, I decided I was better off with just the Coke.

We all left the filling station blazing a trail toward SLC.

I'm guessing that Utah had only four or five police cars in the entire state back then and that, thankfully, they must have been patrolling elsewhere. A trooper could've retired on the speeding citations he might have issued to our little parade. (I won't divulge the exact speed at which we were driving, but I can tell you it exceeded my wildest expectations regarding what I thought a Tahoe was capable of without melting the tires, peeling the paint off the doors, and eventually bursting into flames.)

When we pulled into the game-check station next to the slaughterhouse/ Rental Vehicle Car Wash and Interior Demolition Station, Jon determined that we had made it in record time. (Of course we had! I could've told anybody that just by looking at the amount of smoke rising from the brakes on his Suburban!)

Jon also told us that he had received a call with an update on the older gentleman who had been sick up on the mountain. The man had made it to the hospital, where he was still recovering, but he was expected to be released after a couple days.

It turned out that the emergency-room doctor had told the older man's family that he had been about fifteen minutes from suffering irreversible damage to multiple systems in his body and that he would have passed away without the care that he had received that day.

As one could imagine, the man's survival was very welcome news and brought relief to those of us who had been praying for him. Naturally, Jon concluded that the lesson here was to always listen to him.

We promptly ignored that self-serving wisdom and turned to unloading all the animals.

The game officer immediately started checking tags, permits, and IDs. Once everything was accounted for, we filled out all the donation paperwork and quickly mounted up again to head to the airport—or, in my case, a slightly more conventional car wash than the likes of which I had stumbled upon the season before.

I filled the tank as per my contract with the rental company, had the car run through a car wash and the interior sprayed with freshener, and headed to the airport with my gear and gun case.

As usual, I was pressed for time, but now I had experience on my side. I pulled into the chute at the rental-return lot like Andretti into pit row.

Within seconds I had parked the car, left the keys in the ignition, collected all my things, and positioned myself by the left front fender, papers in hand.

A nice young woman appeared with a bright smile and bright attitude and in a bright voice asked me how my experience with the SUV had been. I was stressed and worried about my flight, but I couldn't take it out on this charming person who was so nice it bordered on criminal. I had a brief, polite conversation with her, thanked her while accepting my receipt, and dashed off toward the ticket counter.

As I approached the desk to check my bags, I was still worried about having enough time to get to my gate.

"Oh, don't worry, sir, you have plenty of time," the agent said. "Your flight is almost two hours late."

My reaction was as surprised as anyone who knew me would have expected it to be. I took it right in stride and thought, *This gives me time to wash up and get some food.*

With that, I turned on my heel, cleared security without incident, and walked down the concourse. I actually had time to decompress. (What a novelty.)

After cleaning up, I found my way to a watering hole. (Heck—if I can find one in the middle of the woods, I can certainly find one in an airport.)

I bellied up to the bar and ordered a tall, cold one and a sandwich.

Sitting at the bar, exhausted and rejuvenated at the same time, I pondered whether I was more excited to be going home to a familiar environment or more saddened about leaving the more-challenging Utah landscape behind. That was indeed the question of the hour.

I sat and enjoyed a leisurely bite while I tried to relax and think of all the experiences I could now credit to these hunts. (I'm pleased to report that they were numerous and greatly appreciated.)

I paid my tab and walked to the gate. The plane, which had finally arrived from somewhere in California, represented the last remaining portion of the adventure before arriving home, and I was moments away from getting on it.

I felt like an entirely different person leaving Utah this time, and, oddly, as best as I can tell, it had very little to do with any one experience I had had at the ranch. Rather, it seemed to be the cumulative result of all of them over the three-year period during which I had enjoyed learning so much.

I boarded the plane thinking of all the funny stories, the people I had gotten to know and the ones who had taken the time to get to know me. I thought, too, about the food, the friendships forged, the camaraderie, and all the things I had learned about sportsmanship and integrity. But what really struck me as remarkable were all the things I had learned about myself. This journey had been nothing short of transformational.

I had changed. Somewhere among eating at the finest restaurants known to man, relaxing at extravagant resorts and luxe accommodations all over the world, and exploring a miraculous piece of property in northern Utah that had left me physically exhausted from the demands of the terrain, mentally exhausted from the required interaction with nature and with my fellow hunters, and emotionally exhausted from facing the absence of simple civilized things such as showers and working toilets, I had become a different person—a better person.

I still loved the best-of-everything lifestyle, but this other existence was amazing as well—and had entirely its own merit. It occurred to me that my head-on encounter with the outdoor life had also been a best-of-everything experience, just one that fit in an entirely different category from anything to which I had ever been exposed. I had expanded my horizons and was grateful for every last moment.

I'm comfortably certain that I still cannot call myself a true outdoorsman for any number of reasons. But looking back, I'd like to think I had earned at least a few stripes over the course of these travels. More importantly, however, is that I know hunting is now truly a part of me—something I never thought I would be able to say.

I took from these incredible experiences the one unexpected facet of the lifestyle that intrigues me the most, and that is that hunting isn't just about taking down game. It's actually so much more than that. It transcends any singular activity and becomes a collective part of who you are. I feel like even though I recognize so many features of it now, I have but merely scratched the surface.

It came as no surprise to me anymore that people spend a lifetime exploring this extraordinary pastime, and I felt privileged to have been introduced to it.

My thoughts were interrupted by the captain announcing our final descent into St. Louis. As the plane neared its destination, I looked back on some of the more practical lessons I had learned on all these hunts. I couldn't help but laugh to myself as I remembered all the fun we'd had:

1. The human stomach has limitations which are surpassed by epic margins when forced to endure Chili con Grizzly; the subsequent expectation regarding the normal and proper function of one's digestive tract is entirely unrealistic. Either abstain from consumption, or be willing to abandon your life for at least a day in favor of remaining in close proximity to a bathroom.
2. Don't pick fights with flight attendants. They remember everything. Forever.
3. The world needs people who are intellectually inferior to make the rest of humanity feel better about themselves.
   3a. Never assume you're not the intellectually inferior person.
4. Waking up when it's still dark outside is fundamentally wrong and should be done only in an emergency — e.g., the bed you're in catches fire.
5. Regarding ATVs and altitude, always listen to someone who knows more than you do.

6. Embrace ABBA.

7. You can never have enough Cinnamon Bears.

8. Don't ever kick a metal bedframe.

9. Whoever thought of using corn as an "indicator" is either brilliant or seriously warped.

10. Try to discourage friends from loading dead animals into your rental car.

11. After you've failed at #10, never let Jon wash the car's interior.

12. Always assume that a deer floating in mid-air over its intestines and other vital organs is already dead.

13. Do a little homework on any prospective adversaries before you challenge them to a shooting contest — or any other contest, for that matter.

14. At the very least, make sure you can differentiate between an elk and a common farm cow before accepting the responsibility of being a hunter.

15. Understand that you don't have to be the fastest person in your group to get away from a predator. You only have to make sure you aren't the slowest. (Tip: A readily available pocket knife can level the playing field.)

16. Whenever you think you have enough bacon, buy more. After you buy more, reread this lesson.

17. Jackrabbits are crazy, and mule deer look ridiculous when they run.

18. Discharging explosives in a tree can save you $3.99 a year in toothpicks.

19. There are no such things as Wolverine bullets.

20. Don't wait for a blinding snowstorm with lightning and thunder to tour your property on a motorized lightning rod.

21. When you have an opportunity to kill a record bull elk the size of a tractor trailer, make sure you hit it.

22. If you find yourself in an environment that resembles that of the North Pole in January, make every effort to avoid disrobing for any reason, including the practical ones. Frostbite is real.

23. If you haven't showered in a week or more, manage your expectations with regard to a hug from your wife at the airport.

24. Be wary of people standing on your front doorstep holding birds of prey. (Although, in some cases, opening the door is well worth the risk.)

25. Don't *ever* say anything about a trailer hitch at a car-rental facility in Utah.

It is important to note that of the twenty-four antlered deer and elk that were harvested on these three hunts from 2001 to 2003, eleven of them were mounted as shoulder mounts or European mounts and remain, to this day, among the hunters' collections representing some of their fondest memories and experiences. And, lastly, of the thirteen guys who were part of our groups during those three magical years, no one is more grateful to them, or as proud to have known them, than I.

Me with my first bull elk. Score: 307⅝ (I'm the one on the right.)

Please remember: Responsibility is critical. Always be safe, lawful, and aware of your surroundings when you hunt. Your life, as well as the lives of those around you, depend on it.

Made in the USA
Middletown, DE
12 July 2024